PRESUMED
GUILTY

A TEACHER'S SOLITARY BATTLE
TO CLEAR HIS NAME

Simon Warr

Biteback Publishing

First published in Great Britain in 2017 by
Biteback Publishing Ltd
Westminster Tower
3 Albert Embankment
London SE1 7SP
Copyright © Simon Warr 2017

ISBN 978-1-78590-181-2

10 9 8 7 6 5 4 3 2 1

A CIP catalogue record for this book is available from the British Library.

Set in Garamond by Adrian McLaughlin

CONTENTS

'Is the accuser always holy now?'

THE CRUCIBLE BY ARTHUR MILLER

FOREWORD

Through a mutual friend, I have got to know a man – I'll call him Chris – now in his early forties, who was sent away to boarding school at the age of eleven. Barely into his teenage years, he was groomed and systematically sexually abused by one of his teachers. That teacher had left a previous school on account of an inappropriate relationship he had had with a teenage pupil there. When Chris's abuse was uncovered, the perpetrator first denied any wrongdoing and then admitted his guilt, qualifying what he had done by saying Chris had enjoyed it. He was sacked from the school and, if reports are correct, he went on to teach at yet another institution, in the south of England, even being supplied with a decent reference.

As for Chris, both on account of those serious sexual offences to which he was subjected and the fact his abuser failed to recognise his own wrongdoing, his life has been pretty much ruined, although recently he has found a partner to love. During the intervening thirty years, apart from his education being spoiled, Chris has undergone many years of therapy and has repeatedly taken overdoses in a bid to end his life. Despite now having a partner, Chris is adamant that he never wants to bring a child into the world for fear he or she might conceivably be subjected to sexual abuse similar to what he suffered. He realises this attitude is irrational, but he believes he would never be able to let any child of his out of his sight. He told me he would, once again, end up a nervous wreck.

Listening to Chris speak, you would need a heart of stone to not be moved. He accepts that abusers exist and that some have absolutely no scruples about satisfying their own sexual appetite by preying on young children. I am amazed how strong and level-headed he is. His abuser was, many years later, arrested by the police and charged, and he had no option other than to plead guilty. He was duly sent to prison. Chris feels that this punishment of his abuser has helped to get his own life back onto something resembling a normal track, although he knows he will never forget what happened to him. He has set up his own company and is at last forging a career for himself. He has certainly not courted publicity about his abuse. He feels what happened to him is very private, something to be shared with only close family members and interested professionals.

Chris is a genuine victim of abuse, reacting, I imagine, how most others do in a similar situation.

At the other end of the spectrum, there are those who take full advantage of ordeals such as Chris's for their own greedy, nefarious ends, particularly since the Savile scandal. They often read accounts in magazines and newspapers and even in court transcripts of the experiences of cases like Chris's and use the information to furnish their own fantasies. They think it is fashionable in modern Britain to join the 'survivors' network', a group set up to help those who have been genuinely abused but which, unfortunately, has now been infiltrated by liars and fantasists. As well as the obvious public sympathy and attention these unscrupulous people receive, they are well aware it is also immensely lucrative.

These liars undermine those, like Chris, who have been genuinely abused.

The furthest thing in my mind when writing this book was to drive victims of sexual abuse back into the shadows for fear they will not be believed. My purpose is to convey a clear message that, while being alert to the needs of those who claim to be a victim of abuse, like the extraordinarily brave Chris, all state agencies must also be mindful that there is a possibility that the complainant might not be telling the truth, which would then make the accused the victim.

When so many people have suffered the nightmare of having been sexually abused, is it perverse for me to focus upon the wrongly accused? In answer to this, I contend that by arresting, charging and even convicting innocent, good, hard-working people, as is currently often the case, this will only serve to diminish the chances of real sexual abuse victims being believed and securing ultimate justice, which is their right.

As author Richard Webster states in his masterpiece *The Secret of Bryn Estyn: The Making of a Modern Witch Hunt*: 'One of the greatest failings of the modern child protection movement is that, in its zeal to believe *all* allegations, it has betrayed the very children it seeks to protect.'

This book is the story of what happened to me when an opportunist duped the police into believing that, when he was at a school at which I taught over thirty years ago, he had been abused by me in a communal shower room after a PE lesson. The fact that I'd never taught him or the subject PE didn't seem to cause the police to consider whether he might be either mistaken or, more likely, lying … although the truth eventually emerged.

I was inspired to write this book having spoken to a number of members of the organisation FACT (Falsely Accused Carers and Teachers, www.factuk.org). One of them recommended that I read *The Secret of Bryn Estyn*. Of the myriad books I have read during my lifetime, this was positively the most shocking, absorbing, detailed, revealing, superbly expressed true story I have ever come across. It was an enormous help to me in writing *Presumed Guilty*.

INTRODUCTION

People believe that where there's smoke, there's always fire.
Yet often nowadays there's just a smoke machine.

— GEOFFREY ROBERTSON

When Jimmy Savile died in 2011, I believe a collective insanity gripped sections of our society here in the UK, to the extent that anyone who was the target of alleged historical sexual abuse was immediately assumed to be guilty. And I do not refer solely to the untutored mob, those zealous internet groups (known commonly as 'Social Justice Warriors') who cannot, can't be bothered to or, usually, don't want to, separate fantasy from the truth; I refer rather to the learned, those in positions of authority, who suddenly became very concerned about historical child sexual abuse and, for this, they are to be commended. Unfortunately, there was suddenly a tendency, post-Savile, to condemn, regardless of the absence of any hard evidence (in my own case even soft evidence). And this is certainly not to be commended.

My arrest for alleged historical child abuse at my school home on 18 December 2012, followed the next day by the publication of my name on the radio and television, which then set in motion a desperate search by the police for similar allegation 'evidence' over the next two years, if not quite a witch-hunt, comes pretty close. The greater the public repugnance against a particular type of crime, then all the more necessary it is to protect those people who are wrongly accused of that crime. But my arrest in December 2012, following 'A"s (his identity is forever protected) absurd, gradually embellished allegations, and my subsequent prosecution the following year, was no more just than the frenzied, partial evidence used with deadly effect in seventeenth-century Salem. (It is ironic that, in 2005, I produced and directed Arthur Miller's well-known, disturbing play *The Crucible*, based on this very topic.)

Whenever supposed criminals are hunted down primarily because of the demonic image we have projected onto them, the pursuit of justice all too easily becomes a witch-hunt, in which the innocent suffer alongside the guilty. I was innocent of the allegations which led to my arrest but I was made to suffer for nearly two years. It seems that all that is now required to devastate someone's life, because these public arrests do exactly that, is an uncorroborated allegation.

The result of this current *modus operandi* is potentially serious for us all. No one is safe from an accusation which will destroy that person's career, his or her reputation and, potentially, take away his or her freedom. This is particularly the case for those like me who have dedicated their professional life to working with children in schools, a group who are usually grossly undervalued and are particularly vulnerable. I believe it is right and proper to praise to the hilt dedicated teachers who sacrifice so much of their private life as they single-mindedly endeavour to give to the pupils in their care the best of all possible starts in life.

I was the victim of state persecution because, post-Savile, traditional safeguards which protect those who are accused were abandoned. The CPS (Crown Prosecution Service) had started bringing prosecutions for sexual offences based upon the uncorroborated and disputed evidence of a single complainant, following the new CPS guidelines: 'Using the lack of corroboration of a victim's [*sic*] account to justify a decision to drop proceedings is flawed.' If that complainant's account was manifestly implausible, then the agents of the state sought to replace quality 'evidence' with quantity. They do this by what is termed 'trawling'. Again and again we are now seeing criminal trials which are manifestly unjust because the accused has such difficulty defending him or herself against incidents which were alleged to have taken place over thirty or forty years ago and juries, naturally programmed to protect children, are permitted to convict even if there is no actual evidence.

Thus, I was arrested and subsequently charged on totally unfounded allegations. I was 'targeted' and a case was built up against me as the 'detectives' ignored any evidence which could actually have proved my innocence. My repeated protestations seemingly did nothing to shake the belief of the main investigative officer or of her colleagues, as I was hung out to dry.

The threshold for charging a suspect is, according to the CPS Evidential Code 4.4, the following:

> Prosecutors must be satisfied that there is sufficient evidence to provide a realistic prospect of conviction against each suspect on each charge. They must consider what the defence case may be and how it is likely to affect prospect of conviction. A case which does not pass the evidential stage must not proceed, no matter how serious or sensitive it may be.

What I am advocating in this book is a sense of perspective; a balance about this sudden flurry of historical abuse allegations. Any gung-ho approach to what is a very serious subject should be resisted and some common sense used (of course, as Voltaire said: 'common sense is not so common'). The eminent barrister, Barbara Hewson, described the prevailing police tactics post-Savile as a 'juggernaut out of control … law enforcement hijacked by moral crusaders'. She believes that the zealots who have created this febrile atmosphere here in the UK 'pose a far graver threat to society than anything Jimmy Savile did'.

In 1215, Magna Carta stated: 'We will not deny or defer to any man … justice'. Six hundred and seventy-two days on bail during 2013 and 2014, which is three times longer than it took to bring the Nazi hierarchy to trial at Nuremberg after World War Two, were a disaster for me. I was left without a career, without a job, banished from my home and community where I'd lived for thirty years, vilified, branded as a pervert and hounded like a criminal.

The police, after staging their early morning raids of both my home in Ipswich and my flat in London, at sizeable expense to the taxpayer, had to vindicate their strategy and seemingly felt it imperative to secure my conviction, regardless of any evidence to the contrary. And if that took them going on for two years, then what or who was to stop them? During this time I felt suspended from life. I felt utterly destroyed for much of my time on bail. I put on a brave face for my family and friends because I did not want them to suffer unnecessarily.

Ever since losing both my parents at the age of six and then being packed off to boarding school, I had learned to be emotionally strong and I have always been fiercely independent when facing life's many challenges and hurdles. The only thing that kept me sane and prevented me from killing myself during the period after my arrest was the knowledge that I was innocent of the allegations. I had spent my entire professional life teaching, tutoring, coaching sports, producing and directing plays and musicals and generally caring for teenagers over and above the call of duty. Some pupils considered me something of a martinet and a number probably didn't like me; I have made errors along the way, which is no surprise, but, overall, I like to think the vast majority of pupils in my care respected me for my professionalism and utter dedication.

This ultimately counted for nothing as I was kept on bail for those two years; basically, I was left in legal limbo for all that time, which is nothing short of cruel, even if I'd been guilty of the offences of which I was accused. Can you imagine the torment in having to survive such an existence? It wasn't as though I'd been accused of a crime as heinous as rape or GBH: I had been falsely accused of touching someone inappropriately in the school shower room in the early 1980s. This didn't stop agents of the state stripping me of my good name, my home, my career, my happiness. As they did everything in their power to coax others to come forward, they left me to suffer month after month, with seeming indifference to the damage it was doing to me. I was frightened every time someone knocked on my front door; totally ashamed of, and humiliated by, having been accused of child sex abuse; desperately tired, yet unable to sleep; always hungry, yet having no appetite to eat; desperate for alcohol but knowing to have even a glass would be the start of a slippery slope. I wish these officers who hide behind 'We have a duty to investigate' stopped just for a moment to consider the effect the uncompromising approach to their arrest procedure has on us, the accused.

After my trial at Ipswich Crown Court, in October 2014, the jury dismissed the seven charges against me officially within forty minutes, although I have since learned that they came to their unanimous decisions in a much shorter period of time, indeed almost immediately. Does this not speak for itself? It certainly does beg the question – why was I charged?

And now that the truth had emerged, which I had to uncover pretty much on my own, was there any apology? Of course not. That would have suggested these agents were wrong to have arrested and charged me without a shred of firm evidence in the first place. Were there any recriminations for the liars? Of course not. For the police to have pursued them for malicious allegations would have compromised themselves in having undertaken an adversarial, partial investigation throughout. Thus, on the one hand, an accused can be taken to hell and back in being the target of totally uncorroborated allegations from decades ago, motivated by the prospect of either financial or psychological gain, while on the other, the latter can repeatedly lie in police statements, even under oath in a court of law, and yet they have nothing to fear; no fear of reprisals; not even the humiliation of publication of their name.

In this book I shall tell you what happened to me and address how we can improve our current way of investigating alleged historical abuse.

Note: Throughout this book I address my main St George's School accuser as 'A' and his associate as 'B'. After they attempted to ruin my career and to trash my reputation by spouting a succession of repugnant lies for their own iniquitous ends, it is only right and proper that they be identified. Unfortunately, the laws of this land forbid me from doing so.

CHAPTER ONE

———

EARLY YEARS AND START OF MY TEACHING CAREER

I've never let my schooling interfere with my education.

— MARK TWAIN

I was born in Haverfordwest, in Pembrokeshire, West Wales, in the 1950s. I was the youngest of three boys; my eldest brother Stephen was ten years my senior, while Nicholas was four years older. We lived with our parents, Walter and Veronica (known as Vernie), in Milford Haven, a small town nestling on the south-west coast of Pembrokeshire, famous for its docks. When I was six, my mother died of cancer and I remember we had a nanny, Mrs Minns, who came to live with us to help Dad out. Very soon after Mum died, Stephen, at the age of seventeen, 'disappeared' off to London and my father spent weeks searching for him in the capital. Without success, he returned to Milford and he too soon died of tuberculosis, an illness directly attributed to his exploits in the war and exacerbated, one can safely say, by his heartache at losing his wife at such a young age and then having to trawl the streets of London searching for his eldest son.

Nicholas and I were fostered to relatives, initially those on my father's side, in Milford Haven, subsequently to relatives on my mother's side, who lived in Cardiff. Nick went to live with Aunty Pat and Uncle Bill, while I was adopted by Aunty Doreen and Uncle Len. The following year, Nick was sent to boarding school in London, while I, at the age of eight, joined him the following September, in 1962.

The Royal Masonic School for Boys, where I was educated for the next decade, catered for the sons of deceased masons. I have mixed feelings about my early years at the junior school. I can remember it being jolly cold, both inside and outside the boarding house, and the discipline even more challenging. In those days, corporal punishment was pretty much a daily occurrence and, as I possessed a cocky, confident character, I was targeted by a number of the teachers. I can remember two members of staff, in particular, who took pretty much an instant dislike to my cheeky nature. On one occasion, when I was no more than ten years old, one of the chemistry masters, I'll call him Ben Stevens, saw me messing about when I was supposedly on punishment (again) sweeping the cloisters. He shouted at me, telling me to report to the master on duty in my boarding house. I knew this was going to be trouble as the master concerned was his close friend, I'll call him Ivan Freeman, one of my house tutors. I was afraid of this man's temper, so I decided not to report to him for fear of his reaction. That evening, while I was doing my prep in the dayroom, I suddenly felt a hand grab a tuft of hair at the back of my head. Freeman lifted me from my seat (he was six feet tall, I was less than five) and screamed in my face: 'Were you told to report to me?'

'Yes, Sir,' I stammered.

'Why didn't you?'

'I forgot, Sir.'

'Forgot?'

With this, he threw me onto the dayroom floor and proceeded to kick me into the masters' duty study, where he picked up a sawn-off hockey stick and thrashed me round my body. He seemed temporarily demented.

That man caned me on a number of occasions (*autres temps, autres mœurs*) and I grew to despise him as much as he seemed to despise me. There was another occasion when, during one lunch break, I managed to persuade the window cleaner to give me a lift around the playground on his motorbike. Freeman was, as usual, in the cricket nets. When he saw me sitting on the back of the speeding bike, holding on for dear life, he blew a proverbial fuse. I was beaten to within an inch of my life, while the poor window cleaner was summarily dismissed. As usual, my friends were keen to see the red marks left on my backside. These incidents were just a couple of examples of the punishments I had to suffer during my junior years. Freeman's pal Stevens taught me chemistry in the third form and I remember his opening line to me as I entered the class at the start of term: 'Oh God, you're in this class. We're not going to get along, are we?'

He put me off chemistry for life. He too caned me on a number of occasions. Did it do me much harm? Did it do me much good? I just don't know if not meeting those two bullies would have radically changed my life. It is often stated that violence begets violence, yet, as far as I am aware, not one of my contemporaries, most of whom were the recipient of corporal punishment at some stage at junior school, has turned to a life of crime or has ever been convicted of violent crimes. The vast majority of us have made a good, honest living despite losing a parent (or both parents in certain cases) at a very young age. The senior school, in particular, taught us the importance of not feeling sorry for ourselves, not to view ourselves as victims just because we had been short-changed early in life and to get out into the world, work hard and use our God-given innate abilities to our best advantage.

One of those two bullies' friends – I'll call him Mr K – who taught French, came into our junior dormitory one night and, stinking of alcohol, proceeded to put his hand under my covers to touch my penis. He proceeded to do likewise to a few of my friends. I remember us boys talking about the incident the next day and, at the morning assembly, the housemaster announcing to all the pupils that the teacher concerned had been merely looking for someone. I can remember to this day saying to my friend Roly Brookman (who went on to play hockey for England) as we lined up for lessons: 'Strange way to look for someone…'

I am almost certain that it was my years locked away at that school with hundreds of other boys that were to have an effect on my sexuality. I vividly remember being attracted to local Cardiff girls at this time and had pretty much a full blown affair with one called Gillian during the school holidays. We would often go for walks and I can remember how sexually excited I would become when we (routinely) disappeared behind the nearest hedgerow. She wasn't the only girl that caught my attention, so I can safely say that I naturally had an attraction to the fairer sex.

As soon as I arrived at my boarding junior school, I was paid attention by some of the older boys. This may have been because of the fact that I had fair skin and red hair. All I know is that a number of boys engaged in mutual masturbation on a pretty regular basis, and I myself was involved. We were simply filling a lacuna – no more, no less. I look back with regret because it was to have a profound effect on the rest of my life. Boarding schools were so different in the 1960s and '70s from what they are now. During my four years at the junior school, we pupils hardly ever left the school premises during term time; to all intents and purposes we were divorced completely from the outside world and this had an undoubted effect on my sexuality.

I didn't particularly enjoy those four years. I missed 'home', such as it was, and I can remember going up to the locked school gates from time to time and looking through at 'normal' life out in the street. I also found the school routine very regimented. We even missed the quarter final of the World Cup, in July 1966, on television, when England beat Argentina by a goal to nil (Geoff Hurst's header), because it was my boarding house's allotted turn for a swim in the outdoor pool between 4.30 and 5 p.m. The routine could not be altered for any event. As we marched in our customary line, the master on duty at the front, carrying our towels to the freezing-cold outdoor swimming pool, we heard a roar from the neighbouring boarding house – England had scored and we'd missed the goal. The only good thing about it, I thought at the time, was at least the teacher on duty had also missed it.

All this stated, junior school wasn't that bad – it was harsh at times, but, on the other hand, there were some kind teachers, the campus had good sporting facilities, I was taught well in the classroom for the most part, no one made me sweep any chimneys, I was not abandoned, I enjoyed the company of my friends and I certainly wasn't living in abject poverty.

I went to the senior school in September 1966 and, with a kind, father-like housemaster, Mr Richard Dilley, I was much happier. The school was less dictatorial and the staff adopted a more caring, friendly relationship with the pupils. It was certainly less brutal. That's not to say I wasn't caned from time to time (even by Mr Dilley, who became a lifelong friend), but at senior school I always understood why I was being punished and I feel, in retrospect, with my character being so mischievous, that I got what I deserved and, ultimately, it was for the best. Any corporal punishment I received at the senior school (commonly known as 'Ston') was administered in a controlled manner, as opposed to the unbridled way it was meted out by some of the staff at the junior school. My experiences at the end of a cane during those formative years were the principal reason why I *never* administered corporal punishment to any pupil during my time in the profession.

I did well at senior school, academically, artistically and in sport. I excelled, particularly in languages, in the classroom. Even though

I didn't take English Language and Literature past O Level, my English teacher, Michael Arthur, was so inspirational and instilled in me a love of books, in particular Shakespeare, for which I shall never be able to thank him enough. I also took on numerous roles in the school plays and I played sports, particularly rugby, for the various school teams. For the most part, I behaved myself at the senior school and, apart from the odd caning (going to a football match without permission one Saturday afternoon to watch Fulham play my team Cardiff City), I created a reasonable impression upon the members of staff. I will be forever indebted to so many of the teachers, particularly those who sacrificed so much of their spare time to coach sports, produce plays and organise trips. Their dedication and selflessness had a profound effect on me and it was because of these teachers and their attitude to their job that I decided to join the profession myself and, once I'd joined, to commit myself wholly during every term for over thirty-five years.

One particular incident that occurred during my time at senior school is marked on my memory. When my mother died in the early 1960s, as mentioned, my eldest brother Stephen disappeared from our family home and my father spent the last months of his own life trying to locate him in London, where it was thought he had gone. After Dad died later that same year and I was fostered to an aunt's care, Stephen's name was never again mentioned in my presence and I thought he had died too. It was only when I was dusting my brother Nick's room (we spent most weekends together where he lived) a number of years later that I came across a letter addressed to Nick from an HM Prison in Suffolk. In the letter, which I surreptitiously read, the writer – Stephen – explained he would soon be released and was going to be living in a hostel in Holland Park Road, London. I scribbled down the address and tucked it away for future reference without telling anyone I'd come across it. The following Easter I travelled to Austria with the school for a two-week skiing trip via the Schools' Travel Service (STS). From Solden in Austria I sent Stephen a card, telling him where I was. He must have done some research because when our group returned to Victoria Station the following week he was there to meet me. He recognised me by the colour of my hair and he immediately broke down in tears. I had to console him. The staff in charge of the trip hastily pulled me away, as the school had been warned that under no circumstances was he to be allowed anywhere near me. It was the one and only time I was to see him before he died at such a young age shortly afterwards.

At the Royal Masonic School there were four of us who studied A Level French, German and Latin in the sixth form: two, Tim Parks and David Blower, subsequently went up to Oxford; I'm not sure what happened to Peter Barclay Jones; while I opted to go to the London Drama Centre in Camden. I was flattered to have been chosen for one of the twenty places available at audition, as hundreds attended. Unfortunately, the South Glamorgan Education Authority, which controlled the grants for those of us who lived in Cardiff back then, would not agree to support me financially, as they considered acting to be a particularly precarious profession, which indeed it was and still is. I nevertheless struggled on in my small shared bedsit in Finsbury Park, cycling to and from the centre each day, but had little or no money, wasn't eating properly and became very down. I hesitate to use that adjective which is so ubiquitous nowadays – 'depressed' – because, until late 2012, I had never been clinically depressed, despite all that had happened to me as a child.

Thus, struggling to survive financially, I decided that it would be better if I used my innate academic ability to go to university, which my family had been encouraging me to do since the previous year, and then join an amateur dramatics group there. I had already been offered a full grant for an academic course.

I applied to Goldsmiths' College, University of London, which had a reputation for being arty, to study French and Education, with the idea of becoming a teacher.

After three glorious years in the capital, probably the most carefree and enjoyable period of my entire life, and qualifying as a teacher, I took up my first post, which was at Crookham Court School, near Newbury, in 1977, teaching French.

Crookham was a delightful little school, set in a Victorian building on the outskirts of the beautiful market town. The boys were well behaved, the staff were friendly and I considered myself lucky to have found such a nigh-on perfect first post. I was there for two years. At the start of my second year, Commander Smithwick, who had appointed me and who was the owner and principal, retired and sold the school to a millionaire called Philip Cadman. The man was eccentric in the extreme and both the discipline among the boys and the general fabric of the place quickly started to deteriorate. I soon decided it was time to seek pastures new.

In 1980, I accepted a post at Cokethorpe School in Witney, Oxfordshire. David Goldsmith, the ex-deputy of Radley College, had just taken over as headmaster and it was he who persuaded me to accept the position of French and English teacher. It was a bigger school than Crookham but I found the staff, most of whom were considerably older than me, very 'cliquey', and when I described one of the clique as a 'pseudo intellectual' (me and my big mouth) behind his back, I was shunned from then on in by a number of colleagues. I never really settled and, despite securing good academic results for my O Level group, coaching rugby to a high standard and producing a first-rate school play (if I say so myself), I decided I wanted to teach in a bigger, more mainstream school, which, coincidentally, Cokethorpe has now become. Their rugby is certainly successful judging by the number of boys who gain representative honours.

The first job I applied for was at Bearwood School, near Wokingham in Berkshire, to teach French and Latin. I was interviewed and appointed within a few days. I was delighted.

Before I left Cokethorpe, the father of one of my tutees, who was the managing director of Tippex UK and who was based in Camberley, Surrey, invited me out to lunch at a very exclusive hotel in Oxford. During the meal, he mentioned that he had heard from Roy Mac, his son, that I was leaving Cokethorpe and had been appointed to teach at Bearwood.

'Are you aware that I tried to get Roy into Bearwood two years ago but he failed the entrance exam?'

'I wasn't aware, no.'

'Mr Warr,' he said, 'I am still very eager to secure a place for my son at Bearwood and I would be most appreciative if, on the next occasion you are at the school, you could put in a good word on our behalf. I would make it worth your while.'

—

I knew what he meant. Naively, I agreed. However, I state categorically that I refused any introductory 'Incentive'.

Having done as requested, I heard nothing more about developments until I arrived at Bearwood late in the summer to deliver my belongings in preparation for the start of the new term, only to find the school bursar waiting for me.

'Mr Warr, please do not unload the furniture van, as our new headmaster would like to see you.'

The hinterland of it all was that when Mr Goldsmith learned Roy, a future Head of School prospect, was leaving to go to Bearwood with my assistance, he read it as treachery and withdrew the superb reference he had written for me. My fate was sealed. Roy still took up his place.

And this was how, instead, I took up a post at St George's in September 1981.

It was in 1981 that I met Hannah, who was to become my future wife. We were introduced to each other by her aunt Barbara who lived (still lives) in Putney, west London. There was an instant mutual attraction and very soon Hannah and I were spending a lot of time together. She was working in London, while I was based in the capital part-time private teaching while scouring the pages of the *Times* educational supplement for a full-time languages post to take up the following September. I was offered a full-time teaching job almost immediately, but declined because the school was too far from the capital. Hannah supported my decisions throughout and was happy when I subsequently accepted a position in Suffolk, which had good access to the capital.

It was not long before we jointly invested in a London property in Hounslow (the proposed sale of which some years later would lead to some acrimony between us).

We were married at Wandsworth Register Office in September 1982 and I am happy to state that, even though Hannah and I divorced a number of years later, her aunt and I have remained very close friends to this day and, as a result of the police's visit to Hannah during their investigation of me, she and I have re-established a good relationship. Every cloud...

At noon on that Saturday in June 1981, I arrived at St George's, a school set in a beautiful Georgian building in a quaint English village called Great Finborough, just outside Stowmarket, Suffolk. The headmaster, who was wearing a tailored suit and a pair of slippers, met me. He was a big man, erudite, with an even bigger personality. We got on immediately.

He asked me during the interview whether I smoked. I inferred from this that he was offering me a cigarette (I was subsequently to learn he wanted to know if I was a smoker). My response was no, but I wouldn't mind a glass of sherry! I was duly given one.

'I'd like to offer you the post of French, Latin and German teacher as from September,' he said.

'I have already been offered a job, as explained.'

'How much are they going to pay you?'

'Seven thousand pounds.'

'We'll give you nine thousand.'

I accepted.

That headmaster, Derek Slade, would in 2010 be sentenced to twenty years' imprisonment for sexual and physical abuse of children in his care.

I can remember him being an intimidating man, not only to the pupils but also to the staff, but also his generous spirit towards me for the most part because he appreciated my hard work and realised my varied talents were good for his business (he was the principal shareholder of the school). He did lose his temper with me on one occasion because he had been under the misapprehension that I had driven the school minibus after drinking alcohol in the local pub. Indeed, he was on the point of sacking me, such was his uncontrolled anger.

I had little or no contact with him on a social level, although it would be subsequently alleged that he and I were friends and had remained friends since he left the school in 1982. This was utter nonsense, but something that was up to me to disprove in a court of law.

Some staff did consider me to be one of his favourites, which I probably was. Why? Because I was young, energetic, enthusiastic and have always, during my thirty-five years of teaching, tried to be loyal to my employers. I gave my all for the pupils in my care at St George's during that brief period in my career. I had been educated at a boarding school myself so I recognised the frustrations that teenagers felt of being away from home, locked within a campus. Accordingly, I tried my best to enrich their boarding experience. To give just one example, on arrival at the school and after setting up the 1st XV rugby team, I set about ascertaining the contact details of the person in charge of Suffolk Schools' County Rugby. I had gleaned from inter-school matches that I had organised that a number of my 1st XV players had a lot of natural ability and I felt that the next step for them would be to be considered for county honours. St George's hadn't even played a competitive rugby match against another school prior to my arrival and, here we were, hardly a term in and already some of the boys were being considered for county representation. I was given the dates of county trials and duly took along a number of players. The day of one of the trials, it happened to be one of the players' birthday, so I arranged to take them all to Rollerbury roller skating rink after the trial match to celebrate.

However, if anyone thinks that my support of the school would include covering up child abuse, let me explain what happened during my very first term at St George's.

I had been at the school for just over a month and I was getting to know a number of the senior pupils. As well as teaching languages, I was also running the 1st XV rugby team, a squad of the oldest pupils, and producing a senior school play. Because of my natural authoritative presence, I was asked to look after the fifth-form (now called Year 11) dormitory, alongside the deputy head and senior master. The school itself comprised pupils from the age of seven up to seventeen. I had little to do with the juniors, other than when I was carrying out one of my school duties in the dining hall. I also taught a few lessons of beginners' German.

I used to enjoy badinage with my fourth-form (Year 10) French group (this didn't change much in my thirty-five years of teaching) and there were a couple of friends in that class in particular who would often enjoy a joke with me during lessons. One morning I noticed that one of the friends (I'll call him 'Nicholas') seemed rather subdued. As he was leaving, I asked him what the matter was. He looked on the point of tears as he shook his head disconsolately and walked out. As his friend was leaving the classroom just behind him,

—

I asked him if he knew what the problem was. He told me that he couldn't really say. It would be Nicholas's decision if he told me or not.

'Just tell him I'm here if he needs me,' I said. 'You both know where I live and you can always visit for tea.'

'Thank you, Sir. I'll let him know.'

Nicholas seemed to have re-found his *joie de vivre* by the next lesson and as no more was said about the matter I put it to the back of my mind.

A week or so later, I was in the local church, at Sunday evensong, and both Nicholas and his pal were sitting in the pew in front of me. As I was singing 'Bread of Heaven' in my usual lusty, enthusiastic Welsh manner, I noticed the two of them were giggling. At the end of the service, I stopped both outside the church, admonished them for their inappropriate behaviour and afforded both a stripe. This was to be added to a chart outside the head's office, which recorded both misdemeanours (stripes) and positive incidents (stars) of each child's daily conduct.

Later on that evening, the head of boarding, Gerard Singer, a French national, came to my room and asked me to follow him to his private accommodation. I obeyed. When we arrived, I saw Nicholas sitting on a sofa.

'Mr Warr,' Singer said, 'could you please tell me why you gave Nicholas a stripe this evening?'

'For inappropriate behaviour, incessant giggling actually, during evensong,' I replied.

With this, Singer erupted in fury at the boy, his eyes staring demonically.

'Do you 'ear that, Nicholas? You bastard! All the things I've done

—

for you and this is 'ow you repay me! You ungrateful bastard!' He proceeded to pick up a half-full bottle of lemonade and hurl it at Nicholas, who held his hands up to his face and curled into a ball for protection.

I swiftly left the scene, trying to make some sense of what I had just witnessed. I had heard rumours about the relationship between this teacher and pupil and what I had just seen convinced me that it was closer than is healthy.

At the end of the following day's French lesson, I quietly asked Nicholas and his friend to stay behind.

'Look, we need to talk,' I told them. 'I couldn't believe what I saw yesterday evening and you need to come clean about what's been going on. I haven't mentioned what I witnessed to anyone in authority but I can't just ignore it. We'll need to arrange a time for a meeting.'

'I have been banned from visiting any other teacher, Sir, so I daren't come to your room,' said Nicholas.

'In that case, next Sunday, the two of you will book out to Stowmarket and I'll pick you up there and we'll go somewhere private to talk.'

So it was that I picked up both pupils and took them to a hotel in Bury St Edmunds for afternoon tea the following weekend.

Nicholas confessed all. He told me about the intense relationship he had been having with Singer for years, indeed, since the time in the late 1970s, when the school was housed in Wicklewood, Norfolk, prior to it moving to its present location in September 1980. He told me that the emotional relationship had become very intense. He also told me that Singer had sexually interfered with one of his brothers.

I was shocked to the core.

'Right, leave this with me. Do not say a word to anyone about this conversation when we get back to school.'

We drove back to Finborough, the two boys chattering away as if they didn't have a care in the world. I drove in silence as I tried to gather my thoughts as to how I was going to deal with this matter. Of course, in any normal circumstances the correct course of action would have been for me to go straight to the head to tell him all I had just learned and leave it to him. However, my sixth sense told me that Slade was too close to Singer for me to trust him completely and that I'd need to hold onto the reins during the next few hours.

However, I knew it was my professional duty to inform the headmaster in the first instance; but I would insist on speaking to the co-owner immediately. I went straight to Slade's study on our return.

'I want to speak to John Sinclair [the joint owner and bursar],' I told him.

'May I ask what about?'

'Something very important.'

'As head, have I not the right to know?'

'All right, I'll tell you. I then want to see John Sinclair.'

I related to him what Nicholas had told me and he stood there open-mouthed.

'I'll call John immediately,' he said.

I waited in his study as he made the call. John duly made his way over.

Gerard Singer had left the country by dawn the following

—

morning. I subsequently learned that the school had given him a grace period of six hours before they would inform the police. Nicholas stayed at John Sinclair's house for the night and he was taken to the local police station by his parents the following morning. Needless to say, Nicholas and his two brothers were withdrawn immediately from St George's and sent to another school to complete their education. Just as the family of Chris (mentioned in the opening pages) was badly affected by his appalling ordeal at the hands of his abuser, such was the case with Nicholas, from whose ordeal his parents never fully recovered. Abuse of one person has a way of permeating entire families like a cancer.

Immediately after Singer's departure, Slade called a whole-school assembly in which he informed the community that Singer had been dismissed for professional misconduct. There was general shock among teachers and pupils but not one other pupil expressed his own personal concern at that time about Singer's behaviour to either a member of staff or a prefect. This was to prove significant over thirty years later as, in 2016, Singer was to stand trial at Ipswich Crown Court for multiple charges of abuse at St George's. That assembly was a perfect opportunity for any abused pupil to speak out: even Slade was clearly on the side of Nicholas, so any complainant would be confident of being believed if he spoke out. In a formal letter to parents, on 19 December 1981, Slade wrote:

> The first major item I have to deal with is one of great seriousness. I regret to inform you that we have discovered that Mr Gerard Singer has … had an affair involving one of the boys.

Not a great deal was 'done', and the boy kept absolutely quiet about the whole thing for a long time; he certainly received vast sums of money from Singer. But eventually he wanted to back out of the relationship. He informed another member of staff, Mr Warr, who at once came to me. At first Singer denied the affair but then, as we pursued the investigation, he admitted it. We informed the boy's parents and they called the police. Regrettably we were unable to prevent him getting out of the country, though he certainly cannot return and attempts may be made to extradite him [which eventually happened in 2015].

Slade left St George's some nine months later, in September 1981, after Roger Cook's Radio 4 *Checkpoint* programme exposed him as a bully, following a variety of complaints by former teachers whom Slade had sacked or 'let go'. Since 2009, the school has been painted as if it were some sort of den of iniquity, which it certainly was not. Most ex-St George's pupils, many of whom are now successful professionals, knew nothing about the routine abuse which was later alleged against Slade. They only knew, just as we teachers knew, that Slade was a bully and, I am sorry to state, in the early 1980s this was not unusual in British schools. None of these other ex-pupils ever heard even rumours that Slade and his personal friends were sexually abusing some of the junior pupils in his private residence, as was later claimed. In such a closed environment as a country boarding school, it is extraordinary that such appalling crimes could be kept quiet among over 300 boys. Any testimonies of the many former pupils who have spoken positively about their time at St George's have been all but disregarded.

—

I knew Slade caned a lot, but in those days caning was legal – part and parcel of the British educational system. No other teachers at St George's caned, so I wasn't that surprised that Slade often had a queue of boys outside his door waiting to answer for their misdemeanours. As for Slade sexually abusing junior pupils, I didn't hear a whisper to suggest this was going on and, as previously stated, neither to my knowledge did any of the other staff, prefects or senior boys. Slade was odd, of this there was no doubt, especially the punishment essay title he often set: 'Whackings I Have Had.' But it would have been impossible for a young teacher with so little power to start accusing my headmaster and employer of abuse when I had absolutely no proof nor intelligence thereof.

Slade himself was a Classics scholar, educated at Oxford. He started teaching in the early 1970s at a school called Duncan Hall, in Norfolk. He then, with a friend, purchased a building at Wicklewood in 1976, also in Norfolk, where he set up a school and installed himself as headmaster. He catered for the sons of servicemen and pitched his fees at precisely the Services' Allowance, to make his own school an attractive proposition. By nature of their job, service personnel were unlikely to be living in one area of the country (or indeed in the country itself) for the length of time their children would spend at school, so a boarding education seemed a sensible option to many. He advertised the school as a cheap, no-nonsense educational environment, based on the best aspects of a traditional British education, focusing on hard work and strict discipline. Starting with a handful of pupils, Wicklewood grew in numbers more quickly than even the confident Slade could have expected, and, in 1980, larger premises were sought. Slade, with banking partner John Sinclair, purchased the former Suffolk Water Board premises, Finborough Hall, near Stowmarket, in Suffolk. In September 1980, Slade transferred all the boys to Finborough and called the school St George's, leaving Wicklewood as St George's girls' sister school. Numbers at the new premises in Suffolk swelled beyond the 300 mark within the first year. Slade's uncompromising approach was admired by many parents and soon word spread that this was an environment in which bad behaviour and lack of respect would not be tolerated. Slade was relishing the fact he had the parents eating out of his hand and was soon administering a regime that brooked no opposition, neither from pupils nor from members of his staff. Indeed, he treated the teachers in his school with the same uncompromising attitude as he did the pupils. Inevitably, by the time I arrived at the school in September 1981, there was a lot of unrest in the staff common room. In my very first week, I was warned not to trust Slade and that, if I crossed him or even questioned his methods, I would be shown the door. One of the bones of contention among some members of staff during the school's first year at Finborough had been the practice, organised by Slade, of bare-knuckle fights between pupils who had a dispute about some matter. Slade, I was told, would referee. When staff members complained, they did not have their 'probationary contract' extended, i.e. they were required to move on. These fights had stopped by the time I arrived. In 1980, the local paper had run a piece headlined 'Bare knuckle fights ban at Suffolk row school', with a sub-heading: 'Parents back disciplinarian headmaster'.

A rumour I do remember which circulated at the time was that Slade had encouraged a ritual whereby a boy who was celebrating

—

his birthday would be stripped naked by other pupils and be made to run around the ornamental gardens. If this ever happened, again, the practice had stopped by the time I arrived in 1981.

Within months of their departure from the school, a number of ex-staff members took their grievances to the BBC and, in September 1982, the journalist Roger Cook, who hosted his own weekly investigative programme on Radio 4 called *Checkpoint*, attacked Slade and his uncompromising, dictatorial *modus operandi* at St George's. It made national headlines; I remember *The Sun* describing St George's on its front page as 'The Wacko School'. Allegations made by the former members of staff, which were broadcast, included descriptions of an autocratic regime; harsh and very frequent punishments; the infamous essay title set by Slade, 'Whackings I Have Had'; the Singer incident; pupils being cowed into not complaining; gullible or unconcerned parents; pupils unable to contact parents, unless urgent; one pupil having bled after a beating; bruising on another boy's bottom; the official bare-knuckle fights; the so-called 'reigns of terror' (whereby the entire pupil body would temporarily lose all privileges); inadequate food; too many hours studying, yet poor public examination results; some dormitories too large; St George's run more as a business than as a school and stringent teaching contract demands.

In a lengthy response to the BBC Board of Governors on 11 September 1982, Slade dismissed each and every complaint, accusing the ex-teachers of dissatisfaction because they could not meet the high standards expected of them by Slade himself. He claimed that they were angry also because they had had their contracts terminated.

Despite this bad publicity, the school continued, albeit with reduced numbers. Slade, however, was relieved of his duties, to be replaced temporarily by his younger and gentler brother Barry. Mr J. J. F. Robinson, MA (Cantab), assumed the reins as head in the summer of 1983. The school did not recover from the crisis of Slade and his departure and I can describe St George's during my final year as arduous – a bit like living in a country that has just had its tyrannical head of state toppled: routine thieving, fires being started, mini riots. I liked to think that, despite all that was going on, I managed to keep firm discipline whenever I was on duty and had the respect of the vast majority of the pupils. Indeed, despite my not being a musician, one of my tasks was to take congregational singing each Friday afternoon in the local church, as the school management felt I was one of the few teachers who could control the body of pupils. And I was probably the youngest teacher there. As was the case throughout my career, I was able to manage even the most unruly pupils by virtue of the fact even these recognised that I was a committed, all-round, dedicated school master.

Looking back, I daresay there are some former pupils who didn't like their time at St George's, who felt intimidated and overcontrolled. I can empathise with their feelings. Slade bullied us teachers as well so I can imagine how frightened the young pupils were of him. I know a number of decent, caring, reasonable ex-pupils now talk to each other regularly on the internet and this coming together is another positive thing to come out of the school. I hope this group continues to offer mutual support and that strong friendships are maintained.

—

CHAPTER TWO

ROYAL HOSPITAL SCHOOL YEARS

He who can, does; he who cannot, teaches.

– George Bernard Shaw

After I left St George's School in October 1983, I took up my appointment as a French and Latin teacher and house tutor at the Royal Hospital School, Holbrook, near Ipswich. RHS is a naval school, set in an idyllic situation on the edge of the River Stour on the Suffolk coast. Its magnificent buildings were built in 1933, as the school moved to the Suffolk coast from Greenwich in south-east London. It catered for the sons of seafarers and the naval traditions were as strong as ever when I joined in 1983. This was a year after the Falklands War and a large number of the boys at the school had had a parent serving in the South Atlantic. The new headmaster was Michael Kirk, whose brief was to modernise the school, which he certainly managed to achieve during his decade-long reign. His very first duty was to interview me on 23 August 1983 (although he always claimed I ended up interviewing him).

One of the initiatives he carried out during his time as head was to change the school's constitution and, following an Act of Parliament, the school was henceforth permitted to accept girls. He looked upon me as a 'modern teacher' as I endeavoured in my own small way to help change the somewhat old-fashioned, insular approach to the running of the school. I organised discos with local girls' schools, as well as regular ice and roller skating trips.

Some of these activities irritated the deputy head of the time, who told me in no uncertain terms that I was wasting my time taking the pupils out of school when the campus facilities were more than adequate. He also told me that, no matter how hard I and the new headmaster tried, the school would never have its ethos changed. He told me repeatedly that a previous headmaster he had worked under, Norman York, would not have allowed me to upset the traditions of the school as I seemed so intent on doing. Basically, he behaved most unpleasantly towards me.

After my appointment as the housemaster of Hawke, one of eleven boarding houses, in 1986, I did all in my powers to broaden the children's horizons by continuing to organise trips out of school whenever possible. For example, I entered the senior pupils of my house into a five-a-side football competition at Portman Road, in Ipswich, to afford them a way of joining in with the local community. I was the first teacher at RHS to organise tutor trips once a term, whereby each tutor would accompany his or her tutees to the cinema, paint-balling, bowling and suchlike. The rather archaic boarding house open-plan, communal shower blocks were replaced by private single showers in my own boarding house in 1989, the first house in the school to be modernised thanks to relentless lobbying by me, supported by the Hawke Parents' Association. Allowing the parents a say in how the boarding house was run was yet another of my initiatives. Due in no small part to my dedication and industry, my boarding house, Hawke, won the Queen's Banner (a competition between the eleven boarding houses based on work, sport, smartness and bearing) five times during my eight years in charge. I impressed upon the pupils in my care the importance of hard work in the classroom and I pushed them to take full advantage of the generous extra-curricular facilities available at school. I wanted them to use their God-given talents at every opportunity. Importantly, my pupils' mental health was always at the forefront of my mind. I was always alert to changes in patterns of behaviour of individual boys. We teach children to be careful of physical dangers they might encounter in daily life to the point we have become very risk-averse as a society, yet we do not seem to understand the mental dangers children are open to. We teach them not to smoke, nor to take drugs; we teach them to clean and floss their teeth and to wear sunscreen on hot days and not to run down narrow corridors, but we don't seem to address the dangers which might arise from inside themselves. I have never been trained in spotting psychological problems but those years in charge of my boarding house taught me to be wary

—

of not only physical but also mental problems, and I became very aware of subtle changes of behaviour. Nearly all the pupils in my boarding house appreciated the care and concern I had for them and responded accordingly. I expected a lot from each and every pupil of my various classes and every member of my boarding house and woe betide anyone who slacked or was obstructive. But, in return, in terms of dedication, I gave my all. In whatever areas I came up short as a teacher, effort and dedication were not among them. I like to think all of my pupils were as well prepared for their public examinations as they could possibly be and my boarding house was a caring, well-disciplined, efficient place in which to live. It was certainly the most popular house among the pupil body. As various houses were closed to be refurbished or to accommodate the entry to the school of girls, the high number of boys in those houses who opted to transfer to Hawke, compared to the others, was almost embarrassing.

In April 1993, nearly ten years after joining RHS, an incident that was to be the genesis to all my troubles occurred. At that time, despite my comparative youth, I was being encouraged by senior staff at RHS, following the outstanding success of my boarding house, to start applying for headships. I was within a cusp of being appointed headmaster of Pierrepont School, in Surrey, in 1992, the very first post I applied for. Educational agents Gabbitas and Thring had afforded me an A grade to the school as recommendation. Had I been a bit older, the job at Pierrepont would have been mine. The following year, just when my career was about to hit the top and I was on the point of securing my first headship, I was brought down to earth with a bang.

In April 1993, two pupils from my boarding house were accused of selling drugs to some of the junior girls. The deputy headmaster sent for me to tell me the news and I was to inform the two concerned that the headmaster wanted to see them immediately. From the tone of the deputy head's voice, I inferred it was about as serious as school disciplinary issues get. When I got back to the boarding house, I told the pair to go upstairs and pack their bags, as they were more than likely to be going home, maybe for good. They were then to report to the head's study. As it happened, both were suspended for the rest of the term and told they would be allowed to return to school for the summer term. I had become overwrought because I loathe anything to do with illegal drugs (the tragedy of my eldest brother having a big influence upon my attitude) and I had erroneously anticipated their expulsion. I should have kept my feelings in check and I have regretted my extreme anger ever since. My card had been marked by the two miscreants.

Both duly returned to school the following term. One of them was in his GCSE year, the other the year below, Year 10. The older one had wanted to return for the sixth form the following September, but I had intervened with the school authorities to prevent this. The boy concerned had been the source of much bullying in my boarding house and was at the centre of a number of house disciplinary problems. That summer term passed by without a hitch as it turned out, and I was surprised that the two hadn't caused problems for me, as I had been warned they were going to by some of their contemporaries. At any rate, this was the case until the final night of the school year, the last day of June, in 1993.

It had been a splendid final Saturday with the usual formal

ceremonies: Speech Day prize giving and, finally, in-house celebrations during the evening to mark the end of another school year. When the party had concluded, I retired to my bungalow with an assortment of guests who were staying with me for the weekend, including my own former housemaster and his wife, Mr and Mrs Dilley. As we were enjoying a 'night cap', there was a knock on the front door and I went to see who it was. To my surprise, the head and his deputy were standing there waiting to be admitted.

'Would you like a drink?' I asked.

'This is not a social call,' was the curt riposte from the head, Mr Kirk.

Anticipating troublesome news, I showed them both through to the kitchen and I closed the door, so as not to be overheard by my guests in the lounge.

'Simon, we have received a complaint about your behaviour in one of the dormitories last night.'

'What? What sort of behaviour?' I asked.

'We have reason to believe you touched two of the boys under their bedclothes.'

I couldn't believe what I was hearing. 'This is preposterous. There is not an iota of truth in this. None.'

'Were you sloshed?' asked the head. I remember the word 'sloshed', which he used, to this day.

'No, I wasn't sloshed. May I ask who the boys concerned are?'

'I'm afraid I cannot say at this stage. The outcome is you will not be allowed to stay in your school accommodation tonight.'

'Oh, yes I am. I refuse to leave my home on the final night of the school year.'

'Well, we've been told by social services that you cannot remain near the accusers in the boarding house.'

'In that case, you're going to have to remove them because I am not going. If they want me to leave, they're going to have to forcibly remove me.' I would not be budged.

The head and his deputy both departed and I returned to the lounge, ashen-faced. When I explained what had happened there was stunned silence.

'It is utterly preposterous, there's absolutely no truth in it.' I could hardly utter my words.

The following morning I learned that one of the accusers was one of the miscreants who had been suspended the previous term. It was beginning to make sense.

Two of the many parents, Mr and Mrs Davies, who were staying locally for the weekend, came to see me before they left for home. By now, everybody had heard about what had happened and there was shock from the entire community (save the conspirators, of course). Mr Davies had been using the outside toilets the previous evening and he informed me that, as he was sitting in one of the cubicles, he had heard two pupils talking in the urinal area – words to the effect of: 'We must keep this absolutely quiet, otherwise we could be in big trouble.' He recognised one of the voices as the second boy who had been suspended and he was talking to a close friend of his, whom I subsequently learned was also involved in the conspiracy. When Mr Davies rejoined the barbecue celebrations, he told his wife that this second boy was once again 'up to mischief'. He didn't know what.

It was now pretty clear what had taken place. There had been

—

a plot – three boys were involved, the two who had been suspended and one other, whose identity it didn't take long to establish. This third boy had first selected a timid Year 10 boy, who had been consistently bullied by some of his peers throughout his time at the school, and who had a reputation of being a very heavy sleeper. He had visited his bed in the middle of the night and touched him lightly under the bedclothes, hanging around by his bed until he awoke. Then the perpetrator walked off. It was dark in the dormitory, of course, and he knew he couldn't be identified, but wanted to hang around long enough for the sleeping boy to come to his senses and realise something had indeed happened and be aware that someone was leaving the scene.

The next morning at breakfast, the first boy who had been suspended announced that someone had put his hand under *his* bedclothes in the dead of night and, of course, just as they hoped, the timid boy said he thought he, too, had been touched. All that was required now was one of the two 'victims' to put in a complaint, which was what happened later that day.

But, even though I knew as early as that following morning what had really happened, with the 1989 Children Act now in force, no one at the school was permitted to make any investigations, as the social services and the police would have to deal with the matter. All the pupils departed that day for their two months' summer holiday.

It took the police six weeks to contact me by telephone – I was at my London flat and it was mid-August, and the words of the officer in charge, DS Corble, will be for ever etched in my mind: 'Could you pop in to see me tomorrow, Mr Warr, so we can get this all done and dusted?'

'Done and dusted' implied to me the police were not giving these allegations any credence and this would be the end of the matter. I drove the following day to the police station in Ipswich and, no sooner had I entered, I realised it was far from 'done and dusted'.

'This is the *Z Cars* bit,' he said, as he started to read me my rights. I had not even organised a solicitor. DS Corble told me that I could have one but I would have to wait a few hours for his or her arrival. But, as I was driving on to Birmingham afterwards and wanted to get away pretty promptly (as DS Corble knew), I decided to answer his questions without representation. I was innocent so I had nothing to hide, was my logic.

I gave over 100 pages of testimony and throughout the interview I didn't falter once, even though Corble attempted repeatedly to catch me out. The only error I made (according to my subsequent brief) was admitting to the fact that I had enjoyed a few drinks on that particular evening, the Friday when the incidents supposedly took place. The police had what they'd been after: a weakness in my story, which they could use to strengthen their case. Although the alleged behaviour seemed totally out of character with how I had run my boarding house for many years, the fact that I had been drinking alcohol might explain the extraordinary lapse in judgement, they reasoned.

I was charged the following November on two counts of indecent assault.

I'm not sure how the truth started to dawn on the timid boy who had been touched, but early in the New Year he withdrew his complaint and I was left to face the charge of assaulting one of the boys who had been suspended. During the nine months

I waited for the case to come to court, the police repeatedly visited him to check whether he was sticking by his claim, that he was sure it was I who had visited his bed that night. He said on each occasion that he was absolutely positive. What he didn't mention at any stage was that his girlfriend had visited the dormitory from one of the other houses that same night – in direct contravention, of course, of school rules.

When the case reached court in August 1994, I had a number of pupils lined up to testify just what had been going on in the dormitory that particular night. I also had the parent to testify what he had overheard in the toilets, although they weren't ultimately required as it turned out, because under cross-examination the complainant finally changed his story and the case was dismissed.

I returned to my post at the Royal Hospital School the following month, September 1994, and was welcomed back with open arms by both my colleagues and the body of pupils. The complainant's parents wrote to the headmaster, Michael Kirk, to express their disquiet that I had been welcomed back despite the fact that my accuser's younger brother was still attending RHS as a pupil (the accuser himself had left). The head wrote back to them immediately to say he fully understood their anxiety and they were free to withdraw the brother straightaway and they would not be obliged to pay a term's fees in lieu, as was standard practice. The brother stayed on, unsurprisingly. It wasn't long before I passed him in the classroom block corridor. Surrounded by his friends, he looked straight at me and, smiling, said loudly: 'Good morning, Sir.'

I inferred from this that he didn't think I was guilty of having inappropriately touched his brother!

—

I was no longer the housemaster of Hawke but decided to concentrate on my classroom teaching, rugby coaching and school
drama productions. Between 1994 and 2012, I went on to coach
another fifty sports teams, to direct and produce over twenty full-
scale musicals, plays and drama festivals and, for a number of years,
to run the whole school extra-curricular activities programme.
I became a Year 11 senior school tutor and I like to think I enjoyed
enormous success in that aspect of my job. Academically, if GCSE,
AS and A Level successes are anything to go by, I feel I achieved
a great deal and helped many pupils to secure grades far higher
than they were originally anticipating. The number of disciplinary
issues I had to deal with, in the classroom, in the boarding house
and among my tutor groups, was minimal. I had the respect of
all but a few of the pupils and I shall never forget those glorious
years post-1994.

It wasn't just my teaching career that was in full swing. After
appearing on *Noel's House Party* on BBC 1 in 1997, part of which
was filmed at BBC Radio Suffolk, the station offered me a Saturday
afternoon sports reporting job the following year. I have worked for
them ever since. I can honestly say I have loved working at BBC
Radio and will be forever grateful for all the help and support I
received from my colleagues at Radio Suffolk during my time of
trouble. Further to being regularly on radio, I was often filming for
various television programmes during the holiday periods in the
noughties. My big break came in 2003, when I saw an advertisement
in the *Times Educational Supplement*. Twenty Twenty Television
was going to make a five-part series for TV entitled *That'll Teach
'Em*, which was planning to recreate school life back in the 1950s.

The production company was looking for seven staff members. This *TES* advert was repeated on Channel 4. Hundreds of teachers applied, of course, and I was one of them. After going through four rounds of interviews and auditions, the producer rang me in June that year to offer me the post of Foreign Languages teacher on the programme. It was an unmitigated success and its audience was the second highest of all Channel 4 programmes that summer, behind *Big Brother*. We staff members had a whale of a time filming at Royal Grammar School, High Wycombe, and we were treated extremely well by the production company, who tended to our every need. I had my own runner and, when asked if I needed any wine to drink (we were not allowed off the campus), I said I'd quite like a box of wine, referring to the cheap boxes you can buy at the supermarket. When I returned to my private accommodation that evening, a case of top-quality wine was awaiting me. The series courted a lot of publicity and from my room I repeatedly caught sight of photographers hiding in the bushes. I loved the experience and obviously impressed my television employers because, in 2005, I was promoted to headmaster. This series was filmed at St Joseph's College in Ipswich. I liked the way that, such was the production company's faith in me, they were even consulting me on major policy decisions. I had recommended St Joseph's. The 2005 series was another triumph. Inevitably, being on television brought me attention from the public, some of it bizarre. One woman kept sending me 'presents' and even turned up at RHS on one occasion. Fortunately, I wasn't on the premises at the time. There is no doubt that my appearances on television and radio are inextricably linked with what subsequently happened to me in 2012.

RHS is situated so remotely that the school is a village in itself, having its own discrete community, a community that accepted me to its heart both in 1983 (save the deputy head) and again in 1994. The thirty years I spent at RHS were immensely fulfilling; I loved the school and, for the most part, it loved me.

The story began circa 2010, when I received an email, out of the blue, from an ex-pupil of St George's School. I'll call him David Praver. He introduced himself to me, letting me know that he had been at St George's. The email he sent was unpleasant and menacing in tone, in which he asked me (I paraphrase), given the fact I could argue rationally and eloquently on TV and radio about various important issues, why I had not used my strong opinions to stand up for him and his contemporaries when they were being bullied by the headmaster, Derek Slade. The first thought to cross my mind was why on earth this person had taken it upon himself to contact me. Being principally a teacher in the senior part of St George's, I had only limited involvement with him or any of his contemporaries. I taught some junior German but, this aside, my interaction with junior pupils was minimal. I did remember 'Praver' as being probably the most anarchic and disruptive pupil I had ever come across in my thirty-five years of teaching. His behaviour was, on occasion, out of control and I was not alone in my view that he should not have been at a mainstream school, such was his delinquency. On 30 December 2008, 'Praver' had posted comments on a former pupils' website, boasting: 'I got 160 stripes [given to a pupil for misbehaviour] in one week, which was the school record.' 'Praver' was the *chef d'orchestre* among the former pupils who subsequently made a multitude of allegations

—

against Derek Slade. He contacted over 200 alumni and arranged a reunion for August 2009 at the school, which a small number attended. The police were aware of this reunion, so there can be no doubt about why 'Praver' had arranged it. He went on to claim that the subsequent statements made against Slade to the police were not discussed during that evening's gathering. He states: 'At no time did anyone at the reunion discuss anything to do with the [Slade] case, nor did they discuss anything to do with any personal statements that may have been made or were to be made.'

'Praver' spent only a short period of time at the school while Derek Slade was the headmaster, but was among those awarded compensation for abuse suffered at Slade's hands. I witnessed him being caned on only one occasion and that was by Barry Slade, who had succeeded his brother Derek as headmaster in 1982 and who had a much less volatile personality. By 'Praver''s account, Derek Slade had not only bullied him, but had also seriously sexually abused him.

In the email sent to me, 'Praver' made it clear that he was not accusing me of abuse. His criticism was dereliction of duty on my part in not protecting the younger pupils from Derek Slade. I thought this was an odd accusation, given that I had been a teacher in Slade's school for a relatively short period of time compared with a number of older, more experienced teachers – many of whom had been working with him for years. I was puzzled, too, as to why he had singled me out because, apart from anything else, my chief responsibility was for the very senior boys. I told 'Praver' that, had I suspected anything untoward, I would have mentioned it to John Sinclair, the joint owner of the school; indeed, John and his wife Sue are still friends of mine. 'Prayer''s response was to tell me I was not fit to be associated with such a fine couple. This is now ironic seeing that he has spent the best part of the past four years attacking John Sinclair's integrity.

One Sunday afternoon in October 2012, I happened to be on duty in a boarding house at RHS when one of the pupils came to tell me that he and some friends had found a blog about me on the internet. Slightly embarrassed, I went to have a look. I saw my photo with the accompanying legend: 'WANTED'. The blog proceeded to explain that I was a danger to children and, what's more, that I had had a homosexual affair with a man who beats up children. The pupils who showed me the blog were laughing but, such was their disbelief, they forgot all about it within minutes and never again mentioned it in my presence. In a closed environment like a boarding school, if those pupils had any suspicion that the blog had any sinister substance to it, the information would have reached all parts of the community within twenty-four hours. I rang the host of the offending site, 'Friends of Crookham Court', on which the blog had been posted, and asked him to remove it immediately. He agreed. He refused to disclose the name of the author of the absurd allegations.

A small band of former St George's pupils spent the next two years attacking former St George's teachers. Among the hundreds of posts on the 'Former Pupils of St George's' website:

> What is the score to date? How many convicted and how many under active investigation?

—

> MP ('Praver'): 'As far as convictions, that would be 2. Soon to be 3 [a reference to me]. It would be great to be 4 and if my mind [is] correct we have had one top himself and another attempted suicide.

'Praver' had shown himself to be totally cold and matter-of-fact when relating reports of those accused of abuse (not yet proven) or who had attempted or committed suicide. The man has spent years complaining of the bullying behaviour of Slade. He was indifferent to the fate which I could suffer, that I could go to jail or myself commit suicide from the shame to which he wished me to be exposed.

Many campaigners against child abuse (even only alleged child abuse) bestow upon themselves a quite extraordinary degree of power, and this role is now well established in British culture. Some campaigners are so zealous in their pursuit of an alleged abuser that they assume that any action they take in their pursuit could not possibly be deemed itself to be bad, cruel or immoral. This was no doubt the reason why the small cabal of ex-St George's campaigners thought nothing wrong in exhorting me to kill myself ('best Christmas prezzie ever') after my arrest. It is described as 'the psychology of righteousness'. Even the most depraved criminals within our prisons take the moral high ground in their attitude towards child abuse offenders. You would think that someone who has slashed another human being's face with a knife over a drugs dispute would consider himself unsuitable to judge the morality of others: not the case. Thus, these feelings of righteousness often overpower moral sensitivity. These people are incapable of even considering the possibility that any action taken in a pursuit to destroy the life and reputation of even an *alleged* abuser could conceivably be wrong or unjust in itself. Such is their mindset that some adopt a sort of 'righteous duplicity', which I certainly think took place in some of the convictions made against Derek Slade. The man acted pretty monstrously, for sure, but was he guilty of *all* the allegations made against him by the campaigners? This is a question that has tormented me over the past three years, unsurprisingly, since two of his accusers blatantly lied about me. We'll never know the absolute truth, though, because Slade died in Norwich Prison early in 2016.

'Praver''s unrestrained expatiation on the horrors of his time at St George's was followed by a number of nasty emails sent to various media outlets by my principal accuser 'A' and 'an anonymous source', all unbeknown to me at the time, which are detailed in Chapter Four.

Thus, I had more than an inkling that dark forces were at work behind my back, and not just 'Praver'. I expressed this disquiet to a friend and senior colleague at RHS just a few weeks before my arrest.

CHAPTER THREE

———

THE ARREST

The road to hell is paved with good intentions.

— JOHN RAY

*(Unfortunately, hell is precisely the place where
most innocent people accused of child abuse quickly
find themselves.)*

The 672 days from hell began at 7.15 a.m. on Tuesday 18 December 2012. I was asleep at my school house in Holbrook, Suffolk. It was the second day of the Christmas holidays.

Suddenly there was loud banging on the kitchen door. I sat up in bed and looked at the clock, trying to gather myself. Half naked but for my dressing gown, I descended the stairs.

The banging continued, becoming progressively louder. From behind the kitchen door, I called: 'Who is it?'

———

'The Suffolk Police – open the door.'

In a state of shock, I struggled to remember where I had put the key. With fumbling fingers, at last I managed to unlock the door and immediately four police officers barged their way past me. The fifth stood at my shoulder, towering above me, as I stood with bare feet.

'Simon Warr, you are under arrest for the alleged sexual abuse of "A", at St George's School, around 1981. You do not have to say anything but anything you do say may be taken down and given in evidence.'

I was stunned yet not totally surprised, having been the recipient of that endless stream of internet vilification during the previous couple of years.

Already the officers were ransacking my personal effects. I looked through the kitchen hatch into the dining room to see a police-woman pulling my carefully ordered books off their shelves and then piling them, in a disorderly manner, onto the dining table.

A mobile phone belonging to one of the officers rang and I heard her say: 'I'll ask him. One of the bedroom doors at your London flat is locked – where's the key?'

I now realised my other home was being searched simultaneously.

'It's in the top-left drawer of the desk in the lounge.'

I was shaking, such was the shock.

I remember saying to one of the arresting officers as he stood guard, 'Do you really enjoy your job? Barging into people's private lives in this way, surprising them when they are asleep?'

'As a matter of fact, I do,' he replied. 'By the way, I also enjoy listening to your football reports on the radio. Now, we'd like you to dress and accompany us to the station.'

—

I went back upstairs, accompanied by another officer, where I was supervised as I washed and dressed. All the while, I heard the sound of cupboards and drawers being thoroughly searched downstairs.

I was then accompanied to a waiting car at the rear of my property at the heart of the school and driven off. I was grateful they had waited for the school holidays to begin before arresting me (even though it was only one week before the usually festive occasion of Christmas). I looked out of the police car window as we made our way out of the school and saw I was being watched by a couple of school maintenance workers. News of my arrest would spread within hours.

On the way down the hill into Ipswich there was heavy rush-hour traffic. The officer sitting next to me, trying to make conversation, asked, 'Is it usually like this?'

'I don't know,' I answered. 'I never drive into town early in the morning.'

I was lost in thought. My friend, Michael Simmonds, was due to come over at lunchtime. Would I be released in time? How would I let him know what had happened, to warn him not to come? There was a local football match that evening, which I was covering for the radio, but this didn't start until 7.45 p.m. Would I be free in time?

Eventually, at approximately 8.15 a.m., the car arrived at the barrier at the entrance of Martlesham Police Station, to the east of the town.

'We have a prisoner,' said the driver into the intercom.

The barrier rose.

I was taken straight in to the state-of-the-art station and led to the main desk, where I was first asked to confirm who I was and

—

then told to hand over my belt, shoes and personal belongings. A desk sergeant booked me in and I then had my fingerprints and DNA taken. I was still in a daze. Could this really be happening or was I about to wake up?

At about 8.45 a.m. I was put into a cell, where I was told to wait until called.

'We have sent for the duty solicitor; we'll return when we're ready to interview you.'

I perused my surroundings: a cell with a single 'bed' and a very small sink where I was able to drink from a tap. Nothing else.

I waited and waited, recumbent on the excuse for a bed, for hour upon hour. I could hear noises emanating from the surrounding cells, mainly from a man screaming to be let out, presumably having been incarcerated for being drunk and disorderly the previous night. Every so often, someone opened the flap on the heavy cell door, peering in to check I was still alive. I lay on the bed, mulling over in my mind the enormous impact this was going to have upon my life. Would it be a short-lived affair? Perhaps someone would come to my cell at any moment to tell me there had been an enormous error; the person who had made this allegation (I couldn't even remember the accuser's name) had called to say he had made a mistake; he had identified the wrong person. Perhaps, on the other hand, all this would lead to my personal and professional destruction. I felt pretty desperate as I kept looking at the clock on the wall.

Finally, at 1.40 p.m., without so much as a cup of coffee, I was called for interview. I was led from the cell into a small room and asked to sit behind a table. Even though I found the entire situation bizarre and distressing, I remained confident that once the police had made all the necessary inquiries and had listened to what I had to say, they would realise something didn't add up and that there'd been a misunderstanding. I submitted to the procedure somewhat confused. I had been arrested, brought to a police station, fingerprinted and had my DNA taken, locked in a cell for hours and was now having to answer questions about something I knew had not taken place – and it was barely past lunchtime.

One of two officers addressed me: 'What I need to tell you at this point is that I am cautioning you that you do not have to say anything but it may harm your defence if you do not mention when questioned something which you later rely on in court and anything you do say may be given in evidence.'

Haven't we ordinary folk always been told that if you are innocent you should answer all the police's questions openly and frankly, as, if you have nothing to hide, it can only help you? What's more, your interrogators will appreciate the fact that you are answering all their questions and afford you the commensurate respect? How wrong to assume this! If I had the experience again, I would say nothing other than 'no comment' to every question. I was treated with cursory respect, even though I answered all that they threw at me both politely and positively. Their response was to listen intently to all I said, waiting for me to say something that might assist their own purpose, which was to prosecute me. Being full, cooperative and frank didn't help me a jot.

I'll give you just one example. During this first interview I was asked who from St George's I had kept in touch with during these intervening thirty years. The reason they asked me this was

—

because I was arrested on the proverbial coattail of the conviction for physical and sexual abuse of the autocratic ex-headmaster of St George's, Derek Slade – all part of 'Operation Racecourse'. As mentioned earlier, the police had been told erroneously by some scurrilous former pupils that I was a friend of Slade and had kept in touch with him during the intervening period. (I realised this was one of the internet group's tactics because a supposed 'author' had contacted me the previous year to inform me he was writing a book about various famous cases and was wondering if I could tell him how to contact Derek Slade. I replied by email to explain I had not seen or heard from Derek Slade since he left St George's.)

I answered this question, like all of the police interrogator's questions, without hesitation: 'I've kept in touch with the senior master, David Harding, pretty regularly over the years, and occasionally I've visited Stephen and Val Land, although not for many years now. I've also visited Derek Sl— sorry, John and Sue Sinclair, the current owners of the school.'

So, I had accidentally said 'Derek Sl', obviously short for Slade. It was simply a slip of the tongue. The police interviewers had mentioned his name to me repeatedly during their questioning, as they seemed determined to establish that Slade and I were friends. Was it so surprising I should make this slight error? Nevertheless, it came back to haunt me at the trial, as the Prosecuting Counsel brought up the fact that I had made this slip and attempted to claim that I was telling the truth, that I had indeed kept in touch with Derek Slade, and that I would not have made this error if it weren't true. He claimed that, in an unguarded moment, I had been speaking the truth.

If I had said nothing at all at that original interview, I would not have been compromised. They used a whole raft of information I had provided them with during various interviews to attempt to build a case against me. I learned all this to my cost.

Here is a transcript of that first interview.

Interview One On Tuesday 18 December, 1.45 p.m.

DC KC: OK this interview is being recorded and it may be given in evidence if the case is brought to trial. I'm DC KC (name withheld), Detective Constable from the Child Abuse Unit at Bury St Edmunds, and also present is my colleague DC HK, based at the Child Abuse Investigation Unit, in Ipswich. Could you state your full name please for the recording?

SW: Simon Roderick Warr.

DC: And also present is…

MS: I'm Michael Stevenson, acting solicitor.

DC: You were arrested earlier this morning at your home address on suspicion of indecent assault on 'A'. So we are going to talk about 'A' and about the specific allegation. But, initially, what I would like to do is just go through some of the background things, just so we can build a picture and find out how you came to be at St George's School. Is that OK?

SW: Yes. I was educated at the Royal Masonic School in Bushey, Hertfordshire, between 1962 and '72. My parents had died when I was six, so I was sent away to school. After that I went to drama school for a short time and then I went to Goldsmiths' College, at the University of London, where I trained to become a teacher. I went to St George's in 1981.

DC: Can you remember what time of year you started?

SW: At the start of the academic year, in September. I had been offered a couple of other jobs but, during my interview with Derek Slade, he offered me more money.

DC: And what did you teach at St George's?

SW: French, Latin and German. I also produced the school plays. I also introduced competitive rugby at the school.

DC: Did you have any other responsibilities apart from your teaching?

SW: Duties, that sort of stuff: looking after the dorms, certain dorms.

DC: When you were at the school, where did you reside?

SW: I had a room in the middle of the school.

DC: I think I should clarify that St George's is now called Great Finborough. You were never at the other premises, Wicklewood?

SW: No.

DC: Would you like to say which part of the school you worked in?

SW: For the short time I was at the school, I worked with Years 10 and 11. I was a tutor in a dorm 11. It used to be called fifth form.

DC: What sort of ages are we talking about?

SW: Fifteen- and sixteen-year-olds.

DC: Did you ever have responsibility for the younger boys?

SW: No. I had nothing to do with the younger part of the school, except that occasionally at weekends, if I was on duty, they'd come and ask permission to go out of school and stuff. What I can tell you is I can't even remember 'A'.

DC: We'll come on to that...

SW: You could give me the names of thirty to forty boys and I would remember them. I would remember people like McMenamin and the Brooks twins because I had daily dealings with them I used to run the 1st XV rugby team. They were mostly fifth formers and the odd sixth former. And this has continued throughout my career. At my present school, Royal Hospital School, RHS, they have a junior house. I've nothing to do with it. I now teach Year 8 in the classroom because of staffing balance but my skills have always been used with the older pupils.

DC: Right, just to clarify and make sure I understand you correctly, what you're saying is that while you were at St George's you had no dealings or responsibilities for the young…

SW: Well, I had some dealings with them, occasionally on duty, you know, you have to go round and make sure everyone is behaving properly.

DC: But teaching, let's just talk about teaching. It was just the older boys?

SW: Mostly the older ones, yes.

DC: When you say that you sometimes had responsibilities when you were on duty, what would that entail?

SW: Well, it was usually at weekends. There was a team of two or three people. We used to take assembly and had to supervise meals and give permission for any pupils to sign out to Stowmarket. I can't remember the exact procedures.

DC: So, did you enjoy your time at St George's?

SW: Loved it. Absolutely loved it and when I left there I remember I was in floods of tears. I had told the school I had been offered another job and they made me stay until my contract expired, at half term. I was supposed to give at least three months' notice.

So I left half way through a term. A group of the older boys, some of my rugby players, they formed a sort of guard of honour either side of the road as I drove out. I cried all the way over to RHS.

DC: Was there a particular reason why you left St George's?

SW: It was just the fact that I was getting involved with county rugby and I was told of a job becoming vacant at RHS, which was a bigger and better school. More secure for my career.

DC: What sort of background did the pupils at St George's have?

SW: Military. I was impressed with Derek Slade at the interview. He was an Oxford graduate. I know he's been in a lot of trouble but when you first meet him… he impressed me.

DC: Would you say you were a popular teacher at St George's?

SW: I think I was, yeah, but I don't set out to be popular. You can talk to any generation at RHS. I am strict. I expect high standards and the pupils are aware of this. Recently a film company was thinking of doing a documentary at our school. I don't know whether you watched *Educating Essex* last year? Anyway, it's the same company. The TV producers took a group of pupils for a walk and they asked them, 'Who is your scariest teacher?' And they replied 'Mr Warr.' They then asked them, 'Who is your favourite teacher?' and they answered 'Mr Warr.' You have to be strict with the pupils otherwise they'll trample all over you. And, don't forget, I was young at St George's and I was put in charge, at times, of three to four hundred pupils. It was a hell of a responsibility. I had to be on the ball. Judging from a few of the emails I have received in recent years, some of them thought I was *too* strict. Some were frightened of me, they claim.

DC: How does that make you feel knowing that some of them were frightened of you?

SW: The context was we were under strict orders ourselves to maintain good discipline. I was in fear for my job as well. Some allege I was a big friend of Derek Slade. I remember one occasion when I went to the local pub before driving the school minibus to Stowmarket station to pick up a group of seniors. He called me in to his study the following day because I had been seen at the pub. I hadn't drunk any alcohol but Slade didn't wait for an explanation. 'If you ever drink before driving the school minibus, you'll be out on your ear, do you understand?' All the staff were sent letters about dress code etc. So, you didn't want to fall on the wrong side of him.

DC: What were the ages of the pupils at the school?

SW: From eight up to about seventeen.

DC: Did you ever supervise the boys when you were on weekend duty? What was the situation when they went for showers and when they had to get up in the mornings?

SW: I don't recall ever watching any boys showering. When I went to RHS it was standard practice, for fear of them misbehaving, but I never stood and watched them, ever. I mean after games at St George's I had to get to my next class. It was only the seniors who I took for games, I seem to remember. I ran the 1st XV. There wouldn't be any juniors involved.

DC: You spoke of discipline. What sort of discipline was issued at St George's?

SW: I was caned when I was at school. Personally, I've never had a reason for it. When I went to RHS, lots of staff were caning: more caning than at St George's because only Slade caned there.

DC: Did you ever see Derek Slade cane anyone at St George's?

—

SW: No. I saw them lined up outside his study. I didn't know what was going on in there: none of my business.

DC: So, how did a child come to be caned by Derek Slade?

SW: I suppose they had been given demerits, or whatever the term was.

DC: Did you ever send a child there for a particular reason?

SW: None that I can remember. I used to deal with my own discipline myself. They usually got the sharp end of my tongue.

DC: You touched upon the fact that Slade has been in trouble. You're aware of his recent court appearances. Have you been in contact with him recently?

SW: I haven't spoken to him for thirty years.

DC: What would you say your relationship with him was like?

SW: He liked me because I was a good teacher. I was good at my job. Nevertheless, as I mentioned earlier, he could blow up like a volcano. You had to be very careful. But, by and large, we got on well. Look what I did there … school plays in the village hall, rugby coaching. Go and speak to the ex-pupils who I taught and directed and coached. I think I was superb on duty considering my age. I'm a very good classroom teacher, which I have proved throughout my career. I organised trips, which they hadn't had before I went to St George's, to Rollerbury and such like. I took them to Clacton ice rink on the pier. I even went with a coach-load on my own. I had been away at boarding school myself and I knew what it was like. I was sent away to boarding school at the age of eight, as both my parents had died.

DC: Did you have a family then, Mr Warr?

SW: I lived with my aunt. My brother went to live with another aunt and then my eldest brother died because he took to drugs when my parents died. We had a pretty traumatic early life. But I'm not making excuses. All I'm saying is I could empathise with them being away from home and I really went out of my way to enrich their lives. If you have enough time, please go and speak to all those pupils who I had daily dealings with at St George's.

DC: You've said that Derek Slade was a character, how do you think the school was run?

SW: Tyrannical would be an appropriate word. Everybody was frightened of him. I certainly was … fearful for my job if I stepped out of line. He got rid of a lot of teachers. He employed them on one-year contracts at a time of recession. I didn't want to lose my job. I toed the line.

DC: Do you recall the names of any other staff who were there at the time?

SW: David Harding was my best friend. Debbie somebody, Katie Heard, Bernard McGuinn…

DC: Were you aware other teachers had been arrested?

SW: Alan Williams, yeah.

DC: And you knew Mr Williams, did you?

SW: I knew him. He was a music teacher.

DC: How did you get along with him?

SW: Great. He was a nice chap, I liked him.

DC: You also mentioned that you remember certain pupils. Do any stand out?

SW: I liked Steve McMenamin, Danny King, Steve Clarke, Donny Cook, Jamie Stannard. The picture that's been painted of St George's is not one I recognise.

—

DC: Are you in contact with any students or teachers from that era now?

SW: I get a Christmas card from David Harding but I haven't seen him for a while. We met in London for a meal. Of course, Derek Sl… I mean John Sinclair. I'm a very good friend of John, John and Sue Sinclair.

DC: He wasn't the principal at the time?

SW: No, he was … that reminds me, his son James was a pupil at the school. John was one of the school governors.

DC: I know you're still in contact with them.

At this point in the interview SW tells the story of Mr Gerard Singer and his relationship with one of the pupils, called Nicholas, described in detail earlier in the book.

The interview subsequently returns to the running of St George's School.

DC: Were you ever aware that Derek Slade was doing some things other than caning?

SW: Oh God, no. I mean, learning of that was a complete and utter shock. I didn't even witness him caning anyone.

DC: OK. If we can talk about the allegation in relation to 'A'. Do you recall 'A'?

SW: No, I don't. I have no recollection of 'A'.

DC: Would you be able to describe him?

SW: No. I haven't got a clue. I don't even know what year he was in, how old he was, what he…

DC: He was born in 1970, which would have made him eleven or twelve.

SW: Well, I had nothing to do with eleven- and twelve-year-olds.

It wasn't within my brief. I was teaching to O Level in two languages. Plus, I ran the rugby and produced school plays, so you can imagine the pressure I was under. I don't know 'A'. What relationship could I have had with 'A'?

DC: Did you take the younger ones for PE at all?

SW: I didn't teach PE. I took senior games, running the 1st XV.

DC: Is there a difference between what somebody would call PE and what they'd call games?

SW: PE is a subject I didn't … I just did games like all the other young teachers.

DC: What would have been the game?

SW: Rugby.

DC: Just rugby?

SW: Well, for me, just rugby.

DC: So you wouldn't have taken any other sort of sports class?

SW: I can't recall any other sport. Cricket in the summer.

DC: Hockey?

SW: Not me. Any games I did were with the senior part of the school.

DC: So, would you ever have supervised the showering after a games lesson?

SW: Do you know what, I can't even remember. If I did, I know what I'm like, it would have been a cursory, 'Come on, hurry up, come on, you've got to get back to class.' Games was done during lesson time, so they had a lesson afterwards, so it was a case of, 'Come on, let's get going, quick', because I, too, had a lesson to go to. I can remember putting my games clothes on in the morning if I had a games lesson during the day but Derek Slade stopped us

—

teaching in our games clothes. So I used to get changed as well, have a shower and get to the next lesson.

DC: So, if you did do that and hurried them along, which group of students would that have been?

SW: As far as I can remember, it's a long time ago, the seniors; the seniors I took for games. If the juniors were doing games at the same time, I can't remember.

DC: OK. And when the students had showers after games, what were they expected to do?

SW: Shower, I suppose.

DC: And games would be what time of day?

SW: I can remember teaching Monday morning from nine o'clock until a quarter past ten.

DC: So they would shower and go into further lessons?

SW: Yeah.

DC: Is that the only time you recall teaching?

SW: It's all a bit vague but I remember thinking how beautiful it was going out one Monday morning and it was September, I'd only just arrived at the school and it was lovely, you know: autumnal crisp. I can remember thinking how lucky I am to be here. I can remember thinking that. That's how I can recall it being Monday morning. Many people dread their job on a Monday morning and here's me in this beautiful part of the world...

DC: Because it's a beautiful building, St George's. Well, 'A' says that after games, PE, whatever you decide to call it, that you would supervise showering and he said that he would be asked to lift up his penis and his testicles and also part his bum cheeks, to ensure he was clean. Did that take place?

SW: No. I wouldn't have done that to one of the older boys, certainly not an eleven-year old, somebody who is pre-pubescent. It's utterly outside my life. I've never asked any child at any time to part their … cheeks; it would be a ridiculous thing for me to do.

DC: He goes on to say that although it happened under those circumstances on numerous occasions, that there was also at least one occasion when you took hold of his penis…

SW: Rubbish.

DC: And his testicles and you lifted them on the pretext of checking he was clean.

SW: Nonsense. I didn't. I refute that totally.

DC: He says that you were then standing in front of him and you got him to then bend forward and you leant over him and again parted the cheeks of his bottom. Did that happen?

SW: No, it didn't. I swear to you it didn't happen – to an eleven- or twelve-year-old boy?

DC: Is there any reason you can think of for 'A' to say that took place?

SW: While I have been sitting in that cell I've been thinking … there is a cabal of ex-pupils led by a boy I knew called ['David Praver'], who sent me an email a few years ago out of the blue, and he wrote: 'I notice on your website you've not mentioned St George's' and then he accused me of covering up, knowing what Slade was doing and covering it up. He said I should have spoken up about it at the time.

DC: Did you respond?

SW: I did. I wanted to meet him to give him my side of the story. I then had another email, this time from a person called

Steve Harris, whom I'd never heard of; he accused me that I had shut a door in his face as he was running down the corridor. The same person rang me on my mobile some months later to say, 'I'm sorry, I was a bit out of order, it was a bit over the top saying that.' He asked if it would be OK for him and another ex-pupil to come and visit me at RHS. That was the last I heard. I would have told him what 'David Praver' had accused me of and explained my side of the story. At school 'Praver' was a constant source of trouble. He was almost anarchic in his behaviour. On one occasion he went AWOL after the usual pandemonium and we were asked to help catch him. He was shouting and screaming and the headmaster, at this point it was Barry Slade, and another teacher cornered him and they whacked him. He put this in his email to me: 'Don't you remember me being chased and why didn't you stop them. Are you a coward?' and suchlike. So, I can understand if he has some antipathy towards me. I didn't know much about his background.

DC: Was that the only interaction you had with him at school?

SW: Yeah. I don't think I came directly across him apart from that. I do remember his name being constantly brought up in the staff room as being a source of trouble.

DC: Going back to 'A', he also says that there was an occasion when you punched him in the head.

SW: I've never punched anyone.

DC: Did you ever use physical punishment at all?

SW: No.

DC: You said you didn't cane...

SW: What other physical punishment is there?

DC: Throwing anything at them?

SW: No.

DC: Have you always lived in the boarding schools where you've taught?

SW: Yes – which brings me to the point I want to make about 'A'. I could've taken him to my room which was in the middle of the school. In the shower room, where was everyone else when I was doing this? I mean, the shower rooms at St George's, I seem to remember, were open plan. There was no door to lock, anybody could have walked in. In my room I had a locking door. If I wanted to abuse, I had a golden opportunity.

DC: Going back to your responsibilities, you taught French, German and Latin. You spoke about doing the plays and rugby. Was there anything else you specialised in at the school?

SW: I ran the activities programme. I would take trips out of school.

DC: Day trips?

SW: Yeah, day trips, that sort of stuff.

DC: Were there any sort of after-school clubs?

SW: Yeah, I organised taking the French group to the Ipswich Film Theatre.

DC: Who did all this before you arrived?

SW: Nobody. All the plays, the rugby, I put my life and soul into it.

DC: And then you said you looked after the dorms. What would you actually have to do?

SW: I would just have to make sure they were in bed on time, 'Come on, chaps, hurry up, it's wash time, get your teeth done.'

DC: So, if the boys were ill in the night, what would happen, where would they go?

SW: They'd go to one of the four matrons.

DC: How were the pupils split up?

SW: In dorms. I had S3 dorm. That was the fifth-form dorm. I never did junior dorms.

DC: And you describe Mr Slade as very strict. Can you be a bit more specific?

SW: He was autocratic. We knew we were in his school and we had to do as we were told. He was also very well educated. He liked me because I was a good teacher and I did a lot for the school. He liked me because I didn't cause any problems apart from the one I mentioned to you – the bus pick-up.

DC: So, you never had a falling out, apart from that?

SW: Nothing. I used also to take school singing practice on a Friday afternoon because of my versatility and I was one of the few members of staff who could keep the whole school in check. The oldest boys, year eleven, respected me, and they wouldn't have done had I been touching little boys' bums.

DC: And you yourself never caned anyone?

SW: Never in my life.

DC: 'A' states that he used to receive the cane from Derek Slade and on occasions he was hit with a jokari bat. Do you remember Slade using this?

SW: Yes. I heard about it. Like a squash-sized bat.

DC: OK, 'A' describes one incident when he recalls himself and two other students, 'B' and (name withdrawn). Are they names you recall?

SW: No.

DC: They'd been sent on a treasure hunt and were sent to his office for digging up some turf and you were actually present in the room, in Derek Slade's office, when he whacked them on their bare bottom.

SW: No, I don't remember. I would've remembered that, I think.

DC: Did you ever see Derek Slade cane anyone?

SW: No.

DC: So, you don't remember this incident?

SW: That would've left an impression on my mind if he'd asked them to take their trousers down. I don't recall it.

DC: Is it possible it could have happened? He says that he received six whacks on his bare bottom and was made to bend over a chair and that you moved seats from the window to then be in a position where you were behind him.

SW: No, I don't recall that.

DC: OK. Is there anything else that you would like to say or anything that you'd like to ask that we've discussed so far?

SW: I just think, if you are going to proceed, I would just like you to speak, to get a balance on this, to the people who actually knew me, those who I dealt with at St George's. I've never dreamed of touching a child in my care and the idea that I would part his bum cheeks is risible. It's so far away from what I would do. I am a boy from a boarding school myself and this has helped me to be a really good teacher.

DC: The clock reads 2.58 p.m.

So concluded my first interview.

I left the interview room realising that, potentially, everything

I had worked for over a professional lifetime was in serious danger of being completely undermined by some fantasist/opportunist. Not an iota of evidence had been presented to me, just the complainant's word. How could this lead to a raid on one's home, being bundled into a police car and being held in a cell for hours on end? Appertaining to raiding a citizen's private home, the 1984 Criminal Evidence Act

> requires police to satisfy a magistrate not only that there are reasonable grounds for believing an offence has been committed, but there is material on the premises relevant to prove the alleged crime. A warrant should be issued only if it is not practicable to communicate with the owner of the house.

And, despite the Education Act 2011 stating that 'teachers who have a complaint made against them by a pupil in the school at the time have a right to anonymity until that teacher is charged', I had my name published on local TV and radio within twenty-four hours. That was convenient for the police as it meant they could start their 'trawling'. (I'll say more about 'trawling' in due course, because this method of 'investigation' was potentially to play such a major part in railroading me into court.)

Having been placed back in the cell, I waited and waited and began to realise I wasn't going to make that evening's local football match, which started at 7.45 p.m.

At 5.05 p.m. I was recalled to the interview room to be questioned about various items the police had found at my two residences – this time by the chief investigative officer of the case

– 'DCi' I shall refer to her as – who had returned from overseeing the ransacking of my London flat. She asked me about a small number of photographs they had extracted from the multitude I had taken over the years; any containing young male adults, of course, were focused upon. At one point, my solicitor interjected to say to me, 'We've discussed the caution and you do not have to say anything and I just make the overall comment the photos we are being shown are neither indecent nor of children. If you feel you don't want to comment…'

'I've got nothing of children, nothing at all,' I repeated over and over again, as they persisted in asking me what various disks contained. The interview concluded thirty-five minutes later.

Little did I realise at that stage that, having committed themselves to a methodology in which one allegation, however unlikely, would trigger a hunt for more, the Suffolk Police would now begin to trawl in earnest. Little did I also realise that the presumption of innocence, the most fundamental principle of British law, had as far as historical child abuse investigations are concerned, already been utterly destroyed here in the UK.

I was not released from the police station until 9.30 p.m. The recently appointed RHS headmaster and his deputy came to collect me. At the station desk, before leaving, I was given my bail conditions and told to answer in three months' time, on 12 March 2013. One of the conditions set was that I was not allowed to return to my home of eighteen years, as it was on the school site.

I protested: 'But it's the Christmas holidays, there are no pupils at the school. Surely it's all right to stay just for tonight?'

The desk sergeant replied in no uncertain terms, 'No, it's not.

There are staff children on the site, are you going to deny that? You will do as you're told, or you'll be re-arrested. You have accommodation in London, you can stay there. As I stated, if you break any bail requirements, you will be re-arrested.'

How humane! How civilised! How shocking, I thought. It also occurred to me that there were children living near my London home as well, so I couldn't follow the logic of them prohibiting me from staying at my school home for that one night.

So, after the emotional upheaval of the day, during which time I had spent the best part of eleven hours locked in a cell – tired, hungry, drained, in shock – I was now expected to go back to my school house, pack my belongings and drive to my London flat, some 100 miles away in west London.

As I was driven back to school, the decision was made that I would stay at a staff colleague's house that night and travel to London the following day.

'Try not to fret, Simon. I am sure this will all be cleared up quickly, once the police realise you didn't even teach this person. What you need now is a good night's sleep,' said the deputy head.

If we lived in a fair, humane, clear-thinking society, which the UK post-Savile was certainly not with regard to historical investigations, she might have been right. What's more, little did I know that, despite being constantly tired, I wouldn't sleep for more than an hour at a time for most of the next three months.

CHAPTER FOUR

BACKGROUND
TO MY
ARREST

If at first you don't succeed, try, try, try again.

— ENGLISH PROVERB

'A', the chief complainant, was first interviewed by the police in 2010 with regard to alleged abuse he had suffered at the hands of St George's headmaster Derek Slade. In an official police report of this interview it states:

> A review of DC Newell's and DC Grimsey's officer books have been conducted (once again) with regard to their visit to 'A' at his home address in February 2010. During this visit

> DC Newell took the notes and it is confirmed that there is no
> mention of Warr within these notes.

'A' spoke to the police subsequent to this interview by telephone, stating he wanted to give an interview to the media and to check what he could and could not talk about. He wanted at this stage to add that I was present on an occasion when he and two other boys were caned by Slade. He explained that my name was not mentioned in the statement he had made to the police earlier because he had thought at that time that they were interested only in Slade.

I would say it seems wholly implausible that 'A' did not see fit to mention to the police either at the interview stage or during this telephone call (or, for that matter, to the journalist) that I had supposedly repeatedly abused him in the shower room after PE lessons at St George's, which he was eventually to claim a couple of years later. After all, to paint a picture of general immorality among Slade's staff would certainly help in any subsequent court case against Slade himself.

Over a year later, on 1 December 2011, 'A' made his first allegation against me. He now claimed to the police that I had checked his private parts after a PE lesson by asking him to lift up his penis and testicles so I could check to see if he was dry. He said he couldn't remember seeing if I'd done this to any other boys. In spite of this new information, 'A' was told by the police early in 2012 that they would be taking no action against me for the allegations he had made, as it did not meet the threshold for a criminal charge: 'SIO (Senior Investigating Officer) deems the evidence against Simon Warr for physical and sexual abuse does not meet evidential threshold.'

Obviously not satisfied with this outcome, later in the year 'A' contacted the police again. An internal report of a telephone message he made to the Suffolk Police on 31 October 2012 reads as follows:

> At 1300 on Wednesday 31 October, I took a phone call from the above person ('A'). He explained that he was a former pupil at St George's School and a witness in the trial of Derek Slade. He stated that during the investigation into Slade he outlined allegations of physical and sexual assaults against another teacher at St George's, naming Simon Warr. He explained that Warr was a teacher at St George's alongside Slade, that Warr was involved in physical assaults against him (punches to the head) and sexual assaults (fondling of the genitals). 'A' seemed angry and disappointed in the apparent lack of investigation into Warr's activities and requests that he is allowed to make a further statement into this matter.

He was duly accorded another interview with the police and, true to form, his account was once again embellished. On 14 November 2012, he now alleged I would grab hold of his private parts after PE lessons (i.e. repeatedly). This time he claimed: 'He took hold of my penis in one hand and cupped my testicles in the other and lifted them up.' He now states he saw me do this to other boys, having said the opposite in a previous interview. The reason 'A' gave for this gradual embellishment, this 'gradual disclosure', was:

Over a period of time I had seen Warr being interviewed on TV
and heard him on the radio. Each time I saw or heard him, it
brought back memories of my time at St George's School and I
started to become more and more wound up … I will have a dream
which will cause me to remember more … I hear a teacher raise
their voice (and) it takes me straight back to my school days. I feel
it's me as a child being shouted at … If I read something in the
paper or see something on the TV which upsets me, quite often
in my dreams that night I am a young boy back at St George's.

This is all very emotional but it still doesn't explain why he kept
embellishing crucial details of his story. Is he suggesting that the
more he remembered about me, the angrier he became and this
caused him to remember details he had previously not been able to
recall? Of course, the most likely answer as to why someone would
take thirty years or more to make an allegation of historical abuse
and then gradually embellish it is because he or she is telling a pack
of lies. It is important to point out that absolutely no empirical
evidence has been found for the validity of the theory of 'gradual
disclosure', a now-discredited theory that crossed the Atlantic during the 1980s. All that researchers found in America with regard to
'gradual disclosure', a theory whereby those abused would gradually remember details of their abuse as a result of professional
prompting, was that the vast majority were not disclosures at all
but fanciful constructions which had been made up in response to
deeply biased interviewing techniques. The complainants knew the
interviewer was expecting allegations of abuse and were prepared
to oblige. Thus, what is left is a theory that claims that the more

inconsistencies, contradictions and repeated embellishments that a series of allegations contained, and the more inherently implausible it all was from a common-sense point of view, the more credible it was likely to be. In this discredited theory, ordinary scepticism and logic seem to have been suspended.

The senior officer in charge of my case had two options: either to put his faith in the theory of gradual disclosure or dismiss 'A''s changing accounts as pure fantasy. He evidently went with the former and subsequently gave the order for my arrest.

Not only did 'A' make increasingly serious allegations about me to the Suffolk Police throughout 2011 and 2012, he was also blackening my name (all unknown to me at the time) to the media.

This is an email (just how it was written) that 'A' sent to ITV's *Daybreak* producers after I had appeared on their morning show in September 2011:

> Once again i am having to contact you with regards to simon warr who you aload to appear on your program after i had sent you an email with photo proof and had a reply. You said you would pass the email on but it looks like have not done so. I am discusted that you feel the feelings of child abuse is not important to listen to I have asked to appear on you program to give the side of those who have been through this form of abuse but you would let an abuser or a person knowing of abuse and doing nothing about it have a say. I hope when this man is held accountable for what he done 30 years ago and what he new was going on but did nothing about you will feel the pain that we went through. You discust me.

This was followed by another email (again, exactly how it was written) sent to ITV after another appearance I made on ITV some months later. This one came from the wife of 'B' (subsequently, 'A' and 'B' claimed in a court of law they had never discussed my supposed abuse of both of them at St George's):

> I have been asked to contact you on behalf of 'A' and 'B' with regard to you once again having Simon Warr on your show talking about corporal punishment and canning. 'A' has contacted Daybreak before regarding Simon Warr appearing on the programme and even his emails from them regarding the matter … Simon Warr abused children at the same school as Derek Slade, 'A' has copies of his police statement verifying this and his solicitor also has details of what Simon Warr done to him personally. This morning Simon Warr sat on your sofa and said he'd never used corporal punishment against any child at the school he worked in that did use it, he lied.

The email continues along the usual lines of the distress caused to 'A' and 'B' at seeing me on the ITV sofa. But, from the date on the email, at this stage in time 'A' had only made a complaint of my having checked to see he was dry after those phantom PE lessons (before the invention of the grasping of the private parts) and 'B' had made no complaint at all of my behaviour at the school in any of his interviews to police. They both also subsequently stated in a court of law that neither EVER discussed between them my supposed abuse of each of them. One can only suppose, therefore, that 'A' and 'B' told 'B''s wife independently of each other and she was sworn to secrecy about the matter and had not told them she was writing on their behalf to ITV.

Another email was sent shortly afterwards, this time from 'an anonymous' source:

> You had Simon Warr on your programme on Friday. In August I took the stand against Derek Slade. Mr Warr is a thug and master of the backhanded slap. He is a socio-psychopath who is a lunatic who canes children. If you go to YouTube and search Simon Warr and George Galloway you'll find a phone-in tyrannical rant. Also, in the East Anglian Daily Times, search for Simon Warr, and there's an article about his book with a swastika on the cover. This man has never taught in the public sector. He's lied on your programme both times.

When I read this email, which was disclosed to me after my 2014 trial, I could not comprehend how someone, who obviously enjoyed his role in securing Slade's conviction, seemed also to be imbued with a feeling of narcissistic superiority in that he was prepared to repeatedly spew forth libellous comments without having any direct knowledge about me other than that based on hearsay. He alleges I knew Slade was abusing children (which is a classic example of guilty by association). As stated earlier, this was not the case. I did know, as did every other member of the St George's community – teachers, matrons, secretarial staff, maintenance staff, kitchen staff, cleaners, gardeners and the parents – that Slade administered corporal punishment, just as about every other headteacher in the UK did in the early

1980s. I was aware he caned a lot but, as no other teacher in the school was permitted to issue the cane, as a young, inexperienced teacher, at no stage did it occur to me to challenge my employer and headmaster about his punishment *modus operandi*. Indeed, I was told at my job interview that the reason why the school had grown in numbers so quickly was because the vast majority of the parents, mostly Services' personnel, wanted strict, uncompromising discipline exerted. I was at the school for only a short time under Slade's regime (one year), while other colleagues had been in his employ for over five years. Why was I being targeted? Part of the reason, I suspect, lies in the part of 'A''s statement in which he says: 'There was talk amongst the boys about Warr being gay.' This was surely the reason I was now being singled out of course, coupled with my high media profile. As I mentioned earlier, much publicity surrounded my various media appearances and recordings of a number of them subsequently appeared on the internet. When the cabal of former St George's pupils assembled some years later 'to bring Slade to justice', I was, of course, in their consciousness. It is strange, therefore, that my principal accuser, 'A', failed to point any finger of accusation of abuse at me until 2011.

I am of the firm opinion that 'A' not only wanted, via the school's insurers, to try to secure a second slice of generous financial compensation from his time at St George's, but was patently relishing the attention his 'suffering' was bringing him from the police and the system. Am I totally surprised that he made these outrageous claims? No. It must be understood that when Slade was finally brought to justice for his abuse while he was headmaster (and probably subsequently), an atmosphere was created by the investigating authorities that suggested everything that this cabal of former pupils alleged would be believed.

Slade was guilty on some counts, yes, but I am convinced he was sentenced to extra time behind bars as a result of lies and exaggeration. I have been told by a former pupil that one of the complainants against Slade told another as he was leaving court: 'You lied about Slade in there.' The answer he received was: 'Fuck him, he's a pervert, he deserves all he gets.' Some of those Slade was found guilty of abusing have been awarded enormous sums of money. Under these circumstances, I am not entirely surprised that 'A' decided to accuse me.

The anonymous source claimed I was a thug, yet during a career spanning thirty-five years I have never caned or struck a child in my care, including any 'backhanded slaps'. Indeed, I ran a successful boarding house of some seventy adolescent boys for many years with little more than my forceful personality and loud voice as a support in resolving the myriad disciplinary issues I had to deal with. I doubt this could be applied to many boarding school teachers of the 1980s.

The interview on the radio with George Galloway was not 'a tyrannical rant', as the source suggests, but a heated discussion between me and Mr Galloway on the topic of the benefits system, which was set up in 2010 by Talk Sport radio, for which station I had been a regular contributor over the years. Indeed, Talk Sport considered it to be such an intelligent, charged, entertaining discussion that they put it onto YouTube. This is how the 'anonymous source' had access to it – not, as he subsequently claimed, by stumbling accidentally upon it as he was searching for Magic radio (which is on a different frequency to Talk Sport).

It is true that my novel, *Howson's Choice*, does have a faint swastika on its front cover, intended to be an allusion to the Nazi sympathies of the main character's family, which has a direct bearing on the entire plot. I presume the message 'Mr Anonymous' was attempting to convey to the producers at *Daybreak* was that I, too, was a Nazi sympathiser. In a similar manner, I suppose, that an author who writes about murder is a potential psychopath. Had he bothered to read the book, which he patently had not (no surprise there), he would understand why a swastika was featured on the cover.

Then there is the allegation that I was lying when I stated on television that I had taught in state schools. I have in fact taught in a number, having spent two full terms in two London state schools when I was training to be a teacher; further to these, I spent part of my gap year teaching in a state school in Surrey; and finally, as a lecturer with the Learning Performance Group during the 1990s and 2000s, I have taught study skills in a whole host of state schools in England, Scotland and Wales. Of course, the anonymous emailer would have been unaware of any of this because he knows so little about me.

'A' stated after seeing a YouTube clip of me on *The One Show* caning Adrian Chiles, the presenter, during a light-hearted look at the pros and cons of corporal punishment in schools, that he felt 'enough was enough'. I had been approached by the BBC following my appearance on television, playing the role of a 1950s headmaster. If he found the caning of Adrian Chiles so upsetting, why did he bother to watch the clip on the internet? It had been there since 2007, so there was no reason for him to complain some four years later. 'I decided enough was enough'. *He decided* – this suggests narcissism masquerading as an act of altruism which 'A' claimed was for the good of society.

And so, after 'A' had changed his account yet again of what I had supposedly done to him all those years ago, a policy decision was made by the Detective Inspector at Suffolk Police overseeing 'Operation Racecourse' to arrest me.

To quote from an official document, a copy of which I have in my possession:

Policy Decision

29th November 2012

Further evidence now from witness 'A' regarding allegations of hands on abuse – Indecent Assault.

Arrest and search of premises controlled by Simon Warr to be actioned.

Now it is an offence it requires to be fully investigated.

Thus, an investigation lasting nearly two years was set in motion, even though there was not a smidgen of factual evidence that any crime had been committed.

CHAPTER FIVE

———

WARR CONTRA MUNDUM

Lie travels the world while truth is putting on her boots.

— MARK TWAIN

The day after my arrest things got even worse for me. I was well aware of the Education Act of 2011, which prohibits the publication of the name of a teacher if a pupil in the same school makes an allegation against him or her; nevertheless, the following morning, I received a phone call from the editor of BBC Radio Suffolk.

'Hi, Simon. So sorry to hear about what's happened. You realise we are going to have to broadcast details of your arrest in our afternoon show? If we don't, we could be accused of favouritism.'

'You aren't allowed to mention my name, Peter, under a recent law, introduced by the "Condems" (in fact, it was the first law the coalition partners passed, in 2011).'

'We can, Simon, we have checked with the lawyers and they say this doesn't apply to historic cases.'

'They are wrong.'

'Well, we are going to publish your name, so we would like a statement from you. This is your chance to give your reaction to these events.'

'In that case, all I've got to say is I repudiate these allegations utterly.'

'Thank you.'

News of my arrest was duly broadcast that afternoon on both local BBC radio and TV. The Rt Hon. Chris Grayling said in October 2015 that 'the police and the Criminal Justice Service need to think very long and very hard before they put the name of any suspect into the public arena'. The press could well consider this statement in their desperation for scoops.

As I was leaving Ipswich to start my journey to London, I decided to pop in to see a good friend of mine (I'll call him 'Brian'), who was a BBC radio colleague. He was not at home, so I put a note through his door to say I'd called. I wanted the reassuring smiles of his and his partner's faces. I felt desperately lonely and was dreading the drive down to my empty flat in London. I had got to know Brian well during recent years and considered him a close friend. He and his partner treated me almost like a member of their family.

Thus I began the trip back to the capital that Wednesday 19 December, tears streaming down my face as rain lashed against the windscreen. I became so upset I was forced to interrupt my journey after twelve miles or so, pulling over on the Colchester bypass, as I was having difficulties seeing the road ahead. Stationed in a layby on the A12, I made every effort to stop crying but the tears continued to flow.

My mobile rang. I ignored it. Some ten minutes later, I pressed on towards London, fearing that if I didn't I soon wouldn't be in a fit state to drive the car. The fact that I was driving in pouring rain didn't help matters. I negotiated the journey by stopping every twenty miles. The journey took me a good four hours, twice the usual time.

No sooner had I reached my flat than my mobile rang again.

'Simon Warr, this is the *East Anglian Daily Times*. We understand you have given permission for your identity to be revealed by the BBC following your arrest yesterday.'

'I certainly did not. I told the BBC that they were breaking the law but they carried on regardless. I'm at the end of my tether.'

'I see, so you won't give us permission to use your name?'

'No, I'm sorry, no, no. So, I was right in telling the BBC that they weren't allowed to publish my name?'

'You were, Mr Warr. Sorry to have disturbed you.'

This turn of events was soon to be exacerbated as my headmaster was promptly on the phone, pleading with me not to divulge anything else to the media. Obviously he was concerned only with the name of the school being publicised and its reputation being tarnished. In spite of the fact that I had been a loyal and highly successful employee for three decades, it mattered not one iota to the school how *I* was and how *my* name was being dragged through the mud; all they were concerned about was distancing themselves from me as quickly and as effectively as possible and ensuring there was no more adverse publicity for them.

'Simon, I thought we agreed that you would not say anything publicly. Why did you speak to the BBC?'

'I had no choice. They presented me with the fact they were running the story and asked me to make a comment. If I'd not refuted these allegations, it might appear I was hiding something, that perhaps there was a grain of truth in them.'

During this desperately difficult conversation, the head's manner was cold and detached. This was a man who used to refer to me in school by the title of 'maestro'. Any affectionate tones had now gone and his manner had become very formal. On an official school document, issued a few months later, the BBC's mistake ended up being presented as my fault: I had 'made the school subject to disrepute' as a result of the press coverage, which had 'the potential to continue to cause further damage to its reputation'.

To sum up then, some narcissistic, greedy, pernicious inadequate relates to the police a series of lies; I'm then arrested without a shred of proof to substantiate the lies; the BBC subsequently breaks the law by publishing my name and I am held responsible for the entire sorry episode by my school employers.

I told the head in no uncertain terms: 'Look, I know this is hard on the school and I'm sorry its name has been publicised but I can assure you I didn't want my name or the school's name mentioned. I told the BBC they were breaking the law but they proceeded anyway. It has made a desperate situation for me even worse.'

He seemed unconvinced.

Realising their mistake, the BBC withdrew my name the following day from their online articles but the cat was out of the bag:
the damage had been done. And, even though my name had been
withdrawn, if anyone Googled 'Simon Warr', the first thing he or
she would read was the account of a teacher's arrest for historical
sexual abuse, with some details of this 'teacher' (who was the same
age as me). It didn't take an awful lot to work out to whom the
article referred. They may as well have included my name.

This marked the beginning of a vicious campaign against me by
internet trolls; a few of them I knew from the distant past, albeit
vaguely, but the vast majority I did not. Nietzsche was correct when
he said: 'Distrust all in whom the impulse to punish is strong.'

The insults poured in thick and fast: 'You fucking paedo, go
to an underground sewer and kill yourself'; 'I trusted you with
my son and was taken in by your supposed professionalism and,
all along, you were a pervert. You disgust me' (this from a former
school parent); 'If Warr kills himself, it'll be the best Christmas
prezzie ever.' And so on and so on.

It wasn't long before the headmaster of RHS had formally written to the authorities to express his 'deep concern' about my arrest.
To quote directly: 'The details relating to the arrest of SW are in
the public domain ... I consider that the relationship of trust and
confidence between the school and SW would be highly unlikely
to be able to continue...' I had been well and truly abandoned.

In that awful week leading up to Christmas, by chance I read
an interesting article in one of the Sunday supplements about
training to join the SAS, which stated: 'The selection process aims
to test psychological resilience. Recruits are deprived of sleep and

drained of energy before their personality is tested to the point of destruction.'

This is exactly how I was feeling during this period of time. I'm not sure how long those potential SAS recruits have to endure that psychological pressure but, as it turned out, I had to sustain it for nearly two years.

It was (supposedly) the festive season but I couldn't go home to my family in Wales; I had no intention of burdening them with this crisis. I decided to ring a dear friend of mine from my school days, with whom I had kept in touch since the 1970s, Dave Hill. How will I ever be able to thank him and his wife Carolyn for their support throughout?

I telephoned David on Christmas Eve: 'Hi, Dave, do you think it would be OK if I joined you and Carolyn for Christmas?'

'Of course you may,' he responded. 'We'd be delighted to see you. Ben and Matt and Lisa [his children] will be here, along with Carolyn's dad.'

I drove up to Preston, a village not far from Hitchin, Hertfordshire, on Christmas morning. I decided I was going to make a real effort to appear normal for as long as possible.

The lunch passed in a blur and I think they must have known something was wrong as usually I was the life and soul of any group wherever I went. On this occasion I had difficulty even concentrating on what was being discussed. (As Paul Gambaccini, whom I have now got to know, stated in his diaries *Love, Paul Gambaccini: My Year Under the Yewtree*: 'Every time you are not doing something else, you are thinking about your plight.') Carolyn's father took a particular interest in me that day, asking me a series of questions about my dual careers of teaching and working in the media. I tried hard to concentrate but my mind was full with the problems of my personal situation and it took enormous effort just to 'compute' his questions. What I failed to realise at the time was this was only *my* crisis and I was going to have to get used to forcing myself to hold conversations about matters other than my personal nightmare. I had to make efforts at some point to engage once again in normal life. If all I talked about was my situation, people would soon start to avoid me. Nevertheless, I had every intention of sharing my secret with Dave as soon as possible.

After lunch the party settled down to a game of Scrabble, a game I usually enjoy. Only, on this occasion, I had much trouble focusing and couldn't wait for the game to end. Late in the afternoon, wanting to be alone with David, I suggested we take a stroll.

He sounded surprised. 'It's pretty unpleasant out there.'

'Please, Dave, just a short walk.'

As we took a stroll around the village, I thought now was the perfect time to tell him why I hadn't been myself all day.

After I had explained the whole story, David was flabbergasted. I told him about how these incidents had allegedly taken place after junior PE lessons and how that couldn't have been true for the reasons stated earlier. He couldn't believe that the allegations were being taken seriously. 'The trouble is,' he said, 'this sort of allegation has such stigma that, instead of being more cautious as a result, the police are, in practice, more gung-ho, knowing they'll have the public on their side, regardless of the outcome.'

I shall never forget his wise response. He summed up the situation perfectly.

—

On Boxing Day, I drove to Diss on the Suffolk/Norfolk border to visit my dear friend and BBC colleague Mark and his wife Kerry. Mark had been my boss in the sports department at BBC Radio Suffolk and I had been the Master of Ceremonies at his wedding in December 2010. Kerry had transformed Mark from an introverted, middle-aged curmudgeon (albeit superb broadcaster) into a happy, outgoing friend, who had at last found his missing link.

It was so good to see the two of them but, inevitably, the tears flowed from my eyes as I was so warmly welcomed. I felt at the time I didn't deserve any friends at all.

On New Year's Eve I was back at my London flat, depressed and unable to sleep. It was early afternoon and I was still in bed – a sure indication of the onset of depression. Why get up? The only time I was not worrying myself sick was on the rare occasions when I was asleep. I decided I had to do something with the day. I dressed and walked to the local Tube station and caught the train into central London. I walked around for an hour or so, contemplating what to do next.

There was no relief from the mental torture. There was really only one way out, I thought. I descended the escalator to the Piccadilly Line and caught the train going to Heathrow. Inevitably, there were more tears. By the time the train reached Acton Town I was in a visible state of distress. A man sitting opposite in the carriage came over to me.

'Are you OK, sir? Can I help?'

This was the conduit for howls of anguish bursting from my lungs. Those in the carriage looked away, embarrassed. He helped me off the train and sat with me on a platform bench. He held my hand. His tenderness made me all the more upset. We sat together for a good ten minutes.

'I'm feeling better. Thank you for helping me.'

'Are you sure you'll be OK?'

'Yes. Thank you.'

With obvious concern, he stood up and boarded the next train. Here was an example of humanity at its best.

I remained on the bench. If I was going to do it, then now was the time. But what of the commuters on their way home, at the end of a long working day and looking forward to their evening out? Why should they be inconvenienced? I thought. And I had to consider the reaction of, and effects upon, my family members, still oblivious to the crisis that had beset my life. Besides which, it was only recently that my friend and colleague Paul McCaffery had taken his own life in March 2012 after losing a battle against 'the demon drink', and I was mindful of the upset and misery he had left in his wake. Indeed, I had described it at the time as a selfish thing to do.

Such suicidal thoughts were fleeting. I soon realised that I had to be strong, after all, I had the truth on my side. It'll be all right in the end, I thought … or will it?

I returned home and went back to bed for a few hours, desperate to catch up on some desperately needed sleep.

I tossed and turned for a few hours but it was no good. In my present state of mind, I was not going to sleep restfully for the foreseeable future – there was too much to think about.

Over and over in my mind I turned thoughts of all the emails I had written, photos I had taken, texts I had received, DVDs I had bought. They were all going to be looked at by a third party.

There was nothing illegal among them, but some of the material would cast me in a certain light, a light I had tried to keep hidden from the world as best I could.

I had had sexual experiences with both men and women in my life but, as mentioned earlier, I had always felt my attraction to my own sex was because I had attended an all boys' boarding school between the ages of eight and eighteen and had hardly seen a girl during this period. When I did, for example when my school's choir joined up with the girls' school for our regular Oratorio concerts, I was as desperate for relations with the opposite sex as any straight person would be. But there is no doubt that sexual experiences with some of the other boys, the only people available to me at the time, had an effect on me in later life. This can't be such a rare thing, surely. I had never discussed my feelings and desires with anyone, although because of my outrageously extrovert personality, people have sometimes asked me if I'm gay.

As for the allegations, I couldn't figure out how such palpable inconsistencies in the accuser's testimony could be given any credence at all. But, then again, I had inferred already that the police were more interested in ruining me than securing the truth. It was evident it was going to be me versus the resources of the local police, which seemed substantial. It has perplexed me since the beginning of this process that, while there seems to be an unlimited budget for pursuing historical investigations, police budgets are continually being cut when it comes to investigating modern-day crimes. I was innocent of the allegations but now I had realised that ultimately this might not be enough.

I lay in bed until the early hours and then rose to eat a morsel or two – loss of appetite being another side effect of depression. I could hear the revelries and fireworks continuing around the neighbourhood: it was torture to think of everybody else rejoicing at the start of a new year, as it only compounded my own misery. I later discovered that it was on this day, New Year's Eve, that the police visited 'B', the second complainant. Unsurprisingly, he backed up the testimony of his close friend that I had supervised junior showers after PE lessons and he also claimed that, on occasions, I asked him to part his bum cheeks to see that he was dry. It was nonsense, of course, but the police had to have some corroborative 'evidence', even if it was the words of a close friend of 'A'. The high likelihood that there had been confabulation between the two witnesses was simply brushed aside by the investigating officers.

I received an email some months later from a third party which stated: 'Lawyers inform me that "B" at no time mentioned your name in any part of his 2011 claim [against the school] nor is there any reference to you in his medical reports.' It wasn't hard to work out why not. Ongoing contamination of evidence between 'A' and 'B' was obvious to anyone with even a modest IQ. The police ignored it all.

It was New Year's Day 2013 and I drove to my brother's home in South Wales. This would be another day of anguish. I felt awful. I wondered if 'A' had any idea what he was putting me through, or if he even cared. If the internet comments were anything to go by, he, like the members of the cabal, was probably securing maximum satisfaction from his malicious lies. If I were found guilty of his trumped-up allegations, he could get his greedy hands upon more money from the St George's insurers and become the centre of some attention once again. If it all went awry, even if it was proven he was telling lies, he knew he had nothing to lose.

It was late afternoon when I finally arrived at my brother's home, just outside Cardiff. As soon as he came to the door, he knew that something was wrong. I sat down in the kitchen and explained in detail the events of the past fortnight, as my brother and sister-in-law listened, aghast.

'Why? How can someone be so evil? So cruel?' This was what my family wanted to know. In answer to that, I gave them my own conclusions. I had inferred that he was primarily after money. He had also tasted the spotlight following the Slade trial. He must have enjoyed that short period of time having the police at his beck and call, and seeing his story splashed in the media. Attacking me gave him another opportunity to become the centre of attention. Was he in it for the money? Getting me convicted would bring him more compensation and likely payments from the media. It's good if you can get it. As far as I could tell, he had shown no obvious talents and no ostensible gifts to speak about; how he must have appreciated the attention when people were taking an interest in him and in what he had to say. These were the factors, I believe, which led to him making these false allegations. This was what I told my family.

I remained at my brother's home for a couple of weeks. At least I was finally eating properly but my depressed state was exacerbated in the early part of 2013 by daily news appertaining to the arrest of Stuart Hall, the veteran BBC sports' reporter, as well as a number of other ongoing celebrity child abuse investigations. They were ubiquitous in the press at that time, as 'Operation Yewtree' flexed its muscles. It did nothing to alleviate my state of mind.

The first main practical issue I had to address was legal representation. I had been a member of the NAS (National Association of Schoolmasters) since 1993 so I rang the union's main offices in Birmingham and explained what had happened. I was told that someone would ring me back in a few days. When the call was made to me a week or so later, it was more bad news. As the allegations referred to something that purportedly happened in the 1980s, and I had not joined the union until 1993, they were unsure whether they could represent me. I would have to wait for a decision and it would take a few months for the issue to be resolved. I had been paying annual fees to the union for just short of twenty years and now I was potentially being left to fend for myself. It was yet more to worry about.

Two weeks passed and I finally had the emotional resources to return to my London flat. When one's home has been invaded, whether by a burglar or by a group of police officers, the place takes on a different hue. It destroys many of the fond memories associated with living there. In my case, the police had looked at everything that belonged to me – nothing was personal or private any more. It always confuses me when I listen to people banging on in the media about our rights to privacy, their disgust about some members of the press who are involved in phone tapping; others complaining that they have been stopped and searched and how they feel violated and how their human rights have been infringed upon. Yet no one seems to address the fact that our current system permits the police to invade *everything* that is precious to someone. All that is required for the police to do so is to seek permission from a local magistrate, which is nearly always given, few questions asked. I had been treated with maximum invasiveness and minimum respect by agents of the state and no one in authority seemed to care.

As I stepped through the front door of my London home, there was an envelope on the mat. It contained a copy of a letter, written by the new headmaster of RHS, to the parents and guardians of all the pupils at the school:

4 January 2013

Dear Parent/Guardian,

I am sorry to begin the New Year by writing to you with difficult news but I felt it is important that you hear about this matter directly from me. Mr Simon Warr, who teaches French and Latin, will not be returning to RHS at the start of the coming term. Mr Warr is the subject of a police investigation following allegations relating to his conduct at a previous school over 30 years ago. The allegations do not involve any current or former pupils of RHS. I should add that Mr Warr denies the allegations.

Given that the police investigation will continue through most of this term, it was decided that it is better for all concerned that Mr Warr stay away from the School while this matter remains unresolved. The School is giving full assistance to the relevant authorities as they carry out their inquiries.

I am sorry that I cannot elaborate any further at this time but will endeavour to keep you informed of any further developments. Should you have any questions, please do not hesitate to get in touch with me.

    With all best wishes,

    Etc.

I sank into a chair and stared into space. As I was supposed to be protected by anonymity, I had been naively hoping that the reason for my absence from school might remain a mystery, even though many would be aware of what had happened from that first day's revelations. The sentence the head had written about 'any current or former pupils of RHS' combined with 'conduct of more than 30 years ago' made it clear that I had been arrested for historical abuse. So much for the law introduced in 2011 to protect teachers! (This would be followed up, a few months later, with another letter that included: 'He is subject to a police investigation following allegations relating to his conduct at a previous school some thirty years ago.')

A few days passed and I was beginning to feel slightly better with the aid of a daily dose of fluoxetine. The trolls continued to send vicious messages, of course, encouraging me to commit suicide, and one even offered to dig a grave on my behalf to save my surviving family the expense. I received many distressing messages and I felt under attack from so many fronts but I had to keep going. What these trolls lack in basic literacy skills they certainly make up for with a seemingly endless supply of menacing bile and crude invective. It reminded me of what Jim Davidson states in his book *No Further Action*: 'All this stress just because the police have let anyone with a grudge have their say.

—

It's so unfair but I must keep trying to not feel so bloody sorry for myself.' Wise words.

A week later, as my alarm went off at 9 a.m., the news headline on national radio was then Director of Public Prosecutions (head of the CPS) Keir Starmer announcing to the listening press that 'victims who complain about historical abuse must be *believed*'. Does Keir Starmer know the definition of the verb 'believe'? I wondered. It means 'accept as true or conveying the truth'. It is *not* the police's job, nor has it ever been or will be, to believe or not believe a complainant – belief shouldn't come into it. It is the police's job to investigate without fear or favour. Further to this, in the moral panic that descended upon the UK post-Savile, a trend had come into being whereby 'complainants' or 'accusers' were referred to as 'victims', even before the complaint had gone to trial. The NSPCC's paper *Giving Victims a Voice*, a joint report made into the sexual allegations against Savile, stated:

> On the whole, victims are not known to each other and, taken together, their accounts paint a compelling picture of widespread sexual abuse by a predatory sex offender. We are, therefore, referring to them as 'victims' rather than 'complainants' and are not presenting the evidence they have provided as unproven allegations.

This almost blind belief of accusations is palpably dangerous.

Similarly, as part of 'Operation Outreach' (why does my heart go into my mouth whenever I come across this word 'Operation'?), which was set up to investigate alleged abuse by Savile at Duncroft

School in Surrey, the police contacted former residents, stating: 'Please be assured that the welfare of victims is the primary concern of both Surrey Police and Barnardo's. This is a search for the truth and you will be *believed*.'

When an 'operation' is set in motion ('Operation Racecourse' in the case of the investigation of St George's), it is seen as the duty of the police working in that operation to try to nail down every individual against whom allegations are made. In my case, the police officers in charge invested a seemingly total belief in 'A' (my principal accuser)'s claims, with the result that, in their own minds, these claims took on a kind of reality. They appeared so determined to have me prosecuted, it seemed almost a psychological necessity. Justice is certainly not served by a one-sided search for evidence to convict. Instead of the police acting on behalf of the general public to ascertain whether or not allegations of historical abuse can be substantiated, nowadays they are, along with the CPS, seemingly advocates for the complainants.

Child abuse allegations require a balanced, fair inquiry and it is all the more important at the moment, as any person even accused of such abuse will face the vengeful, lynch-mob atmosphere which is so prevalent here in the UK today. The untutored Twitterati respond to 'undefended', 'untested in court' claims as absolute truth. Any allegations will be re-tweeted, posted on various websites; blogs will appear and what is written will be automatically accepted as what actually took place. Yet so many allegations have no more veracity than stating England has the best football team in the world. If the defendant is found guilty in a court of law, nothing less than hanging will suffice as a punishment. What's

—

more, in my own experience, even a 'not guilty' verdict will fail to silence the most ruthless, cruel trolls: 'What does the jury know about it? I know the truth,' they state, even though, in fact, they base their immature viewpoint on salacious gossip, founded on half-truths and lies, and, of course, on what they *want* to be the truth. After my acquittal, someone I had never met and who had no connection with either St George's or RHS posted the comment: 'What the fuck? He's fucking guilty.' Nothing short of rearranging reality until it conforms to the delusory, untutored opinion they have adopted will be sufficient.

Imagine being accused of an alleged crime, committed on an unspecified date over thirty years ago. How to go about defending yourself against a police incident room team with generous state resources working tirelessly to ruin you, while at the same time an internet mob is baying for your blood? All you can do is grit your teeth and say truthfully it didn't happen. That was my fate throughout the whole of 2013 and most of 2014.

With hysteria gripping the country, what chance did I have of a fair, unbiased investigation? Over-correcting for systematic disbelief of complainants in the past by now, in 2013, systematically believing them all was creating new injustices. The posthumous verdict that Savile was a serial child molester, who got away with it because people turned a blind eye or were foolishly naive, had become the justification for treating even the most unlikely accusations as credible. The determination that there will never be another Savile fiasco has galvanised aggressive police operations that can terrorise suspects and has led to procedural changes which make it easy for the police to arrest, detain and charge accused people on merely the words of a complainant. Under the CPS leadership of Keir Starmer and, at the time of writing, Alison Saunders, the accuser was now being referred to as the 'victim', thereby logically defining the accused as the perpetrator. To exacerbate matters further, with historical accusations like my own, dating back decades, mounting a defence is extremely challenging, as I was to find out.

As I listened to Keir Starmer on Radio 5 Live that morning, I convinced myself that, if this was the prevailing mood, what chance did I have? I couldn't believe that a supposedly civilised society could become so hysterical so quickly. Of course, you couldn't blame only the police; they were just very ordinary people who had suddenly been handed extraordinary responsibility. But, nevertheless, child abuse allegations had suddenly become a subject seemingly out of bounds for proper scrutiny. The general attitude that was prevalent was 'those accused of child abuse are evil and, consequently, there was no need for proper inquiry'. In his 2008 book *Evil Incarnate: Rumours of Demonic Conspiracy and Satanic Abuse in History*, David Frankfurter cautioned that 'the real atrocities of history seem to take place not in the perverse ceremonies of some evil cult but in the course of purging such cults from the world'.

I had no choice but to struggle through each day and it was good to know that all the former RHS pupils I met in London from time to time during the early part of 2013 had summarily dismissed the allegations as pure fantasy. Indeed, it struck me that no one seemed particularly interested, which I took as a compliment. The only references that were made to my face were along the lines of, 'If there's anything I can do, Sir.'

I was due to report back to Martlesham police station, in Ipswich, at noon on 12 March 2013, day eighty-four since my arrest, which was now only a fortnight away. Unsurprisingly, in the run-up, my anxiety started to return with a vengeance. What were they going to stump up next? If I had been arrested on totally spurious claims and had lost my life as I had known it for no reason at all, what were they now going to stitch me up with? After all, I was part of 'Operation Racecourse', and the police had been afforded generous funds to cover this project. Funds may have been reduced in most other areas of policing but there seemed to be an unlimited budget covering historical child abuse investigations, which had struck me as paradoxical. What possible reason could there be for the authorities to consider the investigation of historical crimes more important than investigating present-day ones? It was certainly in the investigative officers' best interests, if the funding was to continue for 'Operation Racecourse', to secure another conviction to follow the previous two, thwarted as they had been by a possible third prosecution when Alan Williams committed suicide.

I had taught thousands of pupils in my career and, of course, some of them had not been particularly fond of my forthright approach, and this was playing on my mind. After all, anyone can claim anything about anyone to anyone else at any time. What was to stop a couple of ex-pupils who disliked me from coming forward under the cloak of anonymity to stitch me up? They would be welcomed by the agents of the state with open arms, no matter how implausible their allegations. And I was aware during those horrendous days that the police were trawling in earnest for further complainants from the thousands I had taught.

'Trawling' is the method used by the police to search and, in some cases, advertise for fresh complainants, under the premise that the more complainants who come forward, the more likelihood of a conviction. Moreover, allegations made as a result of trawling are treated as though they have been made spontaneously by unrelated individuals. But, of course, there is an enormous difference between spontaneous complaints and those which have been manufactured through collusion, often via social media which is becoming increasingly prevalent. When the authorities 'fish' for allegations, of course they will attract false accusations from fantasists and opportunists.

Trawling operations are the most dangerous development in the history of police investigations. They have been allowed to become more and more widespread to the point of being standard practice, despite Parliament having legislated to put a stop to such investigative procedures through the Police and Criminal Evidence Act of 1986.

One thing is for certain, trawling is a sure method of destroying the presumption of innocence. What is more, because of the particular characteristics of trawling operations, potential witnesses might well be pressurised into making exaggerated or even false statements. In my case, during the police's operation to find more allegations against me, I subsequently learned that some witnesses whom the investigative team interviewed were asked leading questions, which could have potentially created the allegations the team were actually seeking. More than one person who was visited has subsequently told me that the start of the interview went along the lines of 'Mr Warr has been arrested on account of multiple child abuse allegations…' The interviewee was left in no doubt that the police were not after any positive comments about me. I was repeatedly informed subsequent to my arrest that if those interviewed had anything slightly critical to say, this was written down with due diligence by the interviewing officers; if they said anything particularly positive about my enthusiasm and kindness, this was dismissed as 'grooming'. Evidence-gathering can so easily be conducted in the medium of suggestive or leading questions, even unwittingly, and the behaviour of the officers will of course influence how questions are answered.

The ethics of police trawling were recently considered at some length by the Home Affairs Select Committee and it was emphasised: 'Any initial approach by the police to former pupils of boarding and care establishments should – so far as possible – go no further than a *general* invitation to provide information to the investigative team.'

This was not quite how the 'Operation Racecourse' investigative officers went about their business. They made it clear they were after negative comments about my conduct, which is contrary to established police practice. There is little doubt that police trawling has become entirely unregulated.

It can be argued that if a number of spontaneous, similar allegations are made by independent witnesses, then a case to answer should be the result. However, recent history has taught us that these allegations of historical abuse are rarely spontaneous, unprompted or independent. So, in this type of case, any punctilious exactness upon which any good legal system is based has been, to all intents and purposes, abandoned.

Now trawling is used by all police forces in the UK as a means of convicting suspected child abusers. Trawling is the reverse of normal police procedure. Instead of starting out with a crime and setting out to find the perpetrator, the trawling procedure starts with the suspect and then attempts to find his or her crime or crimes.

In historical abuse inquiries, the police must be wary of the fact that there are some adult complainants who, living unproductive lives and with an opportunity to get their hands on more money than they could ever have imagined, are prepared to make false allegations, regardless of the consequences for the person they are accusing. There are some who claim to have been abused as children who are convicted criminals themselves or else are facing criminal charges. Once again, the dangers of trawling are obvious. Quite honestly, if people who are by nature dishonest or struggling financially are interviewed and given the opportunity to claim to have been abused in the past, it would be surprising if they did not allege some sort of historical abuse. Yet, still these trawling operations continue with the full backing of our judicial system and the Home Office and the Ministry of Justice.

The day finally arrived. I had almost made myself ill worrying in the week leading up to this day of reckoning and, as I made my way to London Liverpool Street station, to catch the 9.30 a.m. train to Ipswich, I felt very anxious. Settled into the compartment, I rang my solicitor, who was due to meet me at the police HQ in Ipswich at 11.30 a.m.

'Oh, yes, I was going to ring you; they told me this morning they don't want to see you today; they have further inquiries to make and they now want to see you on Wednesday 8 May.'

The train had pulled out of the station and I was now on my way to Suffolk.

I couldn't believe that I had been informed so late in the day. I had been building myself emotionally as best I could for this date for the past eighty-four days. Eighty-four days of mental torture and, almost as an aside, I had been informed there would be a postponement of a further fifty-seven days: fifty-seven days of more worry, with nothing to live for, but simply to exist and worry. There were only so many times one could walk aimlessly around the countryside of Wales or the streets of London. The heartlessness of the process astounded me. There didn't seem to be anybody in authority who could recognise, or was bothered to recognise, the suffering I was enduring in this cruel process. This was abuse but, of course, I was a suspected paedophile, so abuse inflicted upon me didn't matter.

Looking in my near-empty diary, there was one event to look forward to and that was Jonathan Gold's wedding. Jonathan was the son of my good friends Michael (who had recently died) and Rosemary, and was now a practising barrister. This would be in three weeks. That same week was a dinner in honour of the retirement of a good friend, the Director of Music at RHS, Peter Crompton. It was somewhat ironic that such a (deserved) fuss was being made of the retirement of a dedicated teacher who had spent many years in service at the school (in Peter's case, nigh-on forty), yet I myself, who had devoted myself wholeheartedly to RHS for three decades, was required to leave the premises in disgrace overnight: no celebration, not even a goodbye: nothing.

All this would revolve in my mind day after day, the sheer unfairness of it all. Just because of some cock-and-bull story, I was in exile, being tortured daily, which was now to continue for another couple of months at least. And nobody in a position of authority seemed to care, while all my friends and allies were powerless to assist in righting the wrong. All I could do was sit back and wait.

I returned to my flat in west London and, not for the first time, undressed, got back into bed and sobbed my heart out in total frustration: another fifty-seven days to endure. How was I going to manage? How and when was it all going to end?

CHAPTER SIX

———

SECOND POLICE INTERVIEW

Sometimes life hits you in the head with a brick.

— STEVE JOBS

An alumnus of RHS, James T, was a major support to me. James, one of my ex-drama students, was at this point performing in a touring production of *Walking with Dinosaurs* and I was given a ticket for the production when it reached Wembley Arena. If it weren't for this sort of welcome event in my life, who knows what may have happened to me? Who wants to live with no purpose, nothing to look forward to, with the sword of Damocles hanging over one's head? This applied especially to someone like me, who had lived such a full, creative life.

———

I was being hurt, damaged, humiliated and there was nothing I could do to alleviate the situation. Knowing my family was suffering too only compounded matters. I just had to take each day as it came and invitations to shows like *Dinosaurs* helped immeasurably.

Another person who was kind to me following my arrest was *Times* journalist Libby Purves. I had taught both her children at RHS and, being the person she is, Libby had moved to ease my pain. She even wrote in my defence (without naming me, of course) in various articles she wrote about the current trend of automatically believing any historical sexual complainants, no matter how unlikely their allegations seemed. She also wrote to the NAS on my behalf stating a strong case why the NAS should represent me, which, much to my relief, they duly did. I accompanied her to a number of shows in London, most notably *The Judas Kiss*, starring Rupert Everett, where I was introduced to screenwriter Richard Curtis. These were brief outings but they meant so much to me and broke up the tedium of my existence.

The days marched by, albeit slowly, and the new interview date of 8 May moved inexorably closer. Once again, my sleep patterns became increasingly interrupted. When the day finally arrived, I met my union solicitor, Jeremy Guy, at Martlesham police station in Ipswich, at noon. The Chief Investigative Officer, 'DCi' as I shall refer to her, came to the door. I had not set eyes on her since that fateful day in December, when she and her colleagues had altered the path of my life for ever. In the meantime, I had discovered how cold she could be from her reaction to my request, via my solicitor, for the return of my mobile phone. 'You'll get your mobile back when we have finished with it,' was the curt response.

She knew she was in the driving seat in this whole matter and she wasn't going to let me forget it. She had made up her mind that, as part of 'Operation Racecourse', she was going to deliver me to the wolves and nothing was going to force her to deviate from this path. I was guilty, nothing more than an unmarried pervert.

The second interview commenced at 12.30 p.m. on 8 May 2013.

I was told by DCi first of all that no more complainants had come forward other than 'A''s close friend 'B' and that no child pornography had been found within my possessions. She then recapped the salient points appertaining to the complaints against me, most of which had been discussed during the first interview in December.

After the usual legal formalities had been covered, a recap of the first interview took place:

DC: In respect of the allegation made by 'A', you stated you had no recollection of him, you were not able to describe him, and confirmed you had nothing to do with eleven- and twelve-year-olds, the approximate age of 'A' at the time of his allegation.

SW: Never heard of 'A', don't know who he is.

DC: OK, when asked, you stated you couldn't recall taking any sports classes except rugby, but then you went further and acknowledged you may have taken cricket and hockey but it would have been…

SW: with the seniors. Because it was timetabled for the whole year – when the juniors were playing games, I was teaching and when I was doing games the juniors were in class. What he says is impossible.

DC: You couldn't recall if you ever supervised the showering after a games lesson but said, if you had, it would have been a cursory 'hurry up', as they would have lessons afterwards. You also said that Derek Slade had stopped staff teaching in their games clothes, so you would also have had to have a shower and get changed for the next lesson. You again stated it was the seniors but couldn't remember if the juniors may have been doing games at the same time.

SW: No, they didn't do games, they couldn't have done games…

DC: It's what you said, is there something we need to change?

SW: Yes.

DC: Then we'll do that. 'A''s allegation was put to you and what he said was that he was asked to lift up his penis and testicles and part his bum cheeks, to ensure he was clean.

SW: Liar.

DC: 'A' also stated that on at least one occasion *you* took hold of his penis and his testicles and you lifted them up on the pretext he was clean. Again you denied this totally.

SW: Totally! He's a liar.

DC: You also denied leaning over him and parting the cheeks of his bottom; you also denied punching 'A' in the head as he'd described. 'A' also alleged that there was an occasion when he was punished by Derek Slade and was being hit with a cane or jokari bat with his trousers and pants down, and he states that you were present. You stated that you didn't recall that.

SW: Yep.

DC: 'A' spoke about them being in a communal shower but, from your recollection you can't really remember [*sic*].

SW: No.

DC: They weren't partitioned off into single shower areas…

SW: In those days you didn't have single showers.

DC: OK, so a group of lads would've gone in after a sports lesson and piled into the shower and piled out the other end.

SW: Yeah.

DC: 'A' now states that Simon Warr would sometimes cover for our absent PE teacher and would stand and watch us whilst we were there naked and looking back now, as an adult, he would take too long looking. That's what 'A' is saying, he is saying you were supervising showers for him and other classmates and he is saying you stood and watched while they were having a shower.

SW: 'A' is saying that, is he? I see.

DC: Would you have stood watching the lads have their showers?

SW: I never watched 'A' shower, I don't know 'A', I've never watched him shower, I don't know anything about 'A' and I don't think I've ever watched a senior boy shower at St George's. I can't ever remember watching when I took senior games. I don't know why we're having this conversation because I didn't take junior games. Speak to the seniors, why don't you go and speak to…?

DC: What about supervising the children when they're having their showers? What would teachers do at St George's when students…?

SW: Again, I don't know what the PE teachers did, but for games, as I said to you, it was really a question of 'get in the shower, let's get on with this'. I would then go back to my room, have a quick wash and get myself ready for the next lesson. I would then go back to check they'd all gone. That was standard procedure. I wouldn't have had time to stand there watching. Can I say that if one of the seniors at St George's, and there were hundreds that came through my hands while I was there, if one of them had alleged that I took an inordinate interest in them, then I would say to you all this would be worthwhile. I'm not blaming you because you've got a job to do. I know where this is coming from. I know exactly the basis of all this and I just think it's so unfair that I'm being put through this, that this boy, whom I don't know, I didn't teach, I had nothing to do with, is making these allegations for whatever his personal reasons are. I didn't watch 'A' shower, I repeat I didn't watch 'A' shower, I've no interest in 'A' and I don't even know who 'A' is, quite honestly.

DC: OK, if I can carry on with his statement. Then he goes on to say that whilst Simon was in the showers he got me to bend over; I lifted my testicles and penis, which he says was to check that I was clean. He would also ask me to part my bum cheeks and lift my arms and feet up. Have you got anything to say about that?

SW: Well, you know what I'm gonna say, he's either mistaken, it's mistaken identity or you should be arresting him and interviewing him because this is corrupt, this is evil.

DC: OK. He went on to say that on each occasion after PE, when they had a shower, this process would take place.

SW: What you mean, then, is this happened on all those occasions when I was covering PE. At my own school we cover lessons regularly but in thirty years I've covered about two PE lessons in thirty years, if that. But, of course, at St George's I'm covering regularly: according to 'A', it's a weekly occurrence. This is rubbish.

DC: He hasn't said that in his statement.

SW: But the impression is these lessons happened pretty regularly and this is what I infer from what you are reading out to me. And it shows he's lying.

DC: He says that he remembers Simon Warr coming into the shower area and insisting on checking his genitals again, to check he has cleaned himself properly.

SW: What, just him?

DC: But this time *he* took hold of my penis in one hand and cupped my testicles in the other and lifted them up. He was facing me when he did this. He then goes on to say that he was standing and you were squatting in front of him. He then goes on to say that you let go of his genitals and asked him to lean forward where you allegedly went across over his back, parted the cheeks of his bottom, to check he was clean. He says that the incident lasted about ten seconds. Have you got anything to say about that?

SW: Only that if he is maintaining that it was me who did that, he should be arrested because I think the crime that he's committing, even if I'd done this, which I didn't, the crime he's committing is way beyond the crime he's alleging that I did to him.

DC: OK, he goes on to say that he wasn't able to say at what point during his time at St George's this happened but he believed it was during the first or second year there, when he was between ten and twelve years old.

SW: What, maximum money if he was between ten and twelve years of age – maximum payout, is that the idea?

DC: He goes on to say that this happened on at least one occasion but maybe more. He said, 'I did see him do this to other boys but I can't say who they were, as I don't remember. I think it's important to explain that my time at St George's was not good and it is upsetting remembering some of my experiences.' He goes on to say sometimes he remembers bits when something will be on the television or he'll have a dream which will cause him to remember more. He was quite a small boy, he's only five foot three now, and at the time you seemed a big chap. He called you a bully; there was an incident when you punched him in the head, although he accepts that he had probably been cheeky. He claims you punched him with a clenched fist, your right hand he thinks, as you were to his right. 'It knocked me back,' he states, 'it was forceful enough to do that.' Do you recall doing that to 'A'?

SW: No, I don't recall punching any child in the head, ever.

DC: OK, there was also an occasion when he received either the cane or the jokari bat as punishment from Derek Slade. 'B' and [name withheld] were also there. Have you heard of these two before?

SW: Never. The only connection I have with any of these characters is I just happen to, unfortunately, have been in the same school as them. Presumably they're boys at the school; never heard the names.

DC: They got into trouble for digging up the garden during a treasure hunt. Whilst 'A' is receiving the cane, which would have been on his bare bottom, he says that he was bent over a chair; Simon Warr was sitting in a position behind him. After the whacking he was allowed to leave. Then he goes on to say his friend, 'B', and (name withheld) went in after him.

SW: I don't know these other boys, I don't know if they're friends of 'A' on this Facebook group but did they say I was in the study when they were caned?

DC: And clearly what he is saying…

SW: I think it's evil.

DC: Thank you. Now going through 'A''s statement, we briefly touched on the showers, OK? In the first interview you stated that you don't recall supervising the children in the showers. Having been given time to reflect on that, is this still the case?

SW: I didn't supervise 'A''s showers, no. I don't know anything about 'A', I'm sorry.

DC: Right, OK, that's fine. Now Derek Slade stopped teachers from teaching in their sports clothing.

SW: Apart from the PE teachers, I think the PE teachers did though.

DC: Right, OK, but teachers like yourself that would teach French and German and Latin would have to have a shower. So, where did you go and have your shower after your sports?

SW: My room, I had a bathroom next to my room. I just used to have a wash, a quick wash and put on my jacket and tie and go to teach the next lesson.

DC: OK, fine. And then you said about the showers within the school being a communal shower block, with a door at either end.

SW: A swinging door, I seem to remember.

DC: Right, the kids piled through the door, showered and out again to the next lesson. Where were the showers within the school?

SW: On the far right from the main entrance as you look at it.

DC: Were there any other showers that children could use within the school?

SW: I can't remember but I don't think so, not for games, I think they all changed together for games.

DC: Were the showers they used before they went to bed and

when they got up in the morning the same showers they would have used for sports?

SW: I think that was the case. I think the school also had a new block; this is where I used to do my duties because I was in the S3s, which is year elevens, and there may have been some showers over there as well for the seniors. But I can remember now that seniors did shower down there in the old part after games.

DC: You stated in the first interview that you've never caned anybody in your life.

SW: Never. I know the picture that's been painted of St George's and how history has been rewritten by this group. Can I say, first, that when I left St George's to go to RHS that the latter was more brutal than St George's. At St George's only the headmaster, as far as I can remember, administered corporal punishment. At RHS they had dozens of people caning. Slade aside, I considered St George's gentle in comparison. You child protection officers would have given the matrons a medal, all four of them. They were absolutely superb, in some ways I used to tell them they were too soft, they needed to toughen up a bit; they were really motherly. They were really good to those kids, so whatever 'Praver' and his lot have told you about the atmosphere at St George's, actually when Slade went away, and I speak on behalf of the vast majority of senior boys and the vast majority of staff, it was a good school. I caned no one at either school, just Adrian Childs [sic] on The One Show, in 2007.

DC: Why did you want to leave the school to go to RHS?

SW: Obviously, there was the Slade thing and St George's wasn't part of the pension scheme. Also, it was a major challenge at

St George's after Derek Slade, like what has happened in North Africa, you have a dictator and the dictator goes – the despot goes and it leaves a vacuum.

DC: I need to go back to 'A'. 'A' has made the allegation. Now we've got statements off two other boys, a man called 'B' – do you know him?

SW: No.

DC: And another one called 'Y'.

SW: No.

DC: You might recognise that 'B' was one of the names we referred to previously as being part of the punishment with Slade. 'B' gave a statement about his time at St George's and he spoke about Mr Warr, who wore a black robe. Did you wear a black robe at St George's?

SW: Yeah.

DC: He said he was a very strict teacher and describes him as 'old school'. He says in class you'd throw items at the children, such as board rubbers, or wrap knuckles for misbehaving in class. Is this something you'd do?

SW: I don't remember chucking board rubbers.

DC: He said that he had two or three sports lessons each week and after these lessons 'the other pupils and I would shower in the communal showers in the changing room' and he goes on to describe the changing room and the shower set-up, which is rectangular, two doors leading back to the toilets and the showers were within a rectangle room with no partitions, just a line of showers. He states that he remembers Mr Warr fully clothed when he was standing in the showers observing the boys. He checked each child to see if they had cleaned themselves sufficiently and that our bottoms were clean. He would do this by making us bend over and pull our bottom cheeks apart. Now this is another boy who is at the school at a similar time as 'A' and he's describing quite a similar activity.

SW: Of course he would do, presumably he's a friend of 'A'.

DC: He says that he couldn't understand why he was making us do it but he does know that he wasn't touched in an inappropriate way. What he's saying is that he had to part his bum cheeks for you to check…

SW: Nonsense, nonsense, nonsense, nonsense.

DC: … that his bottom was clean.

SW: Absolute nonsense.

DC: So, from the information we have thus far, you say it's nonsense.

SW: Yes, I do.

DC: OK, so you've got another lad saying that he had to expose his bottom to you, to make sure that the children are clean. That's what they're saying and 'Y' is saying similar. Then we have the treasure hunt and the boys were called into Slade's office and you were in Slade's office when the boys were being caned. 'B' is saying, whilst his bottom was being hit by a jokari bat, Slade was telling you about his bottom and saying, 'Look how it's getting blistered.'

SW: That is nonsense.

DC: And then he says that you took hold of the jokari bat, whilst Derek Slade pushes his head down into a chair, and you administer some strokes of the jokari bat onto 'B''s bottom.

SW: Nonsense – absolute nonsense – total fabrication.

DC: So you say that they're lying.

SW: Yes, I'm saying they're lying, I'm saying they're lying, I'm saying they're lying. I promise you, I promise you they're lying.

DC: Could there ever have been any occasion when you ensured a child had washed correctly?

SW: Well, I only dealt with seniors. If you speak to one of the junior teachers who dealt with all these boys; I had nothing to do with any of these boys. I taught seniors, I can't recall ever checking any of the senior boys to see if they were dry but ask the seniors. We're spending all our time talking about three boys who I had nothing to do with. All the ones I did coach for games, why can't we get these people? These ones don't know me. I didn't have anything to do with them, I was not their teacher. I didn't take them for games, they're all juniors. And the other thing is if I was interested in blistered bottoms why, when I had the opportunity of caning, did I not cane anyone? I've never caned anyone in my life.

DC: 'B' said you hit him with a jokari bat.

SW: Is there any chance of asking Derek Slade for confirmation either way?

DC: Well, as you know, we investigate, we look at the whole picture. Right, just to clarify then our concern is the statement we've got from 'A', we've got a statement from 'B' saying similar to that allegation you used to check pupils' bottoms. We've got 'Y' supporting that. We have allegations you were present in the study of Derek Slade as he whacked them. So, I'll put the allegation to you again, did you touch 'A''s penis?

SW: No, I did not.

DC: Did you touch his scrotum?

SW: No, I did not.

DC: Did you part his bottom cheeks?

SW: No, I did not. I did not do any of those things.

We reached the end of the interview and it seemed to me the police had made little, if any, progress with this investigation since my arrest. Nothing of substance had come to light in the intervening six months other than a vague allegation by 'A''s best friend 'B' and another statement made by one of their cabal, 'Y', who'd stated simply that I had supervised showers after junior games (which he was later to retract). I finished proceedings with a flurry, telling the officers they should be arresting my accusers; it was they who should be sitting in front of them in a police station answering questions. All they would say at that stage was that I was to report back to the station on Tuesday 18 June, six weeks hence, and I would then be told whether or not the Crown Prosecution Service would decide to charge me.

After four hours in the interview room I was mentally exhausted. As I had travelled up to Ipswich by train and didn't have my car, my solicitor dropped me off at a pub adjacent to the A14, where an ex-colleague and dear friend, Don Hawkley, came to pick me up and drive me back to Holbrook, where I was staying with friends for the night before travelling back to London the following day. As I got into the car, I saw Don was dressed in cricket gear, having just left 'nets practice' with the school cricket 1st XI, and it suddenly brought back a rush of memories of an activity that had been such a part of my life during the past two decades, coaching and umpiring 3rd XI school cricket, an activity I had loved and now very much missed. As polite conversation was made, I managed to conceal my true emotions until I got out of the car. Finally on my own, tears streaming down my face, I crumpled into a ball behind a wall, just out of sight, and sobbed my heart out. I had cried more tears during the past six months than I had cried when I had been sent away to boarding school at the age of eight, just after both my parents had died. Now back in Holbrook, happy memories of the past thirty years flooded my mind and it was all too much. I had some time before my hosts returned from their school day, so I took myself off for a walk to try to compose myself as best I could before seeing familiar, friendly faces. I knew I would have to be strong in order not to embarrass myself and upset them.

The following day, the headmaster of the school, ascertaining that I was staying briefly in the locale, came round to visit. There was, of course, a specific reason, and it wasn't to check how I was coping. Very quickly I was told that I would be reported to the National College of Teachers and that the head would be required to carry out a separate, internal investigation of the allegations and this would be concurrent with the police investigation. I was told in firm terms that, to ease this ordeal, it would be advisable for me to resign from my post as from the end of the current term, so avoiding a second ordeal. So, after thirty years' loyal service, I was being, in effect, asked to quit, while sitting in someone's garden over a cup of tea. The thought of more interviews, more pressure, convinced me I hadn't the energy to face up to a second investigation, so I took the easy option and resigned my post there and then. I wrote my letter of resignation the moment the head left to return to his school duties. In it, I did add that I would like to be able to keep on good terms with the school, to the service of which I had given the majority of my adult life, and that it would be nice to pay a visit from time to time. The letter back, in characteristic blunt style, informed me that my resignation had been accepted but added that it would not be prudent for me to return in the foreseeable future.

Was I being weak in resigning so readily? No, just realistic. If I could find myself in this desperate situation for absolutely no good reason, what would the school make of innuendo about my sexual tendencies? I was too fragile at this point and thought it would be too much emotional baggage to carry around on top of all the mental anguish I was already enduring.

A doctor's appointment had been made for later that day and I had to present myself in stoical manner. My GP, Dr Dineen, who was a credit to his profession in his supportive dealings with me, had been very concerned about me when I had attended his surgery in December 2012, just after I had been arrested, and had feared, at that stage, I would take my own life. Initially, he would ring me on pretty much a daily basis to check I wasn't going to do anything 'silly'. I had learned to portray myself over the phone to him as being able to cope with the emotional turmoil in which I found myself. I shall never be able to thank him for the kindness and support he afforded me during those dark times. After a warm, unhurried chat in his surgery, he prescribed more anti-depressant pills and off I went.

I took a taxi bound for Manningtree station and, as we were driving past the school, I saw a number of pupils returning in their sailing equipment from the reservoir, Alton Water. I recognised all of them and was eager to open the window and hail them but decided not to, just in case it would break the terms of my bail. One of them recognised me and started shouting and waving. I ignored the gestures and dropped my head. I felt utterly frustrated and very sad.

CHAPTER SEVEN

POLICE TRAWLING PRODUCES ANOTHER COMPLAINANT

Injustice anywhere is a threat to justice everywhere.

– MARTIN LUTHER KING

Then it was back to my empty life in London: nothing to do other than record my feelings as events unfolded (or lack of events, as it happened). I found even this recording onerous on my own, with just a computer keyboard for company. The last time I had spent long periods of time on my own was during the summer holidays of 2011, when I wrote the bulk of my first novel, *Howson's Choice*. As another negative side effect,

---

these allegations had ruined any chance of *Howson* selling any more copies.

The following week, my dear friend Peter Crompton, the Director of Music at RHS, had a retirement dinner at Milsom's in Colchester, to which I was invited. I was honoured even to receive invitations to events, such was my state of mind. It would have been quite natural, I reasoned, for friends and colleagues to keep me at arm's length until the outcome of this investigation. I readily accepted, of course, and it was good to see former colleagues and even better to know that they were all supporting me, seeming confident that I was innocent of the allegations that had been made. Peter and I had produced many full-scale school musicals and we had loved working together. We are both proud to have directed and produced hundreds of pupils in our plays and musicals over two decades.

My close friend Michael Gold had died at the age of sixty-one in 2011 and Jonathan, his barrister son, was getting married. The day had at last arrived, 1 June 2013. It was so uplifting watching Jonathan wed Lil, who was also a barrister. It was such a shame that Jonny's dad, Michael, was no longer with us, as he loved his family so much (this was the same man whom it had been alleged in that blog that I had had a homosexual affair with!).

Michael Gold and I had met in 1993. He was a Balliol, Oxford, scholar, probably one of the most academically brilliant and most heterosexual men I have ever met. We shared a love of literature and music and became instant friends. Like me, he was a confident man and had a good eye for business, although he spent all his profits as fast as he made them, due to his rampant profligacy.

Michael had been headmaster of Crookham Court School, in Berkshire, (where I had started my career) and after Crookham he had become director of the London Bridge Club. I invested in a number of business ventures with him; some successful, others not. Michael even helped me write my first novel, *Howson's Choice*, although he became ill during the course of the project and I was left to write most of it on my own. He would certainly have been very proud of his son on that memorable summer's day and of his subsequent career as a London barrister. I'm only glad he had not lived to see that filthy insinuation posted on the internet.

The next date for me to answer bail was to be on Tuesday 18 June, when I would learn if the CPS was going to charge me or not. In normal circumstances, I would be confident my ordeal was about to end but I had come to realise that the police had established a stance and were concerned only with confirming it. This is known as 'confirmation bias'. There is nothing open-minded or balanced or fair about this type of 'investigation'. In my case, they had their preconceived ideas and nothing was going to alter their course.

So 18 June approached – day 190 since my arrest. The weeks leading up to these 'answer to bail dates' were always stressful, to put it mildly. That knot in the pit of my stomach returned, the same feeling I had experienced during the early months of 2013. A good night's sleep was not an option – all I could do was to grab the odd couple of hours now and again. Dog-tired throughout the daytime, I found it impossible to relax; impossible to find anything approaching peace of mind.

On the morning of the 18th, my solicitor telephoned: they didn't want to see me that day as they had further 'inquiries' to pursue. The first thing that crossed my mind was the possibility that the police were deliberately wearing me down so I might possibly accept some sort of caution, just to end the torment. If they hadn't found the proof they were desperately searching for after 190 days, what could they still be looking for? It beggared belief. The new date was set for 13 August – another fifty-six days. So, my life would remain on hold for at least another couple of months. Another fifty-six days under suspicion of child abuse; another fifty-six days for the police to trawl for other 'victims'. As they say with terrorists, they need to be lucky only once to secure 'victory'. It is the same with police trawling – of the hundreds of pupils I have taught/tutored/coached/directed, they needed just one to make an allegation, anything negative, to help their prosecution.

At least Suffolk Police had got around to returning my mobile phone, which arrived by post during this time. They had had it for half a year, and I couldn't quite work out why it had taken them such a long time to extract any information they required from a single phone. And quite what a mobile phone had to do with an alleged sexual assault of thirty years earlier, before mobile telephones had been invented, puzzled me even more.

Tuesday 13 August approached and the usual increase of anxiety set in. Then, just the day before, I received a phone call to advise me that the police were not ready to see me the following day and that I was to report two weeks later, on the 27th. No reason was given for the delay this time, and I was forced to endure another two weeks in purgatory.

En route to Ipswich on the 27th, day 260 since my arrest, I

received a telephone call from my solicitor's office to explain that the police wanted to interview me again that day, as they had received a letter 'out of the blue' from an ex-pupil of RHS. When told of this news, I had presumed the letter could in some way exonerate me, or, at least, once again suggest that what had been alleged couldn't possibly have happened. I must have been deluded in thinking the police would bother even to keep such a letter!

On arriving at Bury St Edmunds police station, I was met by a substitute solicitor, as my usual representative, Jeremy Guy, was away on holiday. The first thing the new man told me was that he had represented Alan Williams, the-ex music teacher at St George's, who had been the previous teacher to be accused as part of 'Operation Racecourse' and who had committed suicide prior to being put on trial, in February 2012.

'It was a shame he killed himself,' said the solicitor as we chatted in the police station waiting room.

'I can understand why,' was my response. 'I defy anyone to have to go through this process and not consider suicide. Was it the same DC who pursued Williams?'

'It was – DCi. I know her well.'

Moments later, DCi entered via a heavy, locked door into the reception area from the station beyond. All smiles, the two greeted each other like seemingly long-lost friends, even though their mutual connection was a man who had recently killed himself. I was staggered at the coldness of it all. This woman who was leading the investigation against me in such a forthright manner had previously been investigating another teacher who had committed suicide. She must have been well aware that there was no actual evidence against me other than a few blatantly unreliable allegations, and that this ordeal might cause me to consider taking my own life too. I appreciate police officers have to have thick skins to operate efficiently and dispassionately but, surely, if someone had killed himself during an 'operation', one would be as careful as possible when dealing with the next person accused.

I was put into a cell while my solicitor was given the details of the letter, a process which is referred to as 'disclosure'. (The word 'disclosure' is routinely used during police investigations, yet something that is not true cannot possibly be 'disclosed'. Disclosure means something has definitely happened.) After twenty minutes or so in a holding cell with DCi for company, I was then taken to an interview room where I was subjected to further questioning. A former RHS pupil, 'C', of Hawke House, had alleged that I had chased him around a packed social area attempting to pinch his bottom and would, on rare occasions, endeavour to remove his towel from him as he walked past me into the shower room. No sexual angle was alleged, the complainant telling the police 'he [Warr] had thought it to be a big joke'. The complainant himself was someone I had helped beyond the call of duty when he was a pupil in my boarding house and it was staggering that he would want to complain to the police in this manner over twenty years later. Even if the allegations were true, it was hardly the crime of the century, if a crime at all (in his summing up to the jury at my trial, the judge stated: 'Even if you're sure "C" has given you accurate evidence, was that conduct … actually indecent?'). Nevertheless, I was obliged to account for alleged horseplay that had apparently occurred over two decades ago.

One of the ongoing themes of this investigation was that I had a propensity for hovering around the shower area as the boys were washing: such an easy and convenient allegation to make against a teacher working in pastoral care in a boarding school, particularly a man who is unmarried or divorced. I had already stated forcibly to the police I had never supervised showers at St George's and certainly not in the junior part of the school. As for RHS, as would later come out at the trial, it was my boarding house, Hawke, which was first to have its open-plan shower room demolished and upgraded, thanks to my own relentless campaigning. Of course, the complainant 'C' had no knowledge of any of this, so his lies and exaggerations appertaining to my shower supervisory habits were ultimately shown to be what they were.

The interview started at five past four. After the initial formal warnings with which I was now familiar, I was told: 'I need to arrest you on suspicion of indecent assault of "C" at Royal Hospital School between 1989 and 1993.'

On learning his name, I remembered immediately who 'C' was, but was at that time totally unaware that the person who had accused me in 1993 just happened to have been the best man at 'C''s wedding and they were still firm friends.

We had reached this point after the police had spent eight months visiting various former pupils in the hope they would make a complaint about me and also advertising for further complainants to come forward via social media.

After the usual legal formalities, the DC commenced the interview in the presence of stand-in solicitor Mr Bridge, from the NAS.

DC: I need to arrest you on suspicion of indecent assault of 'C'.

Up until your arrest you worked at the Royal Hospital School. How long did you work there for?

SW: Thirty years.

DC: What was your role when you went there?

SW: French teacher.

DC: From my understanding there were eleven houses.

SW: Yeah, to begin with I was assistant housemaster in Hawke and taught French and Latin, like at St George's. I was appointed housemaster of Hawke in September 1986.

DC: Did you have an assistant?

SW: I didn't have a live-in assistant, only matron, Hilary Gibson, who lived in the house. After living in a flat in the middle of the house, when I was appointed housemaster I moved into the attached bungalow. I did eight years in this role in the house. Then I became Head of Drama.

DC: Can you explain to me the set-up of the accommodation for the seniors and juniors within the house?

SW: When I took over they had two open-plan dormitories, about twenty boys in each. There were some study bedrooms for the prefects. In the open dorms they slept in ordinary single beds but in the early 1990s cabin beds were introduced.

DC: It was quite antiquated then.

SW: The showers were open-plan in the middle of the house and the teacher on duty'd have to turn an archaic wheel to turn on the water. First the juniors would come in, then later the seniors. I did feel this was one area of the school which needed changing and the one thing I was reluctant to do was to stand there watching, which was a school rule, while the adolescent kids were showering.

What I used to do each morning was turn on the water, get the juniors in, go out to wake up the senior side of the house, then come back and tell the juniors to get out, then call in the seniors and leave them to finish, as I went into the junior dorm to hurry them along onto their morning cleaning jobs. We called them 'stations', as they do in the navy. So, technically, I was breaking the rules. If they had games in the afternoon, I would do the same. You had to have a teacher there.

DC: And in the evenings?

SW: The duty master supervised. One of them would cover me when I was off duty, Wednesday and Friday evenings and times at the weekend. I worked really, really hard and my house won the Queen's Banner five of the eight years I was in charge. The Banner was won by the house which received the most points based on work, sport and smartness and bearing. I was pushy, I was strict but I went out of my way for those boys, even organising trips when I was off duty. I gave them my life. That sounds dramatic but I've been brought before you because of implications about my integrity and after this I wish I'd never gone into teaching. I gave my heart and soul. My house was so well run that if pupils were causing a problem in another boarding house, Michael Kirk, the headmaster, put them into my house.

DC: Going back to the daily routine, when you wake the pupils up, put the lights on and everybody gets up, what do they do when they get out of bed?

SW: They immediately put their towels around their waist and file past me into the shower room.

DC: The juniors, what age are we talking about?

SW: Eleven to fourteen.

DC: How long did they get to shower?

SW: About four minutes.

DC: Do you remember a boy called 'C'?

SW: Yeah, I do. He was a nice boy. He was a good laugh, a great sense of humour; he used to make me laugh enormously.

DC: How long did he live in your house for?

SW: Four years, I suppose.

DC: OK, 'C' talks about the refurbishment being in 1991, is that correct?

SW: About that time.

DC: He describes you as an exuberant personality, outspoken with a strict disciplinarian attitude. He claims that 'on certain occasions when we made our way past him towards the showers, he would attempt to whip the towels from some of the boys, exposing their naked bodies'.

SW: Why would I want to do that because part of my duties is to stand there and watch them naked? What possible reason could I have for doing it moments beforehand? I mean, very occasionally one of them used to say my nickname 'pecker' as they walked past and I would feign to grab the towel but it was a joke.

DC: Did you ever take a towel off a boy as they walked past?

SW: Never. Can I just get this in perspective, over eight years on about forty thousand occasions they have filed past me and on a rare occasion in all that time 'C', having a sense of humour, he was quite cheeky, a bit of high jinks, there's nothing sexual in it. If you're suggesting I did that so I could have a good look at his bum, well they're about to stand in front of me anyway.

DC: OK, he goes on to say that 'Simon Warr would laugh when he did this; it certainly humoured him.' He goes on to say that 'He attempted to remove my towel in this manner on several occasions' and I'm getting from you that it wasn't a one-off. He says this happened during his junior years, when he was aged between eleven and fourteen. He goes on to say, 'On other occasions Mr Warr would randomly pinch your bottom, for example, when you walked past him in the day room or in the corridors in the boarding house.' What have you got to say about that?

SW: Once again, I don't know if I did, I can't remember ever doing that but there would have been a reason for it, he'd have said something.

DC: He goes on to say that 'This was completely unprovoked and he felt unsettled and embarrassed by it, yet, because the acts were carried out very publicly in front of the others, most boys felt that this was part of the eccentric nature of Mr Warr.'

SW: I didn't mean any harm to him, I didn't mean to embarrass him and, if I'd ever detected that, I would never, I didn't want to hurt him in any way.

Mr Bridge (read out by DC): The issue here is whether there was any sexual content and what my client's saying is there is absolutely no sexual content whatsoever.

DC: That's fine. 'C' then says, 'I recall Simon Warr had a habit of standing and watching us shower rather than leaving the room. I know that on occasions I turned my back on him, as he made me feel uncomfortable.'

SW: If you speak to any other teacher at RHS, they will tell you we were meant to stand there, that was part of the job. Furthermore, if you could measure the amount of time I spent in front of them, compared with other teachers, I can tell you now I did not do my duty properly because we were meant to stand and supervise throughout. One teacher was telling me only recently how he was told off by a previous head, Mr Worswick, for not supervising showers. My boarding house was the first to be converted, to get rid of those showers because I pushed for it. Now, if I enjoyed standing there watching the boys in the showers, why did I then push the head, Michael Kirk, kept on at him, until he finally said to me, 'Look, you've badgered me so much, you'll be pleased to know Hawke will be the first house to be converted to have more private arrangements. Your house will be the first to have them.'

DC: 'C' goes on to say that 'I can't recall other teachers staying within the shower area once they had turned on the main hot water valve.' He goes on to say that a group of boys who achieved eight pluses or more for their school work were invited to his house for a fish and chips supper three or four times a term. He states: 'Nothing untoward or inappropriate happened to me whilst I attended his house for these fish and chips suppers.' On one occasion, however, he claimed you placed your hand upon his shoulder or onto the back of his neck while he was doing his prep in the dorm. Would you have done that? He says the behaviour was subtle but 'his hand remained on me for too long, a sort of lingering, inappropriate touch'.

SW: If I did touch him, it was because I liked him, not that way, because he was a first-rate boy, he never caused me any problems. I'm a very tactile person.

DC: OK, so when you put your arm onto 'C', would that have been a sexual touch?

SW: Don't be ridiculous. If I wanted to touch him sexually, I had every opportunity of asking him to see me after prep in my home. 'C' was outstanding in his work and I was probably reading what he'd written and I just wanted to convey the message, '"C", that's fantastic work.' I have dealt with hundreds and hundreds of children but since 'A''s allegation my whole reputation has been absolutely ruined and whether or not he's now interpreting what I did in a different light because he never said anything at the time. He knew me well enough to tell me how he felt.

DC: I've no further questions.

SW: Finally, I would like to state that 'A' should be arrested; 'A' should be sitting in front of you because 'A' is a liar and whether or not you're going to charge me today, I'm going to prove it to you. I'm going to prove I couldn't possibly be in a shower room with 'A' on his own and all I'm saying is he's a liar. He's a liar, he's a liar, he's a liar and I'll carry on saying it.

As the interview concluded at five past five I was taken back to a cell, where I was told to wait until a decision was made by the CPS down in Chelmsford as to whether I was going to be charged.

'How can the CPS be expected to make a decision about this if they have not watched the interview?' I inquired.

'They'll make a decision based on what I tell them,' was the DCi's response. She added that she was keen for a decision to be made there and then because she was flying out to Greece the following day for a couple of weeks' holiday.

So, the CPS would be under pressure to come to a decision within the hour for the benefit of the DC going off on her annual holiday and, if it were to be a hasty decision, I decided it could go only one way – 'charge him'. Until I had been immersed in this whole affair, I had naively presumed that the police worked independently from the Crown Prosecution Service. The Crown Prosecution Service, I had always thought, is the guardian of the British public, its duty being to tackle criminality in a totally unbiased, intelligent, analytical manner, ensuring they have all the relevant information they need before coming to an informed decision whether to charge or not, a decision the CPS takes totally independently. Its guiding spirit, in my mind, was the figure of justice that stands upon the Old Bailey, the most famous criminal court in the world: justice, fairness, the truth. The CPS, I thought, stood for 'we're all equal in the eyes of the law'. Yet this policewoman was telling me that she was about to advise them to decide on whether to turn my life upside down by means of a second-hand report of an interview that had taken place seventy miles away from those decision-makers – and be quick about it.

This astonishing answer from the DC made it abundantly clear to me that the two, the CPS and the police, work hand in hand. How can this *modus operandi* lead to a fair investigation? The police present what they have found to the CPS and the latter then tell them what else is required for them to be able to take the defendant to court. So the police do more trawling, attempting to fill in any gaps. They then return to the CPS and await direction from them about what they need to do next. This process continues until there are sufficient grounds for charges to be brought. If there's no direct proof, the police have to find a series of complainants to tell roughly the same story. In this particular case, the DC would tell the CPS her opinion and, presumably, expect them to comply. But, it was precisely to ensure an innocent suspect was not railroaded by the police to a criminal trial that the CPS was set up in the first place, in 1986.

I realised from what she had said there would be little chance of me walking free from these allegations that day because, if the police were prepared to make a fuss over such pettiness as these latest complaints, I presumed they needed these to go through as charges to suggest a pattern of behaviour, without which the other two allegations would have little chance of standing up in a court of law. There had to be some corroborative complaints from the institution where I had taught for the last thirty years and, in the absence of anything else, these would have to do.

What the police were after was 'evidence' cut from the same cloth. I discussed this dangerous *modus operandi* earlier in the book. How can similar 'fact' evidence be introduced into a criminal investigation when those 'facts' are yet to be established as true? In my case, all the police had was similar 'allegation' evidence, which, of course, is not evidence at all. Although different alleged offences are usually tried separately in order to protect innocent defendants against the presumption of guilt, there are exceptions to this rule. The law has long held that in certain circumstances, if crimes are sufficiently similar, they can be tried together under the rules governing 'similar fact' evidence. Testimony about one alleged crime can then be offered as corroboration of another. This approach to prosecution is, of course, fraught with dangers.

These dangers were significantly increased by a change in the law that made it much easier to secure convictions purely by advancing a sufficiently large number of uncorroborated allegations. The police use this similar allegation 'evidence' to sway the jury into believing 'this is a dirty old man because more than one person is alleging the same propensity'. In the case of 'A' and 'B''s allegations against me, it is my contention that the striking similarities between the two complainants (close friends) points more to the likelihood of collusion than to any pattern of behaviour on my part. An *allegation* of inappropriate conduct with a child is in no way tantamount to *proven* inappropriate conduct with a child: there is an enormous difference between the two. What's more, the police had been trawling for nine months, spending vast amounts of taxpayers' money, so, unsurprisingly, they were pretty desperate to find some, any, similar inappropriate behaviour on my part. They had, at the eleventh hour, rather conveniently received a letter from a 'disgruntled' former pupil, 'C' (who had certainly never been ostensibly disgruntled when a child). He had proffered innuendo against me with regard to 'shower rooms' and the police were hoping this would add weight to the lies propounded by 'A' and 'B' of what is alleged to have happened in the shower room at St George's. Besides which, I was all but sure this wasn't a letter out of the blue, rather, 'C' had been prompted to write to the Suffolk Police by a third party. Once I had learned that 'C' was a close friend of the complainant who had taken me to court in 1993, I then knew for sure that none of this was spontaneous.

Even a saint could be made to resemble a sinner if enough time, effort and money is spent dissecting his or her entire life, ignoring the multitude of good things that person has done but focusing only on any negative points that can be found. How easy it is to build a case on innuendo, suggestion and prejudice, so to sway a jury that the person on trial is disreputable. And how much easier it is when that person has dedicated the whole of his professional life to working with children! Prejudicial evidence should, of course, be excluded as 'one of the most deeply rooted and jealously guarded principles of our criminal law. Judges can be trusted not to allow so fundamental a principle to be eroded.' (Boardman v DPP, 1975.) This fair principle, of course, has long gone.

After a further hour in a cell, I was told that no decision could be made on this occasion and that I would have to return to Bury St Edmunds police station in two weeks' time, 10 September, which just happened to be the day after my birthday. What timing!

Another fortnight's anxiety would have to be endured. The police were unlikely to be aware – probably couldn't care a fig – that this 'investigation' was about to reach day 274.

CHAPTER EIGHT

CHARGED ON
SEVEN COUNTS

Sorrows come not as single spies, but in battalions.

— WILLIAM SHAKESPEARE

The plan was for me to drive to my friends, who lived in Stowmarket, on my birthday, 9 September 2013, to be ready to go on to Bury St Edmunds police station for 10 a.m. the following morning. En route to Stowmarket, I called in to see one of my ex-school friends, Denis, and his wife Ros, who had both been amazed by just how strong I had appeared to be during this *annus horribilis*.

At about four in the afternoon, as I took tea in the couple's lounge, my phone rang. Feeling it might be my solicitor, Jeremy Guy, with some police news, I took myself into the bathroom.

'Hi, Simon. I'm afraid it's bad. I have just spoken to the detective. They are charging you on seven separate counts.'

'Seven? How the hell did they find that number?'

'Three counts of indecency with a child and four counts of indecent assault.'

Actually, I wasn't that surprised the bastards had charged me on so many counts because, as mentioned, each was singularly so unlikely that the only way they would have had a chance of getting anything favourable for themselves would be to pile on the charges and hope something stuck.

'I know this is difficult for you,' Jeremy continued. 'We're going to have to fight this with all our resources. The truth will out.'

I returned to the lounge, looking like I'd seen a ghost.

'Are you all right? Who was it?' Denis asked.

'Oh, nothing much.'

I had got used to dissembling.

I doubt most people realise just how psychologically damaging just being arrested is. No crime has been admitted, not even levelled at this point. Even when one is charged, an accused person is still supposedly innocent in the eyes of the law but, in reality, the masses have already judged that person as guilty. To be arrested and then, after months of waiting, to be charged, is about as psychologically challenging as it gets. It represents absolute proof in the minds of the trolls.

I proceeded on my way to Stowmarket, staring at the road ahead, unable to stave off those feelings of depression that had engulfed me in late 2012 and at the start of 2013. I was about to be charged with offences of which there couldn't be even a smidgen of proof because they were false and malicious. By this time tomorrow, my name would have been put out into the public arena for a second time and I would be facing yet more humiliation and the concomitant internet abuse. How damned unfair the whole business was. I was having my life ruined on the back of some malicious lies and there seemed nothing I or any of my supporters could do. In reality, the only person who was being abused was me, over and over again, with the state's blessing. And today was my birthday. Day 273 since my arrest.

The birthday champagne that I had purchased to drink with my hosts in Stowmarket was opened upon my arrival but no one had much of an appetite for celebration. I phoned my brother to deliver the news and, once again, it was difficult to stop the tears from rolling down my cheeks.

That night I hardly slept a wink, although I had become used to interrupted sleep patterns over the previous nine months. I was due to meet my solicitor, Jeremy Guy, at Bury St Edmunds police station at 9.30 a.m. the following morning.

As I walked into the station, the detective was waiting with the charge sheet.

The seven counts were read out:

Charge 1
On an occasion between 01/01/1979 and 31/12/1983 at Great Finborough, in the county of Suffolk, you committed an act of gross indecency with or towards Child B, a boy under the age of fourteen.

Charge 2
On an occasion between 01/01/1980 and 31/12/1984, at Great

Finborough, in the county of Suffolk, you committed an act of gross indecency with or towards Child A, a boy under the age of fourteen.

Charge 3

On an occasion between 01/01/1980 and 31/12/1984, at Great Finborough, in the county of Suffolk, you indecently assaulted Child A, a boy under sixteen.

Charge 4

On an occasion between 01/01/1980 and 31/12/1984 at Great Finborough, in the county of Suffolk, you indecently assaulted Child A, a boy under the age of fourteen.

Charge 5

On an occasion between 01/01/1980 and 31/12/1984 at Great Finborough, in the county of Suffolk, you indecently assaulted Child A, a boy under sixteen.

Charge 6

On occasions between 01/01/1989 and 31/12/1994 at Holbrook, in the county of Suffolk, you committed an act of gross indecency with or towards Child C, a boy under the age of fourteen.

Charge 7

On occasions between 01/01/1989 and 31/12/1994 at Holbrook, in the county of Suffolk, you indecently assaulted Child C, a boy under sixteen.

The first five were from my time spent at St George's, where I'd been a teacher between 1981 and 1983. Yet the charge sheet said the alleged offences occurred between 1979 and 1983 or, just as confusingly, 1980 and 1984.

'It doesn't matter,' I muttered sarcastically to the charging officer. 'Why not put between 1969 and 1973? For what the paper's worth, it'll make little difference.'

When the charges had been read out, I was offered a 'support sheet' by the desk sergeant, with numbers to ring if I needed emotional help. I was so disgusted by this piece of hypocrisy I threw it back at her in a fit of pique.

'I don't want any help from you people. You have shown me no reasonableness, not even respect. You lot were set on a predetermined course from the outset. I'll do this on my own.'

I had prepared myself for this moment. I was going to have to be strong. I knew that the cards would be stacked against me, particularly now that the state had decided to charge me. I was fully aware that, despite the fact the burden of proof was supposed to be the responsibility of the prosecutors, in these child sex cases it is not. Due process has been effectively reversed. A defendant facing allegations from more than one complainant about historical sex abuse has a steep hill of prejudice to climb, particularly when you factor in the police's zeal in character assassination when interviewing possible witnesses, encouraging them to provide accommodating statements. Add to this jurors who are understandably loath to acquit where they think there is even a chance that a crime has been committed, and you end up with a pretty toxic, biased cocktail. The national position of innocent people serving time behind bars for historical abuse doesn't bear thinking about.

I was also to appreciate fully within the next thirteen months just what an unequal battle defending criminal charges is. The prosecution has almost unlimited resources at its disposal, while the defence has virtually none. In historical cases, apart from the obvious advantage of the prosecution having the benefit of an incident room team of police officers, the defendant has to set about defending him or herself alone against allegations that were supposed to have taken place many years before, in my case over thirty. The police in this instance had decided to 'believe' a couple of opportunists to whom all that mattered was the short-term pecuniary benefit and some media attention; who were being mollycoddled, put at ease and even being actively encouraged to spout their unconscionable lies. To me it confirmed once and for all a perversity in the UK's justice process, which, until my arrest, I would never have thought possible. Another fact that would occur to me as I prepared myself for the forthcoming criminal trial was that people like me who had little to do with the police and the justice system have a harder job in coping within the demands of a trial preparation than hardened criminals who had regular experience.

Within ten minutes I was back in the car park with my solicitor. Inevitably, the topic of the barrister's fees was immediately on the agenda. I was required to sign a cheque for £11,000 immediately, as per the NAS's rules. This was just another example of just how unbalanced these cases are. I was forced to deal with one taxing problem after another, while my accusers had everything served on a plate. They were covered by their 'Personal Injury (PI) No Win

No Fee' solicitors. Not only would my accusers not have to outlay a single penny, but they also stood an excellent chance (particularly complainant 'A') of securing a vast amount of compensation money if I were to be found guilty.

The possibility of gaining financial compensation from these PI claims, which are usually paid out in tens of thousands of pounds, may well prove irresistible. In the case of the motor industry, we refer to PI lawyers as 'ambulance chasers' and, finally, the government has made attempts to curb the seemingly endless number of 'whiplash' injury claims. PI lawyers now realise they are on much safer ground when they are dealing with alleged child abuse because the whole issue is so sensitive that no government is likely to interfere. Indeed, few people are prepared to speak out against compensation for alleged historical abuse for fear of seeming heartless, even cruel. (I tried to on a recent radio broadcast on Radio 5 Live and was immediately shouted down by the presenter.) The result is these lawyers work under the pretence that they are 'riding white chargers' in defence of abused individuals, all of whom have a right to substantial compensation for their 'suffering'. The lawyers do not advertise the fact that their fees are often in excess of the damages awarded to the claimant. They rarely tout for business in low-profile abuse cases within the family, where most abuse occurs, because there is no insurance on offer and the family itself has few, if any, financial resources. So much for PI altruism!

In *No Further Action*, Jim Davidson states that Chris Davis, a celebrity agent, told him 'that a law firm had called him to ask if he had any female clients of a certain age. If they worked with Jimmy Savile and claimed he touched them up, he could get them fifty grand each – less his commission, of course.' It is not just the police and social services who are involved in sustaining the modern-day moral panic; these PI firms are also playing their part.

Had I been convicted, there would have been civil claims against the fully insured company, 'Anglemoss', which owned St George's during my brief time there. Damages would have been paid out with little resistance and awards would likely have been in five figures. In a local newspaper, straight after the 2010 convictions of flagellomaniac Derek Slade, the following was written:

> ... other pupils who were involved in the police investigation, but whose allegations did not proceed to Crown Court, can also make a successful claim. If you were in an abusive school and were seriously abused, there is a watermark of £30,000. This is the average pay out and goes up from there. The psychologists are the ones that give the opinion on the damages that resulted and often that is more than meets the eye...

The PI lawyers themselves have a 'production line' process in the form of a ready-made claim letter, altering the odd word to adapt to that particular claimant. Claimants can, of course, also maintain their anonymity. (This stated, my two St George's complainants fed their stories to the media after Slade was convicted because, to paraphrase, 'they wanted to show the world how brave they were and how they wanted to do something to help other survivors'. Unsurprisingly they did not engage with the media and dropped out of sight after the jury immediately rejected their claims against me on Tuesday 21 October 2014, at Ipswich Crown Court.)

Thus, it is not only the police who propagate and drive forward this post-Savile panic. PI lawyers are also involved and money is at the heart of it all. Are some PI lawyers blind to the fact that some alleged victims are not victims at all? The situation has got so out of control that some PI lawyers are actually acting as a pressure group for people to make allegations of historical abuse. Is every teacher in England to lie awake at night wondering which child they might have offended decades earlier, who might suddenly decide to go to the police to complain?

I started to make my way back to Stowmarket and, as I pulled out of the car park, news of my having been charged was already being broadcast on BBC local radio. I'd hardly had time to leave the police station. How do the media get hold of the news so quickly? Another battle I had to face was the police being able to use the media outlets as an aid in developing a hinterland of public prejudice, which in turn, they hope, will help them secure an ultimate conviction.

Of course, the police could now lawfully publicise my total humiliation with society's blessing. They could now start unhampered advertising for more disgruntled ex-pupils to come forward with their individual stories about my 'perversions' and it wouldn't matter a jot if it were all a pack of lies. As in so many similar cases, the police were going to trawl the country in a bid to find anybody else who was prepared to make an allegation against me. As I drove back to Stowmarket, I hated my accusers, I hated the police, I hated the media and I hated my existence.

The next few days were about as bad as it got. As I arrived back at my London flat, a letter was awaiting me from the headmaster.

———

This is the school whose previous head had described me in an official reference as 'one of the outstanding school masters of his generation'. Nothing had changed in the intervening period, I had just been the unfortunate target of malfeasance from a few lying opportunists. The letter read as follows:

> Your employment with the school terminated on 10 September 2013 and there are a number of practical issues which I would like to address. Firstly, you still have possessions in the house you lived in whilst working at the school. Bearing in mind the conditions of your ongoing bail, I think it would be best … to have the contents of the house packed up. Secondly, I am aware that since your arrest and while you remained an employee of the School, you have been in regular contact with the Chaplain, who has been providing pastoral support. You are no longer employed by the School but I can confirm that the Chaplain would be able to continue to provide pastoral guidance and support going forward on the basis of an entirely personal arrangement. Finally, you made reference in your letter of resignation to attending events at the School in the future. On the basis that you have now been charged and that some of the charges relate to your time at the School and are in the public domain, I do not think this would be appropriate.

It was clear that I was now persona non grata at a school where I had spent thirty illustrious years.

The expected torrent of abuse came flooding through via Facebook, Twitter and emails. The press reported the allegations as if they were facts, over and over again. Needless to state, there are many in our society who don't wait for verdicts – once you're arrested, you're fair game and, if you're subsequently charged, that's the death knell as far as they're concerned. They're like vultures, desperate to feed on the carcass of the accused.

Of the myriad emails I received, some in support, a number exhorting me to kill myself, one was from an ex-RHS parent whose sons I had taught, telling me what a disgusting hypocrite I was. How dare I preach about good behaviour to his sons while simultaneously abusing other boys in my care: 'I've spoken to my two sons and they assure me you didn't abuse them. Thank God for this. If you had have done, you would have been answerable to me. You disgust me. I hope you pay for your filthy sins with a long prison sentence, you pervert.'

I had steeled myself for this outcome. Most people who are charged on false allegations do not lose complete faith. I still placed some hope in the fairness of the British court system, even though I had lost all faith in the police. I still had some belief that I would not be convicted of crimes I did not commit. At the same time I was wise enough to realise that the police were attempting to secure at least one conviction on prejudice through volume. The first five counts were based on patently contaminated statements and yet the agents of the state didn't seem to care.

CHAPTER NINE

FIRST COURT APPEARANCE

There's nothing that cleanses your soul like getting the hell kicked out of you.

— Woody Hayes

My first court appearance was scheduled for Tuesday 24 September – Day 288 – at Bury St Edmunds Magistrates' Court. This is the usual first step whereby someone charged with a crime is required to appear before a magistrates' bench, who then decide if they have the power to deal with that particular offence. In the case of alleged child abuse, they don't, and the case is referred to a Crown Court.

Since I had been charged, my depression had re-established

itself: I couldn't sleep, couldn't concentrate, had lost my appetite and I couldn't even read, one of my favourite pastimes. As had been the case throughout the previous nine months, I enjoyed the unalloyed support of the school chaplain, the Reverend Philip McConnell (he under no professional obligation, as I was no longer a member of staff), who accompanied me to the courthouse in Bury St Edmunds with my dear friend, organist Michael Simmons. Both these friends were an enormous support to me throughout the ordeal and their love and kindness I will never forget. Philip certainly practises what he preaches. I am so sorry that Michael suffered a massive stroke just prior to my trial and I still wonder how much the worry and sadness he endured on my behalf affected him. He is now bedridden in a nursing home in Colchester.

I was met at the courthouse by an acting solicitor, Mr Tariq Tayara – an impressive young man, just starting out on his career.

'You don't need to enter a plea today,' he said. 'They're not expecting one.'

'I am entering a plea, whether they're expecting one or not. "*Not* guilty." I want it entered formally.'

'Very well. If that is your wish.'

'It certainly is my wish.'

By chance, one of the court solicitors on duty that day was a parent from RHS. As soon as he saw me, he made his way over.

'Mr Warr, on behalf of my son and me, we are so sorry about what has happened. You were his favourite teacher and I know that is the feeling of so many pupils. Thank you for all you did for him.'

Those few kind words were indeed welcome at this awful stage in my life.

I entered the courtroom, eyes lowered at all times. I was forced
to stand behind a glass partition, like some caged animal. Was this
usual practice, I wondered, or just reserved for 'hardened' criminals
like me who were accused of touching somebody inappropriately
over thirty years previously?

As the magistrate addressed me, I continued to look at the floor,
my only way of trying to convey my deep pain and anger and my
lack of respect for these proceedings. This was a miscarriage of
justice and, in my mind, these magistrates were voluntarily par-
ticipating in it. The three magistrates sent the case to Ipswich
Crown Court for a preliminary hearing on 10 October 2013, in
accordance with practice, and a provisional trial date window of
10 February to 21 March 2014 was given, which would be 420 days
from my original arrest.

The court proceedings, of course, attracted more media attention and, once again, the allegations were repeated in the press,
on radio and TV. As I was to find out, however, the media want
the allegations to be true just as much as the police, because the
more an accused person is humiliated and destroyed, the more
copies they will sell. Add the fact that the person is a teacher, and
the press has a juicy story.

To give an example of how these things operate, *The Independent*
was swift to report fully my being charged in September 2013 but
failed even to mention my acquittal in October 2014: this tells
a tale. The viewers/listeners/readers quickly convince themselves
that there's no smoke without fire, particularly as the allegations
are repeated over and over again. The masses love reading about
alleged perverts, particularly if they are professional men, and the

more disgusting the allegations, the more the likelihood they will buy that paper, listen to that radio bulletin, watch that television report. For the person accused, it is catastrophic. In the arena of public opinion the presumption of innocence no longer applies as the headlines are dressed up to be as salacious as possible. The presumption of innocence used to serve not only to protect a particular individual when he or she was the subject of an investigation but also to maintain public confidence, at least in the minds of those of us who think rationally, in the enduring integrity and security of the legal system. Some people nowadays even believe that it is better for an innocent person to be convicted than permit someone who is guilty to evade justice. If only they could spend just one day living the life that I had to lead during 2013/14. That night I went with my friend Denis to watch West Ham (his team) play Cardiff City (mine) in a League Cup match at Upton Park. He had just read about my plight in *The Independent* and continued to be surprised as to how strongly I was dealing with the nightmare.

'Simon, how can you be so calm? You've just been to court on child abuse offences.'

'Is there anything you suggest I do? Hide somewhere?'

'No. But it's no small matter.'

'So you think I ought not to be going to a football match?'

'No, I didn't say that.'

'Then what precisely are you saying? What positive advice can you give me? Do you think I should stop cracking jokes and look miserable the whole time?'

He had no advice, of course, because all of this was out of the realms of anything he had come across. He was visibly shaken, yet he wasn't the person who had to live with the nightmare. This was someone with whom I'd been a close friend since schooldays, in the 1960s and '70s. He and I had shared all our intimate secrets for nearly half a century and, yet, I had little desire to share the full details of this ordeal with him. Now he knew I had been charged, he was understandably dumbfounded by both the allegations and my ostensibly calm response. We walked to Upton Park in virtual silence as he tried to arrange his thoughts. Like so many of my friends, he found enormous difficulty in knowing how to respond, how to have a simple conversation with me. For my part, I wasn't blasé, of course, but when life throws crisis upon crisis at you, gradually you become immune. You stop feeling as a normal person feels. It is the body's way of coping with an ordeal that would send most of us to an early grave. The anxiety permeates your whole life and yet somehow you become used to it; you have to in order to survive. Even though West Ham beat Cardiff City that night by three goals to two, I actually enjoyed the game as, for a couple of hours, I was transported into another world. God bless Association Football and Cardiff City's one and only season in the Premier Division, which came at just the right time for me.

I was due to move my belongings out of my school home at the earliest possible occasion. I was suddenly informed by the school that Monday 7 October was the date set. My niece, however, was getting married in Cardiff on 6 October and I would not be able to drive from Cardiff to London after the occasion to pick up the hired van and then travel to Ipswich. I would then have to load all my belongings from my house, continue to the lock-up near Colchester, where I was storing most of them, and then return to London with the rest. To complete the task I would then have to unload them at my flat and finally to return the hired van, all by the following evening. This was an impossible timetable for me. The school, nevertheless, would not change the set date, as I was told that residents would be moving in to 'my' house within a short space of time and it needed immediate redecoration. They wouldn't postpone it even for twenty-four hours. (The house was eventually occupied the following September, eleven months later.) So, I was unable to attend the wedding. The disappointment would have ordinarily played on my mind but, with all the other things that were going on in my life, this matter seemed trivial. Nevertheless, it painted a picture – my school wanted an immediate end to any relationship it had with me and cared not one fig for any of my personal issues. I had embarrassed the institution and could potentially cost them pupils. They needed my belongings removed immediately, like a surgeon removing a cancerous tumour.

Thus, the house was cleared on the day set. It was an emotional experience, clearing out a house I had lived in for over sixteen years, leaving a community of which I had been a part for thirty. It would be bad enough if I had simply retired after such a long time, but the circumstances surrounding this made it so much worse psychologically. There were to be no goodbyes, no assemblies to praise me for my dedicated professionalism, no public thanks for all those superb public examination grades I had secured for my pupils: nothing, no 'send-off', which every other leaving member of staff enjoyed. I was damaged goods. I was even told as I was packing up my belongings that I had to get the job done by the time classes ended at four o'clock because the school authorities didn't want the pupils to see me. What a way to end my thirty-year career at the school.

There was no hiding place – the press had announced my name and home location. It wouldn't be long before everybody knew. Before I'd been charged, I had some privacy in London. Now the full story was widely available. Obviously, one of my neighbours had heard all the salacious details via the local grapevine because a few days after my return to my London home, I met him on the stairwell: 'We're moving,' he announced. 'I've heard what's happened to you and I don't feel safe living here as I have a son.' And he stalked off.

Another local resident recently told me that, at the time, my ordeal was the talk of the neighbourhood and many parents were telling others that they were not going to allow their children anywhere near me. When you consider the average age of these children is five, you see the hysterical reaction someone who is charged with child abuse has to face.

I decided that the only way I was going to survive this latest trauma was to keep out of sight as much as possible, but I knew this was going to be difficult as I was chairman of the Residents' Committee. If I were approached about the case, I would have to brave it out. That stated, I realised that, whereas on the one hand, human beings are very outspoken on the net, when it comes to face-to-face interaction, only a few are quite so brave as to spit their poison directly, as that neighbour had done (he has since apologised profusely). Indeed, those who are most cruel in front of a computer screen are generally those who find it the most difficult conducting any sort of coherent, intelligent, rational discussion when physically faced with the target of their abuse.

On 10 October, I received a letter from the 'Disclosure and Barring Service', based in Darlington, who explained that my name had been referred to them by the Royal Hospital School and that they would be making their own enquiries and would be writing to me again to inform me of how they would proceed. So, at my lowest ebb, I was now being told that a second government body was undertaking investigative procedures about my good character. I had not been found guilty of any crime, but I was now being attacked by yet another organisation. I wasn't allowed to work with children as part of my bail conditions, so why was it necessary for the Royal Hospital School to refer my name *before* any trial?

The following morning I was awoken by the sound of my mobile ringing. I looked at the screen and saw it was voicemail. I listened to hear the sound of my friend Brian from Ipswich. We had been good friends for a number of years and I had regularly visited him the previous year when he was battling ill health. 'Hi, Simon, it's Brian,' he said. 'So sorry, mate, to hear about all the problems, I just wanted to say I'm thinking about you and anything I can do, you can count on me. I wanted you to know your friends are right behind you and anything I can do, don't hesitate to ring – thinking about you, mate.'

The message he left was obviously recorded in a public place, a café I presumed, because, as he was speaking, I could hear other voices in the background.

Though his message seemed to end there, he had obviously failed to hang up properly, as I then heard him presumably addressing others sitting at the table with him. It went something like this: 'Well, you know, there's no smoke without fire. He's done this sort of thing before, so there's obviously some truth to it all.'

Brian's opinions continued to be voiced for the benefit of his audience but I was so upset I stopped the message before I became more hurt. I could just about cope with all the poisonous vitriol directed towards me by those trolls who didn't know me but it was harder to deal with listening to 'friends' telling people I was a paedophile behind my back. Needless to say, Brian and I have not spoken since that day.

The St Joseph's Schools' annual weekend rugby festival was approaching, 19 and 20 October, an event in its twenty-seventh year. It was the biggest schools' rugby festival on the national calendar and I had attended every day since its inception in the late '80s. Indeed, I had been one of the original helpers in the setting up of the tournament and had done much in recent years, via local radio and newspaper, to help publicise and report on the event.

On the Tuesday prior to the start of the 2013 tournament, I received a letter from the headmaster of the college informing me that I would not be welcome to attend.

St Joseph's College
16th October 2013

Dear Mr Warr,
I am writing to you in connection with the St Joseph's Annual Rugby Festival, which will take place this weekend.

It has come to my attention that you intend to attend the Festival but, given recent events and the publicity surrounding your arrest, you will understand why I do not believe it would be appropriate for you to be present.

———

Please treat this letter as confirmation that you do not have
permission to enter the school site, which is private property.

Yours sincerely,

Etc.

There was nothing to do but to bide my time until the next court
date, which wouldn't be until January 2014. I knew what my prior-
ities were: I had to build my own defence, but this would be easier
said than done. I was up against the wealth of resources available
to the police and the CPS but my own solicitor had numerous
other cases upon which to concentrate and I met with him only
occasionally. I was effectively alone. I didn't even have my diaries,
address books, letters or emails – all had been confiscated and were
being held by the police on a long-term basis (until after the trial,
as it turned out). Re-establishing contact with people from over
thirty years ago was going to be difficult.

And I was going to have to contact as many people as possible
who were contemporaneous with the three accusers – that meant
any colleagues and ex-pupils of St George's (1981–83) and of Royal
Hospital School (1986–93). The details of the very few with whom
I had kept in contact during the interim period were in one of the
two address books of which the police were in possession.

I remembered the names of a couple of pupils from St George's
in the early 1980s and this was as good a place to start as any. One
I remembered as owning a hairdressing business in Norfolk in
the 1990s. I had had spasmodic contact with him since leaving
St George's, and, after searching the internet, I finally found the
name of the person I was seeking: he was still running his own

hairdressing business in Norfolk. I telephoned him (I'll call him 'Dave') one Saturday morning in December 2013:

'Hi, Dave, it's Simon, Simon Warr.'

'What do you want?'

'I don't know whether you've heard but…'

'Yeah, I've heard, and I think it's fucking disgusting. You should have your balls cut off. Why are you contacting me?'

'I was hoping you'd say something nice about me, after all the good times, in court.'

'If you don't hang up, I'm going to phone the police; in fact, I'm going to phone them anyway.'

He hung up and he did.

Within days, my solicitor received a phone call from the Suffolk Police to inform him that if I was to continue interfering with possible witnesses, I would be re-arrested. I had not been told, however, that this person was either a complainant or a possible witness (which he turned out not to be). In other words, if I attempted to take steps to defend myself, I would be breaking the law.

How was I to continue if contacting former pupils was potentially going to lead to more trouble? After re-reading my terms of bail, I could see no reason why I could not contact former pupils and staff from St George's, providing they were not witnesses for the prosecution. I would just have to make sure that my solicitor kept me abreast of anyone who was joining the ranks of the prosecution team. Besides, if I made no effort to mount a defence for fear of breaking bail conditions, I would be going to prison anyway, so I had to take my chances. A few days later, when I had refound some strength, I sat at my desk and, via information I found on the web, I wrote to a number of people who had the same name as another of the pupils I remembered from St George's, whom I shall call 'Danny'. Danny had been one of my star rugby players and I'd helped and supported him throughout my time at St George's. I realised that I would need to be prepared for a hostile reaction but I had little choice. Danny's surname was quite a common one and I had to send out more than thirty letters to all parts of the country. He could have been living abroad, of course, as he had been keen as a boy to join the army.

A few days later, I received a call from the Danny I was looking for; he was now ex-army and was living in West Wales, coincidentally in the same small town where I was born, with his disabled son. I was relieved that he was both sympathetic and outraged on account of my plight in equal measure. He said he would be prepared to come to court to testify, if required. At the very least he agreed to send a character reference to the court.

Within twenty-four hours, Mike Callander, another of my rugby players and a friend of Danny, called:

'Hi, Simon. How are you? I heard about your arrest and I've been trying to find you. Danny passed on your details.'

Mike, whom I hadn't spoken to since the day I left St George's in 1983, was to prove an absolute rock in my fight for justice during the ensuing months, for which I shall be eternally grateful. He and his family will be my friends for ever.

The following week, I was invited to a dinner in Ipswich with my colleagues in the sports department at BBC Radio Suffolk. It would have been so easy for those colleagues to keep me at arm's length, particularly as they worked in the media, but they showed me unqualified support throughout my time on bail. The phone calls from Danny and Mike, and the fact that my BBC colleagues were right behind me, helped to pull me out of the depression which had gripped me in recent days, and I started to rebuild my strength.

As the new year dawned, my next court appearance approached. It would take place at Ipswich Crown Court on 24 January 2014, day 402 since my arrest, and would be the committal hearing to set the date for my actual trial in front of a jury.

I took the train on the morning of the 24th to Chelmsford and my solicitor and I drove together to Ipswich. On arrival at the court, I met my barrister, Matthew Gowan, for the first time. I was most impressed: Mr Gowan was refreshingly thorough and had already got hold of the fundamental facts of the case.

The two policewomen who had started the attack on my life on that fateful day in December 2012 were also in attendance. I'll refer to them as DCi and DCii. The judge stated that the trial was to commence the week beginning Monday 12 May. This would make it 504 days between the time of my arrest and my opportunity to tell my side of the story in a court of law. It seemed an extraordinarily long passage of time.

The end was in sight, though – at last – and the fact that I was now on the home straight cheered me up somewhat: just a hundred days to go.

During the ensuing days I contacted a couple of former staff colleagues from St George's, who were both prepared to attend court on my behalf. One of my colleagues, Valerie Land, who was married to the former deputy head, Steven, now lived on the north-west coast of Wales, so she would have to travel from one side of the country to the other.

'I don't mind at all,' she said. 'It's important that I have my say about this, as both these accusers were my tutees.'

She would be backing up my claim that I didn't teach either of the pupils and that I certainly didn't teach PE to any pupils or coach junior games. Neither former pupil ever complained to her about my treatment of them when they were pupils. Indeed, my name was never mentioned, as would be expected.

Another ex-colleague who would be supporting me in court was the former Senior Master of St George's, David Harding. He had also recently been the target of abuse online from the small cabal of disgruntled ex-pupils. Indeed, the abuse towards him reached such a pitch he had to go to his local police station to ask for assistance. I remembered him as a first-rate, dedicated school teacher, who had enjoyed a successful 35-year career. He would support the fact that I had nothing to do with the running of the junior part of the school. He could confirm that, with he himself, I was designated to look after the oldest of the pupils because, despite my comparative youth, I had a strong character and was needed to handle the toughest and potentially most demanding section of the school – Year 11, then known as the fifth form. He would also confirm that I did not teach PE to any pupils. Once again, how will I ever be able to thank both enough for travelling so far to speak on my behalf?

What I now needed was an ex-pupil who was in the same year group as the two accusers (Danny and Mike had both been seniors, whereas my accusers were only eleven years old at the time).

This was going to be difficult because I had had so little to do with this age group. How on earth was I going to make contact with any now, thirty-odd years later? And if I did, why would anyone want to get involved in this whole tawdry process after so long a period of time? None of them owed me anything, after all. I just happened to be a teacher in the school at the time when they were resident as pupils.

The owner of the present school, now called Finborough, John Sinclair, who was the St George's bursar back in the 1980s, gave me a few numbers he had secured from that reunion which had been organised in 2009. I recognised the name of one boy (I'll refer to him as 'Russell') because he had been a very keen sportsman as a child. I didn't coach him on the sports field, but he might well remember who his actual sports coaches were and would be able to confirm I certainly wasn't one of them. Would he want to help me? I rang him on the off chance.

'Hi, Russell. You may remember me, I was one of the teachers at St George's in the early '80s.'

'Yeah, I know,' he responded. 'I heard about your problems and if there is anything I can do to help, please let me know.'

'Well, actually, I was hoping you could talk to me about your games teachers. I'll explain why. Would you be on for a meet?'

'Sure thing.'

Unbelievable, I thought. How human beings differ: after the abuse I had received from someone I had always gone out of my way to help, here was someone who owed me nothing but who was potentially prepared to put his head above the parapet to assist me.

A few days later Danny told me that he had been contacted by the police. They had asked him if he would be prepared to support the prosecution's case at my trial. Quite what they had in mind we didn't ascertain, but since he had testified against Slade, it was obvious the police were hoping he would do likewise against me. This was trawling at its worst and, if Danny was being approached, they were no doubt attempting the same with other former pupils of St George's. Suffice to say Danny told them he had already agreed to support me.

I had made a list of potential ex-pupils from both my schools who I felt would be strong witnesses. I was scouring the web, speaking to ex-colleagues and former parents at Finborough and RHS. I set up further meetings with people I hadn't spoken to for decades but who I felt could paint a clear, true picture of my time as a school master, both at St George's and later on during my time at RHS. I visited Tunbridge Wells, Portsmouth, Guildford, Leicester, Lancaster and Oxford: some of my potential witnesses had heard of the allegations, some had not. One thread emerged from each interview: total incredulity about what had happened. These were all professional men – a couple of doctors, an ex-Naval commander, senior teachers and a former headmaster – and all readily agreed not only to write a testimonial on my behalf, but also to appear in court if need be.

My visit to Leicester was remarkable – I had not spoken to Rufus, now a successful businessman, since he had left RHS in 1993. As a schoolboy, he had proved to be an interesting character. Like me, he was at boarding school because his father had died when he was very young. Also like me, initially he had found boarding onerous and he was so unhappy he did all he could to get himself sent home. At the start of one term he had returned to school with a Mohican haircut, knowing full well this was unacceptable in a traditionally run boarding environment. He was duly rusticated. I had taught Rufus French up to A Level and had got to know him well. I empathised with him about the difficulty in growing up without a father and gradually, with my support and advice, he changed his behaviour. Such was the metamorphosis, he was eventually appointed as Head of School (Head Boy). As part of his duties, he was required to lead the administering of the pastoral care system of his team of prefects. In this capacity, he spent quite a lot of time visiting the boarding house which I ran in the late '80s and early '90s. During this time, it turned out, he had got to know 'C', one of my accusers. Back then, 'C' would apparently tell Rufus all about his friends, and the two would discuss his personal problems. Rufus remembered how 'C' praised me as a housemaster; how enthusiastic and dedicated I was to all the boys in my care; my strictness when it came to high standards; and, of course, my sense of fun. In so many words, as a child, 'C' frequently told Rufus how proud he was to be in Hawke House.

I told Rufus about the charges that had been made against me; that 'C' had alleged I had chased him around a packed common room trying to pinch his bottom and had, on occasions, attempted to remove his towel on the way into the shower block. I explained how the complainant had frequently muttered my nickname under his breath when walking past me, in a jocular manner, in order to incite a reaction, which very occasionally happened. I told Rufus that 'C' had said in his statement that there was nothing sexual intended, it was just me thinking 'I was being funny', as he termed it.

Rufus was stunned and immediately told me that he had frequently heard 'C' calling me by my nickname to my face when he visited my boarding house, even though the complainant later denied he had ever done so when he eventually gave evidence in court.

Rufus listened in astonishment as I informed him of all that I had had to endure since late 2012 and, when I had finished relating the whole sorry saga, he said it was almost Kafkaesque that someone who had devoted such a substantial part of his adult life to his boarding school duties, with such obvious success, should be subsequently hauled before a court of law. He was horrified that 'C' had decided to make these complaints. He told me he would do everything he could to support me.

I returned to London on a late-night train from Leicester buoyed by our meeting. At last, the actual events of decades earlier, as opposed to what had been reported to the police, were finally being confirmed in my mind by reliable sources. This may be a rather strange thing to write but, when confronted with a barrage of lies, one begins to doubt one's own mind. I had fleetingly doubted my own recollection of what had taken place; or had *not* taken place, with 'C', to be precise.

Things got even better in early March 2013 when I met Russell, the ex-pupil from St George's, who was a contemporary of 'A' and 'B'. He was now the physiotherapist at a professional football club. The meeting took place at a coffee bar at Reading Station.

I explained the details of the allegations, that after junior PE lessons I was supposed to have inspected the boys after they had showered, in an inappropriate manner, and had gone on to touch one pupil, and it was he who had contacted the police in 2012.

'A''s close friend 'B' had backed up his story that I would inspect the pupils after PE but didn't see me touch his friend (neither, for that matter, did anyone else in the crowded changing room).

'But you didn't teach PE at St George's,' said Russell. 'PE was my favourite subject, in fact the only one I was good at, and I didn't miss a single lesson during my time at school. There was a separate PE department. I can remember the names of the teachers. These accusers, whoever they are, are lying. You never taught PE or games to us juniors. The only games you did were with the 1st XV, the older boys.'

'Would you be prepared to write a statement on my behalf,' I asked, 'or, better still, to come to court to say this, Russell?'

'I would do whatever, definitely.'

'But you don't owe me anything. I didn't do much for you, if anything at all, when you were a boy.'

'I have to come to court because I need to tell the truth. It's got nothing to do with you or anyone else. It's simply the truth.'

Not for the first time, I was flabbergasted by just how much human beings differ.

CHAPTER TEN

———

ANOTHER POSTPONEMENT

Justice delayed is justice denied.

— Magna Carta

I was in an almost positive mood when I came away from that meeting at Reading station. I had endured darkness for such a long time, when all had seemed hopeless, and gradually, as I had managed to contact more and more professional former staff and pupils, I was able to see a glint of light at the end of the tunnel.

I received a phone call about this time from Roy Mac, a City whizz kid who was the son of the former managing director of Tippex UK. Mac had been a pupil of mine in the early '80s at Cokethorpe School, where I had taught briefly before going to St George's.

———

He had been interviewed by the Suffolk Police some time earlier by telephone and had been asked not to contact me in case he was required to write a statement. Some weeks later, he had emailed the officer in charge and asked her whether it would now be possible to contact me, whom he regarded as a friend and who had helped him as a boy growing up.

The return email from DCi read: 'We have decided not to ask you for a statement, Mac, and, if you wish, you may contact Simon Warr.'

Mac's email response to her was straight to the point:

> I'm not surprised you didn't want a statement from me, as I didn't come up with any dirt that you could use in your case … I will find out from Simon what these 'multiple' claims are, but, in the meantime, it's pretty clear that you are not interested in actually investigating whether these allegations are indeed true, you are just searching for any old scrap to assassinate his character. Very worrying, and in the light of current high profile cases falling down, you should be thoroughly ashamed of yourself, if only for the disgusting waste of public money.

He handed a copy of this email to me when we met up. Mac had hit the nail on the head without knowing much about what had led up to my arrest and is another person to whom I shall be indebted for the rest of my life.

A few days later, an independent TV producer, having heard of my recent ordeal, contacted me. He seemed eager to produce a documentary about the process of being arrested and then charged for a historical child abuse allegation on the basis of little, if any, supporting evidence. He wanted to capture the turmoil that false allegations cause, how they can wreck someone's life. A camera team attended my London flat the following week, where a long interview was conducted, followed by filming in the local park. I had the chance to pour my heart out about the torture I was in the process of enduring and, though it was difficult to put into words, I found it rather therapeutic.

'It's only for another month,' the producer reassured me. 'You have survived the process for well over a year and you have just a short while left.'

It was true. I had been counting down the days to 12 May, which would be day 504 since my initial arrest. I had survived to Day 475. I was nearly there. This period of time I had spent on bail had been not much better, I imagined, than being locked up in a jail. Although I technically had my freedom, it had been a miserable existence. If someone had given me the option on 18 December 2012 of going to prison for eighteen months and then have the whole episode erased forever, I would have preferred that option.

The pre-trial hearing was to be held at Ipswich Crown Court, on Tuesday 29 April. I was getting almost excited. I was dying to explain to the world that these allegations were the workings of cruel, dishonest individuals. I knew that their claims could not possibly stand up to scrutiny and that finally I would be free to resume my life, although I would find it difficult, if not impossible, to get back to how I was.

I took the train to Chelmsford the morning of the hearing and my solicitor drove me to the court in Suffolk. The hearing started at 2 p.m. It was supposed to be a meeting of the interested parties in front of a judge to verify that all the necessary papers had been produced and that both sides were ready for the actual trial.

However, there was a problem. Apparently, a number of papers that the defence were expecting had still not been produced by the CPS, and the judge ordered that they be presented by the following Wednesday 7 May, which was just three working days before the actual trial was due to start.

My solicitor, barrister and I returned to the court on the 7th to learn that the CPS were not ready to go to trial and that the judge would have to set another date. They'd had over 500 days since my arrest to prepare their case, yet it was still not ready. How difficult could it possibly be? Unless, of course, the foundations upon which they had to work were a pack of lies.

The next occasion the court could conduct a possible eight-day trial was the week beginning Monday 13 October – another 160 days.

'Justice delayed is justice denied' it says in Magna Carta, which forms the basis of English justice to the modern day, a system which has had the respect of the world for centuries. Fairness and swiftness of justice are the criteria that have long underpinned British law. I was being denied both.

I now had another five months to endure; the police, on the other hand, had another five months to trawl for more complainants. Within twenty-four hours of the announcement of the postponement, a website, 'The Survivors of Crookham Court', run by an 'injustice collector, specialist subject child abuse' based in Newbury, Berkshire stated:

'I am informed that the trial of former Crookham Court teacher, Simon Warr, will now begin on 13th October 2014. I am further informed that the police in Suffolk are willing to take statements. An email address for a named officer can be provided or you can communicate via me.'

In other words, 'The Suffolk Police aren't allowed to advertise for complainants to come forward, so I am doing so on their behalf. They need more people to come forward if they are to stand a good chance of having Warr convicted in October.' It was staggering, yet unsurprising, that this police agent had been given the job of touting for business on behalf of the Suffolk Police. I wondered how such advertising for complainants could even be legal, a police force 'trawling' in this crude manner via a third party? Furthermore, this Crookham advert followed information I received some weeks earlier from an ex-colleague of mine at RHS, who told me he had alerted the school that advertisements for complainants had been appearing on an RHS former pupils' website.

So, if the police were going to use the next 160 days for a trawling exercise, I would use the time to strengthen further my defence. I decided to contact a former pupil of St George's whose sons I had subsequently taught at RHS. He seemed genuinely pleased to speak to me and assured me he would do all in his power to help reveal the truth. He would confirm I had taught him as a senior boy and that the only team I had coached at St George's was the 1st XV, which comprised only senior pupils. He would be a good witness. During the conversation, he revealed to me that he had been abused by Derek Slade at St George's, and I told him how he could claim for damages against the school. He subsequently contacted the solicitors dealing with the claims against the school and this was the last I heard from him. He refused to take any more of my calls and obviously valued his payout more than supporting me in my quest for justice.

Throughout the summer of 2014 I was receiving regular updates about the internet chats among the group of former St George's pupils. A typical entry was:

> Any news on Warr?
>
> Yup, trial was to start 12th May but it's been bounced to October 13th. Prosecution are gathering more evidence.
>
> Oh, ok, fair enough. Just as long as he gets sent down, er, I mean a fair trial.
>
> … these people never get enough for what they have done. They should be hung upside down by there [*sic*] balls till they fall or maybe slowly boiled mmmm with a bit of salt and pepper…

I had been advised to ignore it all but, in my mind, I was going to have to prepare myself for any possible onslaught when the trial eventually took place. I wanted to know what was being said about me. The police were constantly perusing these websites, so they were fully aware of the level of hostility, yet they did nothing about it. On one occasion, when I asked my solicitor to complain to the police about what had been written, the response was: 'They are entitled to their opinion.'

By chance, I had met at a school parents' meeting some years earlier a former Head of House of mine, Mark Hambly, who had been a first-rate pupil. He had ended up as Head of School. He was at the meeting as his nephew was now attending the school. We had a brief chat and exchanged numbers. After leaving school he had gone the way one would have predicted, studying Engineering at Cambridge and then training to be a medical doctor. He had been a boy of the utmost integrity and diligence and, unsurprisingly, had developed into a successful adult, both professionally and personally.

By pure chance, I came across his number written on a piece of paper stuffed in one of my briefcases. I rang him and we arranged a meeting in Tunbridge Wells, where Mark was practising and living. We met at the railway station and went for afternoon tea. I explained what had been alleged in counts six and seven (the supposed bottom pinching and attempts to take away the towel). Mark said he had never heard anything about this when he was at school and, particularly during the year he was Head of House, he had heard every last piece of gossip among the boys in the house.

'Would you be prepared to come to court to say as much?' I asked him.

'I certainly would,' was his immediate response.

Once again, here was a well-regarded professional prepared to involve himself in a pretty tawdry child abuse case where he had nothing to gain (other than telling the truth to help justice to be served) and a lot to lose.

On my way back in the train to London I was, once again, feeling uplifted, as I had repeatedly felt having met up with someone who was interested only in telling the truth.

* * *

As well as ex-pupils, I had also set about contacting a number of ex-colleagues at RHS to ask if they would be prepared to represent me at the trial. All agreed without a moment's hesitation. This included two young teachers who had originally been pupils at the school and whom I had taught and coached. Once again, their positive, supportive attitude lifted my spirits as the trial date approached. (Unfortunately, they were subsequently dissuaded from appearing by the school authorities.)

I now had a large team of witnesses and character referees who would be attending court, comprising two ex-headmasters, a number of ex-colleagues, ex-parents and pupils, which included a retired Naval Commander and two doctors. I also had a number of written testimonials for my barrister to read out, if needed.

September 2014 arrived, over 600 days since my arrest, and the end was finally in sight. Surely, I thought, there could be no more delays. There was a final potential witness that I wanted to contact, Donny, a senior pupil (and Head Boy) at St George's, who was now a senior teacher at a state school. Indeed, he had for a number of years been its Child Protection Officer.

As a pupil, he had been an outstanding individual, mature and particularly responsible for his tender years. I managed through a third party to secure his contact number. When I rang, he was at a football match with his son. In spite of the ambient noise, we managed to have a productive conversation and we agreed to meet the following week, on 24 September.

'Yeah, they came to see me some months ago,' he said with a look of disquiet. 'It was horrendous. By the time the two officers left I was in a right state. My wife had to comfort me for hours afterwards and I wasn't in a fit condition to go to work the following day. They painted a picture of St George's I simply didn't recognise. It seemed people had been rewriting history. All the allegations of midnight abuse in Slade's house – surely we pupils would have heard something – anything – on the grapevine? There were late feasts but that was all we knew about. Abuse? Nothing. Not a murmur. Not a word. And I liked to think virtually everything came back to us prefects. How could there possibly have been this mass abuse going on and no one get an inkling? It's just impossible.'

'Of course, once Slade had been proven to be guilty on some counts, it was open house, so to speak, and he didn't have a chance on all the other accusations, bizarre and unlikely as they were,' I said.

'They were particularly aggressive when they started questioning me about you,' Donny continued. He went on to explain and his words mirrored what I'd heard from others who had been visited by the police: the interviews were saturated with leading questions and inadvertent cueing. In a statement that Donny subsequently submitted, the following was included:

> In the six years I was at St George's I never heard any rumours regarding Mr Warr and any improper conduct by him regarding pupils … We have discussed the Derek Slade case and on no occasion has anyone raised any suspicions about Mr Warr … Through my professional life I have brought to the attention of the relevant authorities a number of cases regarding child protection … I had nothing to say regarding Mr Warr … I was approached by the police earlier this year who visited

my home and took a statement. They were not impartial. They made it clear that Mr Warr was guilty of abusing children and that he would be convicted without question. After the interview and the statement had been given, they then told me some asides which included divulging that a number of ex-pupils of St George's had committed suicide as a result of the abuse they had suffered.

With regard to the last point, we still to this day do not know of any ex-pupils of St George's who have committed suicide and, if any had done, surely this would have prompted the police to carry out an immediate investigation? Even if this had been the case, it would have been Slade in the firing line, not me.

CHAPTER ELEVEN

DAYS BEFORE THE TRIAL

Spectacular achievement is always preceded by unspectacular preparation.

— ROBERT SCHULLER

With only a few days left, I sat down at my computer and listed a number of points that I felt would assist my barrister during the trial: some bedtime reading for him, if you like...

Firstly, I wrote down a timetable of events that had led to the imminent trial at Ipswich Crown Court:

18/02/2010 'A' contacted Suffolk Police with regard to

allegations against the headmaster of St George's, Derek Slade. No mention of me.

24/02/2010 'A' gave a statement of complaint against Slade. No mention of me. (Compensation in five figures awarded to him.)

21/11/2011 Suffolk DC reports that 'A' is a pupil being represented by Paul Durkin of Abney Garsden and McDonald Solicitors and his disclosure now includes having his genitals touched by Simon Warr, a matter which he did not disclose in his original statement against Slade.

01/12/2011 'A' makes two allegations of sexual abuse and one allegation of physical abuse against Simon Warr. He does not allege in this statement that I touched his genitals but I asked him to lift them up, which is contrary to what he told the solicitor.

13/06/2012 Policy 117 was made by a DCI. He deemed that the evidence against Simon Warr for physical and sexual abuse against 'A' does not meet the evidential threshold as it stands.

('A' informed)

31/10/2012 'A' requests to speak to an officer regarding his allegation against Simon Warr.

14/11/2012 'A' makes further allegations of sexual abuse against Simon Warr, this time touching his genitals is introduced for the first time to the police.

19/11/2012 Policy 126 made by DCI. Further evidence received from 'A' regarding allegations of indecent assault and the decision was made to arrest Simon Warr and search his premises.

1) I told the police during my first interview that I am not, or ever have been, a PE teacher and even provided a list of names of those who were. Why were none contacted? One junior games

teacher was contacted but the police did not bother to ask him to confirm one way or the other whether I taught junior games. Why weren't even basic checks carried out? Val Land was their tutor – why was she not interviewed?

2) I did not at any stage supervise showers, not even with the seniors.

3) The matrons and non-teaching staff supervised evening junior showers, so 'B''s allegations that I supervised on alternate evenings with Slade is palpable nonsense. This can be easily verified.

4) Let's suppose I did supervise showers after junior PE, why on earth would I introduce the added defence of denying I did? After all, I would be expected to supervise as part of my professional responsibilities, so, if I were guilty, I would just say that the complainants were lying in their allegations of inappropriate inspections, I was just carrying out my professional duties. If I were guilty, I certainly wouldn't deny even being there, which could easily be disproved by the prosecution.

5) 'A' has changed his account on a number of occasions, each time embellishing what had been alleged prior: when he was first interviewed by the police in 2010, he tells them he remembers I was there as a teacher but says nothing about my abusing him, yet this was an interview which was focused on him being abused as a pupil at the school. In a later interview he claims I checked to see he was dry on 'an occasion'; in subsequent statements this became 'occasions'; then 'I asked him to lift his private parts' became 'I lifted them'; then 'I didn't see if this happened to other boys' became 'I did see him do this

to other boys but I can't remember who they were'; and 'he hit me because I banged into him' became 'he hit me because I had probably been cheeky'. So, in 2010, when he contacted the police to tell them he had been abused by Slade, in that interview he was asked if he remembered any other teachers at St George's. He mentioned my name (he had seen me on TV) but failed to mention to them I had abused him! Why, if it were the case I had repeatedly abused him? In a subsequent interview he told the police I had been present on one occasion when he had received a caning from Slade but even at this point said nothing about me repeatedly fondling his genitals in the shower room and punching him in the head. Why on earth not? Could it be because he hadn't invented the incidents at that stage?

6) Are we expected to believe, as both claim, that despite their having had extensive contact before and after I was arrested, at no stage did 'A' and 'B' discuss between themselves me having acted inappropriately in the shower room, even touching one of them and parting the bum cheeks of both? According to a statement made by 'B': 'In conversations about Simon Warr we have talked about his TV and radio appearances but only in the way you would have when you have seen someone you have had a bad experience with or you don't like.' He is claiming that the two of them didn't discuss any of the supposed shower room incidents. 'A' stated in official evidence given to the police: 'Obviously, "B" and I have had discussions about what happened to us at St George's. We are aware that we have each given statements to the police but have not discussed the content of these statements.' This is all beyond the realms of credibility.

7) Why do the details of 'A''s original civil claim, after Slade's conviction, differ in a number of crucial points to his statements to the police about me? At the time of Slade both 'A' and 'B' were interviewed by the police and neither mentioned the fact that I had abused both of them. Indeed, 'B' made no mention of me whatsoever other than the fact he had seen me on TV, and stated he could remember only Mr Schoeberl from St George's (who, ironically, was one of his games teachers). Both gave interviews to the media after Slade's conviction. There was no mention of me. Indeed, a DCI, in an internal memo which I have read, was concerned about 'A' appearing on the radio detailing his experiences as a witness (in the Slade case). The DCI stated in an email to a colleague that '"A" exhibited some concerning behaviour before giving evidence [against Slade] and has a police record including assault'.

8) As for Slade, much of the prosecution's 'bad character' angle to be used at trial against me was going to be about my 'close relationship' with Slade. I had little to do with Slade while I worked for him, only socialising with him on one single occasion, when I acted as his taxi driver, and have not seen him since he left in 1982. So much for the 'close relationship'.

9) In 'A''s letters home about all the awful things about St George's, he never mentioned me. This seems extraordinary for a boy pleading that he be allowed to leave. If he had been touched up by one of the teachers, his mother would certainly have withdrawn him.

10) How can someone ('B') go from remembering absolutely *nothing* in 2010 ('I had no recollection of Simon Warr') to later

recalling even the most precise details of some events? In his 2012 statement he says that for many years 'till I was contacted by the police in 2010, I had no memory of my time at St George's. I knew I had been there but my brain had blocked the detail.' He subsequently goes on to remember even precise details like Slade using the adjective 'compliant' to me as he handed me the bat while in his study. Indeed, 'B' goes from this 'I had no recollection of Simon Warr' to 'I have *never* been able to forget what I went through. I can remember these incidents very clearly, Mr Slade and Mr Warr destroyed my youth.' Unbelievably, in a fifteen-point claim form about his alleged abuse at St George's, made in 2011 to the school owners of the time, Anglemoss Limited, 'B' made no mention at all of me.

11) 'C' states that I 'had the habit of standing and watching us shower rather than leave the room'. He is unaware, of course, that it was compulsory for staff on duty to supervise, a regulation I consistently broke, such was the excellent discipline within my boarding house. Furthermore, I almost singlehandedly had the fifty-year-old communal showers replaced by individual units. My boarding house led the way in the shower room refurbishment programme, installing private cubicles, thanks to me, before any other boarding house.

12) 'C' states I 'pinched his bottom in a public place'. If there were a sexual angle to this, I surely wouldn't do it in front of groups of boys. Indeed, he doesn't allege anything sexual. 'C' was, on his own admission, alone with me on a number of occasions and no suggestion of anything inappropriate has been levelled.

13) 'C' states that, on occasions, as he was filing past me on

the way to the shower room (once again, in a very public place), I snatched, or made to snatch, his towel from him. I reject his towel ever came away and assert that this was a game he occasionally liked to play, of calling me by my nickname, in order to elicit a response.

14) One of my witnesses was 'C''s close friend at school and he will state that 'C', in private conversations, had nothing but praise for me as his housemaster and never mentioned any discomfort in my presence.

15) Why on earth did 'C' not make any mention of these concerns back in 1993 after his best friend made that original complaint that I had touched him in the dormitory?

That will do for now, I thought. I have done all that I can with very limited resources. I must now hope and pray.

With time moving inexorably closer to the start of the trial, I was making efforts to find a place to stay for the duration. There was the option of a hotel, of course, but that would be a pretty lonely, miserable experience, sitting each evening in a hotel room with a bottle of wine for company. So, I emailed my recently retired ex-colleagues, Chris and Catriona Herbert, who had been supportive friends throughout the whole ordeal and who had purchased a rather palatial home in Holbrook, the village adjacent to where RHS was situated, some six miles from Ipswich.

'Of course you may stay,' was Chris's immediate response. 'Just bring yourself and your toothbrush.'

Chris and Catriona's kindness proved to be an enormous boost for my mood as those last few days had to be negotiated. It is almost impossible to describe the enormity of the pressure one feels upon entering a period of time which could conceivably end in the loss of one's liberty and the final extinguishing of one's good reputation. I had been here before in terms of mental stress but this time, despite the relief that at last I would be having the opportunity to tell my side of the story, the pressure was exacting. Staying at the home of cherished friends would help enormously.

I drove to Suffolk on Sunday 12 October, leaving London at 2 p.m. How I managed to focus on the road ahead is anyone's guess. I decided to take my time driving the 100 miles. As it happened, I stopped on a couple of occasions and didn't reach Holbrook until 6 p.m. It did occur to me at the wheel that afternoon that driving to Holbrook in the bright sunshine was in stark contrast to the awful journey in the teeming rain coming the other way on the day after my 2012 arrest.

As expected, the welcome I received couldn't have been warmer and I shall always be indebted to Chris and Catriona and their three children for their hospitality. I was given my own double room, with *en suite*, and felt reasonably calm the evening prior to the court case starting. A worry that had been at the back of my mind, however, rushed to the forefront as I lay in bed that final night: homosexual offences against young people were viewed in the worst of all possible lights, a *crimen exceptum*, by the public and such abhorrence can undoubtedly have an effect not only on the jury members but also on the Bar itself. An unguarded judge might be less likely to demand fairness and justice for a defendant (me, in this case) in a child abuse case than he or she would in a case of theft, burglary or even murder. There are powerful pressures to which even a judge might not be immune. He or she might be fearful of allowing a defendant accused of a child assault to walk free if there is even a suspicion that he or she may be guilty. It would ultimately be the jury's decision but the judge in a criminal trial has an enormous influence on the outcome of proceedings. Since Savile, in particular, the pressure to gain convictions in any child sex case which reaches a court of law had increased substantially. I knew I was innocent. I knew they couldn't possibly produce any evidence to the contrary because these alleged assaults were fictitious but, nevertheless, for these reasons, I did wonder whether proceedings could turn against me. I wanted the outcome of the next week to be founded on proof and not on prejudice.

We British have an intense and deep faith in the workings of our judicial system. But, prior to being arrested on 18 December 2012, I had had an intense and deep faith in the working of the police. I no longer had this and I was afraid that the judiciary might be the next to let me down. Could I possibly be convicted of crimes I did not commit? I was unsure. I asked myself whether I wanted to live in a country where accusation was enough.

As I tossed and turned in bed that final night, despite my total innocence, it was clear I might be yet another defendant to be convicted on prejudice alone.

CHAPTER TWELVE

THE TRIAL AT IPSWICH CROWN COURT

The only thing worse than a liar is a liar who's also a hypocrite.

— TENNESSEE WILLIAMS

I would have liked, at this stage, to set out the actual transcript of the seven days' trial but, unfortunately, the company, HM Courts and Tribunal Service, which produces them, wanted to charge me nigh on £5,000 for the privilege of being sent it. When asked if it were possible to provide the DVD only and allow me to type out the text, the answer was negative. I thus rely on memory and notes, save for the full transcript of the various police interviews of 2012/13 and the judge's summing up, which I had in my possession.

Finally, on Monday 13 October 2014 – 664 days after my arrest – it was time for the trial to begin.

I was driven to court by Chris Herbert and was accompanied by Marc Godfrey, a former colleague of mine from RHS. He had been sent by the school to monitor everything that was said in court and to report back, so that the school was fully prepared to react to the press, if need be.

The first thing I noticed when I entered the courtroom was that I would be sitting for the duration of the trial in another glass cage, with a guard sitting alongside me, just as I had at the Magistrates' Court. This would surely give anyone on the jury who was entering a courtroom for the very first time the suggestion that he or she were there to adjudicate on the future of someone already judged to be dangerous. This, coupled with the screen that sometimes hides the complainant from the defendant's gaze, must surely give a distinctly prejudicial impression to any naive jury members. It's the 'perfect storm': the 'victim' behind a screen, so vulnerable; the 'perpetrator' behind glass, so dangerous. The sooner they do away with these cages the better. Defendants in America, after all, sit next to their legal team.

The events of the first day were confined to swearing in the twelve jury members. The court had to be sure that none had a vested interest in or friendship with any of the involved parties. We were told that opening speeches by both the prosecuting and the defending barristers would not be given until the following day. I felt sure I would feel more settled once the trial had started.

As I sat in my room that night, ruminating about the week to come, I was under no illusion that the two principal liars who had dragged me into this nightmare would care a flying fig for the rules of a courtroom. It would be living in a fantasy world to expect them to tell the truth now that they were standing in one of Her Majesty's Crown Courts. I was fully aware of the deception of which they were capable, so for them to swear solemn oaths on the Bible, if they decided to do so, would count for nothing. After all, in official interviews, 'A' had said he felt 'insulted' that the police had asked him a second time if he was sure that these events with regard to me had taken place. 'I know what happened to me, I was there, I couldn't make up something like that,' he said forcibly. Only he didn't, he wasn't and he most assuredly could.

On the second day, we arrived at court in good time, so I had the opportunity to have a discussion with my barrister, Matthew Gowan. Proceedings began promptly at 10.30 a.m. (I wondered why the start time was always so late in the mornings) and presiding over the case was His Honour Judge Goodin. I have to admit I was, to an extent, excited. I was the only person in that courtroom who knew for sure that these supposed 'events' were a pack of lies. How on earth was 'A' going to negotiate his way through interrogation by my barrister, who was furnished with details of how his version of 'events' couldn't possibly have occurred?

Both barristers made their opening speeches. Mr Thompson, for the prosecution, started by telling the jury that what they were about to hear were not the most serious of allegations proffered in a court of law, yet, if true, were a breach of a teacher's professionalism. He was going to show how, in my role as a PE teacher, I had abused the trust put in me by St George's School by abusing two eleven-year-old boys. I had inspected both inappropriately after showers and had even touched one of the pupils' genitals. Some years later, he continued, I had once again acted unprofessionally towards a pupil in my care, at the Royal Hospital School, by pinching his bottom and attempting to remove his towel on his way to the shower room.

Mr Gowan, for the defence, responded by stating that he was going to show clearly that I was not a PE teacher at St George's and had never taught a single lesson of PE at any time in my career and could not possibly have been in a position to supervise junior showers. The only sport I had taught at St George's was in my capacity as coach of the 1st XV rugby team, which comprised the oldest boys in the school. I had little, if anything, to do with the junior part of the school, other than teaching the odd junior German lesson. As for the RHS complaint, if there was an iota of truth in the allegations of bottom-pinching and attempted towel-removing, it was down to high jinks, something that the complainant conceded. Actual contact was firmly rejected by me. Mr Gowan told the jury that I emphatically denied all seven allegations made against me. The events as alleged could not possibly have taken place and his job was to show this.

At about 11.15 a.m., 'A' appeared on the stand. I was intrigued to see him in person. I would describe him physically if I were allowed, but, alas, unlike me, he has the cover of anonymity for ever, even now, after his allegations have been shown to be lies. He started by swearing on the Bible that he would tell the truth, the whole truth and nothing but the truth. However, to inspect closely the court trial system is to enter a grotesque *Alice in Wonderland* world in which opportunists and fantasists swear solemn oaths on the Bible and then give false testimonies that can send decent people to prison. In bygone days, many people were God-fearing, and swearing on a Bible was meant to almost force people to tell the truth. This is certainly not the case nowadays, so I knew that none of these alleged victims were going to pause for a moment to consider being struck down by the hand of the Almighty for telling lies in a British court of law.

The testimony 'A' offered the packed courtroom on that morning was an embarrassing shambles. He appeared to me to be the perfect paradigm of the modern-day historical abuse claimant, where the compensation culture and feelings of very low esteem take centre stage and do all they can to triumph over justice.

After a few gentle questions posed by his own barrister, 'A' glanced over at me, sitting in my glass cage, and suddenly burst into tears. The judge called for an adjournment as 'A' was escorted back out of court and, a short time later, a screen was brought out, so he was out of sight of everyone in the court except the judge, the jury and the barristers. He managed to complete his own barrister's questions eventually, despite repeatedly breaking down while giving testimony. He stuttered and stammered and came across as a damaged, emotionally unbalanced individual.

Then the real problems started for him as my barrister took to his feet to ask him about the events he had alleged. We had repeated breaks in proceedings as he failed to answer even the simplest questions and, sobbing, was removed repeatedly from the court. Eventually, tired by the questions which were strongly suggesting he was an unmitigated liar, 'A' exploded and blurted to the courtroom (I paraphrase): 'I don't care whether he abused me or not, but all I can say is no one stuck up for me when I was being beaten by Slade – not him, not anyone.'

Unmoved, my barrister paused and continued his line of questioning about the circumstances of the alleged incidents of abuse supposedly perpetrated by me. He asked about the layout of the open-plan changing room at St George's and how it was 'A' could name no one else in his class who was abused, other than his close friend 'B'. Why he couldn't name a single person, not even 'B', who had witnessed him being touched. Why he had initially not mentioned me to the police and then had embellished his claims each time he had been interviewed. Mr Gowan set out the timetable of statements which demonstrated the inconsistencies and gradual embellishments in his statements to the police.

Mr Gowan asked him why it had taken him to 14 November 2012 to mention to the police the fact that I had actually touched his genitals. He was unable to offer a reasonable answer, of course.

Mr Gowan then questioned him about whether he had discussed his having been abused by me with 'B'. 'A' said they had not discussed the allegations. He was asked whether we were expected to believe that two close friends, who had allegedly been abused by me, had never discussed their similar experiences in the St George's shower room. 'No,' he answered. 'We didn't need to.'

Mr Gowan asked him why, when writing home to complain about life at St George's, no mention was made of me and what he claimed I had done to him. Why, when he was questioned in 2011 about Slade abusing him and was asked by the police if he remembered any other members of staff, he mentioned my name only in the context of having seen me on TV. His response was he didn't think the police were interested in me, only Slade. He was asked why, when he gave an in-depth interview after Slade's conviction, revealing all the 'terrible things' that had happened to him at St George's, once again there was no mention of me by name or even a general remark about having been abused by another teacher. He continued to stutter and stammer his way through what cannot even be described as answers. One answer he did give, which later proved significant, was to the question asked by Mr Gowan regarding what I had been wearing when supervising showers. His answer was: 'Red track suit bottoms and a white T-shirt,' (which, in his summing up, the judge described as extraordinary attire in which to be coaching rugby).

Approximately one hour after first entering the courtroom, the torture was over for him and 'A' retreated, never to be seen again. After he had left, I asked myself what on earth I was doing sitting in a glass cage in a court of law, 672 days after being arrested, on the 'strength' of what I had just heard.

Next to appear was 'B'. Most in the court didn't see him as he had asked for a screen to be erected from the off. In my opinion, he was even less entitled to a screen than 'A', given his allegation against me. He'd wanted a screen, in my mind, because he was embarrassed: he was fully aware that I knew he was telling a pack of lies and he did not want to catch my reaction.

In court, 'B' was more composed than 'A' and started answering the questions with more confidence. Of course, once again, his allegation was less serious than those proffered by 'A'. He spoke of his time at the school and then focused upon the occasion when I supposedly asked him to part his bum cheeks after games to check he was dry. What had originally been an allegation of events after PE now became events after games. When his own barrister had finished, my barrister asked him how it was possible for this to happen after games, as when he, as a junior pupil, was having a PE/games lesson, I was teaching languages with the senior pupils. 'B' proceeded to claim it happened after weekend games. But, my barrister pointed out, weekend lessons had been abandoned at the school in 1980, before I arrived, so this was not possible. 'B' stumbled and stuttered but maintained I had coached him rugby at weekends. Mr Gowan then reminded him that in his official statement to the police in late 2012 (when he had at last remembered who I was), he had said: 'We had two or three sports lessons a week with Mr Warr.'

He was then asked about an event that supposedly happened in his first or second year at the school, when Slade was caning him in the headmaster's study with a jokari bat, at which he had claimed I was also present. 'B' confirmed that this did occur and that Slade had handed me the bat after he had administered three strokes, saying: 'It's your turn. Don't worry, he's compliant.' I then allegedly hit him three times. Mr Gowan asked him why, when he had been first interviewed by the police about Slade in 2011, not only had he not mentioned my name, but actually stated he could not remember me at all at the school, but was aware that I had appeared on TV. On 16 May 2011, he did indeed talk in detail about his being caned by Slade to the police, but at that point claimed it was only Slade who beat him. Then, in a subsequent statement to the police in late 2012, Mr Gowan reminded him, he had stated that 'I have never been able to forget what happened or what I went through. Mr Warr destroyed my youth.' 'B''s answer included the usual lines, how he had 'blocked it from my mind', the 'memories were too painful', he 'shut everything away'. 'B' asked us to believe that, from remembering absolutely nothing in 2011, he finally managed to conjure up a detailed picture of all the events, including Slade having used the word 'compliant' in his study when handing me a bat, while 'B' was being punished. Quite how he managed to recapture the word 'compliant' from the recesses of his mind is beyond me; unless he was telling lies, of course. The *Journal of Experimental Psychology* recently published an article about remembering details of what happened many years in the past. It stated: 'The higher the level of detail of a childhood memory, the less likely it is that it is accurate.'

As a final question, Mr Gowan asked 'B' what I had been wearing in the shower room at the time of the 'checking' and 'B' was momentarily nonplussed. He certainly hadn't prepared himself for this question, simple as it was. Of course, in his preparation with 'A', the line they had decided to take was that I would walk around the school wearing a black gown, wielding a cane, rather as I had appeared on *That'll Teach 'Em*. After a pause, 'B' answered, 'A suit and black gown.' Quite what Judge Goodin made of this preposterous statement it would be hard to imagine!

So, there I supposedly was, after taking 'B' for rugby practice at the weekend, supervising his shower while wearing academic dress. Presumably I had not been wearing that formal dress out on the field, so I must have rushed to my flat, got changed, putting on my academic gown, and then rushed down to the shower room. However, even if all this ludicrous nonsense were true, no teacher wore formal dress at the weekends. I never once wore anything other than casual clothing, even when I was on duty.

There was no doubt that anyone listening to the day's testimonies would be certain that there was a lot of inconsistency in what the two had had to say. Indeed, it seemed obvious it was a farrago of lies.

'B"s testimony concluded events for day two and the jury was asked to return at 10.30 a.m. the following morning. I met a BBC Radio Suffolk colleague, Brenner Woolley, for coffee in the town centre later in the afternoon (I was barred from the BBC premises itself) and I recounted what had been said during the day's proceedings. I told him the general opinion of my court support group was that this whole process was becoming increasingly preposterous. I felt reasonably content, as what the court had heard that particular day was the main thrust of the prosecution case and it had been fantastical, bordering on the ludicrous. I couldn't see how any member of any jury could possibly be certain that these two had been abused by me all those years ago, as both their accounts were riddled with inconsistencies and obfuscation, not to mention palpably bizarre claims. They had both come across as confused and unsure, desperately trying to fit their lies into a coherent narrative. My supporters in the public seats couldn't wait to tell me that what they had heard seemed nonsensical. The accusers were unable to produce a single witness, I told Brenner, other than 'Y', who would be appearing the following day (and who was to put even more doubt upon their accounts).

The headlines of the local paper that evening were a rather lame 'Suffolk teacher denies indecency in showers'. The ensuing article left one wondering whether the reporter had actually been in the court, as the nonsensical allegations were barely commented upon.

When I arrived at court the next day, my barrister called me into a side room.

'I've got some news about "Y"'s statement,' he told me.

'Let me guess: he's altered it. I didn't teach the juniors PE?'

'Right first time – spot on. He claims he made a mistake in his statement, he meant to say you supervised showers after evening prep not after PE. How did you know?'

'Educated guess. Although you wouldn't need an IQ much above the day's temperature to work that one out.'

It had been evident both during the lead-up to the trial and after the previous day's testimonies that there was a lot of doubt about when the supposed abuse took place. I had no doubt in my mind that 'Y' would have been forewarned that the story about the alleged abuse having happened after PE or games during the working day wasn't standing up to scrutiny, so, unsurprisingly, he had decided to change his story at the last minute. What an utter shambles. 'Y' was supposedly in court as part of the prosecution case, his role being to confirm 'A' and 'B''s line that I had supervised showers after PE lessons. Now he was in danger of ending up as part of the defence case.

Indeed, as 'Y' entered court, one of the first things he stated was: 'Everyone knows Simon Warr didn't teach junior games.'

'Y' had, at no point, accused me of sexual assault ('Simon Warr never ever touched my private parts. I can also confirm he never physically hit me.'). He was called to court only to back up his friends' statements about the PE story. In 'Y''s official statement to the police, on 8 January 2013, some three weeks after my arrest, he stated:

> I remember that there were a number of teachers who would supervise us during shower time after *sport* [my italics] and tell us to wash ourselves properly. One of these teachers was Simon Warr and I remember that he would watch us and check that we had cleaned ourselves properly with soap and flannel. He would point to the areas, for example he would point at our toes and genital areas, and tell us to bend over facing away from him when we washed our toes and feet.

(If there were ever any doubts in my mind about 'Y' being in cahoots with 'A' and 'B', that phrase, 'bend over facing away from him', extinguished them.)

Here he was, in court, now claiming that the shower inspections took place after evening prep (homework). This was his lifeline: he had agreed to support his friends' story and it was now too late to withdraw (he was prepared to be involved in the case against me, having secured hefty compensation for claims against Slade). Now he had found himself in a cul-de-sac, so, as a result, in an effort to cover his own back, he had decided to alter the time of the 'inspections'. Thus, he was of little use to the prosecution case; indeed, he damaged it irreparably by confirming once and for all that 'A' and 'B''s stories could not be true. His own lame final story, designed to extricate himself from this dead end, was to alter the time of the inspections and make out he had initially made a mistake. It was all lies. His original statement was all lies and this revised version was all lies. *At no stage* was it part of my responsibilities at St George's to supervise any evening showers. If I were to have done, it would have been at the senior end of the school, where I carried out all my pastoral duties. There were four matrons and three sets of house parents who ran the juniors' routine, including evening showers. Indeed, 'A', 'B' and 'Y''s tutor, Mrs Valerie Land, would drive some 600 miles round trip from her home later in the trial to confirm exactly this. It was too late for 'Y' to withdraw as a witness and, while disgusted to see yet another person lie on oath, I was pleased his appearance inadvertently strengthened the case for the defence. 'What a tangled web we weave when at first we practise to deceive.'

'Y' went on to tell the court that he thought I was a good school master who had been influenced into being a bully by my 'close relationship' with Derek Slade: 'He was constantly shouting, being intimidating. He was a tyrant.' (The local paper now had its headline for the day, I thought.) In truth, he could remember hardly anything of me from the St George's days, as I'd had so little to do with him. Of course, the junior pupils were aware that they had to behave themselves whenever I was around. Did I have to apologise for this thirty years later? If my being able to control a pupil body of more than three hundred lively teenagers by the force of my personality made me a 'tyrant' in his eyes, then so be it. Rather, I think it was he who had been influenced; influenced by the unfettered bile and lies being churned out by his internet colleagues on the former pupils' website.

My barrister questioned 'Y' about his relationship with 'A' and 'B'. In response, 'Y' told the court that 'A' had got in touch with him just after Slade had been sent to prison, via Facebook. Then, one day, out of the blue, 'A' had called to tell him that he had made a complaint about Simon Warr. He then asked him if he remembered Warr having been present while Slade was caning a group of them in his study after a treasure hunt at the school. When 'Y' affirmed that he did, 'A' then said: 'I must stop you there because I have asked the police to contact you with regard to Warr.' Three weeks later, 'A' contacted him again to ask if the DC had visited him and 'Y' said she had. 'Y' stated firmly in court that he wanted to confirm 'A' had initiated all contact between the two of them and at no point did 'Y' seek out 'A'. When asked by my barrister how many times he had been in contact with 'A', 'Y' replied five or six times. Once again, this is a clear case of contaminated 'evidence', even though the police would have us believe that the three liars' testimonies were spontaneous and had integrity.

It may be a suitable time to explain the details of the aforementioned treasure hunt, after which I was alleged to have administered three strokes on 'B''s backside in Slade's study. This was brought into the case against me in an effort to provide some sort of link between Slade and me. As stated earlier, Slade was a caning tyrant and seemed to take much pleasure in administering corporal punishment. 'A' and 'B' had seen me on BBC's *The One Show* caning Adrian Chiles in 2007 (or, more likely, a YouTube recording in recent years); they were also aware that I had, on a few occasions, spoken on the airwaves in favour of controlled and supervised corporal punishment as a final deterrent in schools, rather than that a particular child be expelled or, heaven forbid, arrested by the police. I have also stated that being caned would be of more benefit to a child than drugging him or her into submission, which happens nowadays in schools. The intellectual nuance of this opinion is, of course, lost on the untutored, and can easily be read as if I am a bully who enjoys caning children. The fact is, during a 35-year career, I have never caned anyone, even though for the first ten years of my teaching career it was legal to do so. Indeed, when I arrived at RHS in the early 1980s, it seemed almost *de rigueur*. I, however, never felt the need. I believed it was the responsibility of the headteacher alone, a viewpoint I have always held. I have detailed earlier in this book, too, my own experiences and opinions of having been caned when I was a boy at boarding school.

As for the treasure hunt, the allegers had obviously discussed their story together (but failed to assimilate the basic details) and they had ended up with a general account of three pupils (or four, depending on who was relating the story) being sent on a treasure hunt. During the activity they had been misbehaving, which had supposedly been witnessed by me. One story alleged I had seen them from Slade's study window, while another stated I had been walking nearby. I had apparently taken them to Slade's study immediately (or they had been summoned to Slade's study after evening school assembly, again, depending on who was relating the story). Slade had caned each one with a bat, while I sat and watched. One pupil, 'B', alleged that after Slade had administered three strokes, he handed the bat to me and said to me, 'You carry on. Don't worry, he's compliant.' 'B' in fact did make mention of this incident in Slade's study in his 2010 interview with the police, but on that occasion all he had to say was: 'On one occasion I remember Slade starting to whack a few of us at the same time and we were then sent out and had to come back in one at a time. I think "A" was there at the time.' Why was my name not mentioned to the police at any point in that interview by 'B' if I had witnessed the caning and even joined in, as he later claimed? For some reason, this incident was brought into the prosecution case on the tenuous grounds to suggest I had a liking for administering corporal punishment and shared my interest with Slade. They were desperate to make a connection between the two of us.

Once 'Y' had answered questions about his involvement with the treasure hunt episode – unsurprisingly, he supported the version of the story that I had been present in Slade's study during the punishment but that I had just sat and watched – he then left the courtroom. He had managed to extricate himself from a situation in which, I can only imagine, he felt out of his depth.

After lunch on that third day, Wednesday 15th, 'C' entered court to give his testimony with regard to his complaints about what he alleged had happened when I was his housemaster at RHS. I had always presumed, when I was his housemaster, that my relation-ship with 'C' had been on secure ground, in that I felt I had done my utmost to provide him and all his contemporaries with a safe, secure, demanding but happy environment. I am utterly convinced that if 'C' had felt any disquiet, he would have felt confident enough to mention it either to me or at least to one of the prefects in the house. I had open, frank discussions with the prefects every Thursday evening in my bungalow, at which meetings they had *carte blanche* to report any worries they had appertaining to any of the pupils in the boarding house.

While answering the prosecutor's questions, 'C' did mention an incident, which I had completely forgotten, about my driving him on one occasion into Ipswich, the local town, so he would be able to purchase a pair of new football boots. He said he was comfortable being in my car and that nothing untoward had happened. Of course it didn't. If there had been an iota of truth in my wanting to pinch 'C''s bottom, I had every chance that day. 'C' also mentioned the fact that he came occasionally to my private accommodation for a fish and chips supper for having been commended for his school work and he confirmed nothing ever untoward happened. (So, anything that did allegedly happen happened only in full view of the rest of the pupils!) The judge, at this point, asked 'C' whether he liked being in Hawke House, to which he answered 'yes'. He was then asked whether he was proud to be in Hawke and he answered 'yes'. Was it well run? he was asked, to which he replied 'yes'.

This brought day three to a close and the case for the prosecution to an end.

That evening I went to the village shop to pick up a copy of the *Evening Star*, to read the local journalist's account of that day's proceedings. Unsurprisingly, the headline ran: 'Teacher Simon Warr was a bully'. As usual, the press preferred to lead with a sensational headline. Once upon a time this sort of reporting was the preserve of the national red-tops, but in recent years it has crept into local newspapers and I think it is to their detriment.

CHAPTER THIRTEEN

THE CASE FOR
THE DEFENCE

If you tell the truth, you don't have to remember anything.

— MARK TWAIN

As the prosecution case had now concluded, I had an early-morning discussion with my barrister to ask him if the trial needed to continue. He told me that, in a case involving child abuse, it would be in my best interests to have the whole evidence heard. The judge obviously agreed. I can't help feeling that, had this been about any other subject matter, the trial would have been halted there and then.

In court that Thursday the entire day was taken up with reading the transcripts of the three interviews for the jury to hear. Tomorrow it would be my turn to take the stand. I had always imagined that this would be a particularly stressful experience but I couldn't wait to have my say in public after more than 670 days on trial. So much had been reported about the whole case and, of course, I was shackled in not being able to respond. Tomorrow would be my chance to show everyone that the disgraceful allegations that had been made by a couple of opportunists were downright lies.

The next day, Friday 17 October, I took to the stand at approximately 11.30 a.m. The prosecuting barrister interrogated me first, questioning me initially about my career as a teacher, focusing, of course, upon my time at St George's. To start, there was a question as to why, having been appointed onto the staff at Bearwood College in Berkshire in 1980, not long after I had started teaching, the job offer was subsequently withdrawn. I explained to the court, as detailed earlier, about the father who'd asked me to put in a good word for his son in an attempt to get him a place at Bearwood.

I was then asked about my time at St George's. As expected, the barrister was eager to associate me as closely as possible with Derek Slade. I explained, once again, that Slade liked me only insomuch as I happened to be a very good school master, and thus good value to him in his business, the school. I was asked about my opinions of Slade as a headteacher and I tried as best I could to paint the whole picture about him, as opposed to the one-sided version we had all heard repeatedly. Slade could be cruel and acted at times in a grotesquely tyrannical manner, not only with the pupils but also with us, his staff, but, as a colleague of mine in the Latin department, he was also a superb classroom teacher and was popular with the older pupils, with whom I worked.

Indeed, my approach at St George's was to work as hard as I could, thereby staying on the right side of Slade. I explained to the court that I had gone out to dinner with him (and the Head and Deputy Head Boy) on one single occasion and I was invited along only as the chauffeur, as Slade had neither a driving licence nor a car. I rejected the notion that we were firm friends and I confirmed the fact that I had had nothing to do with him since he left St George's in 1982. The prosecuting barrister was standing a matter of feet away from me and I noticed he had his right hand on what looked like a birthday or anniversary card.

'Did you not send each other Christmas cards after Slade left the school?' he asked. 'No,' I replied immediately. He then moved on. Whether he was trying to bluff me into thinking he had a card from me to Slade in his possession, I will never know. I thought subsequently, however, what if we *had* exchanged cards at Christmas? It hardly proved we were close friends, let alone fellow abusers.

I was then asked about Mr Singer and his dismissal and, for the benefit of the jury, I once again covered the series of events leading up to Singer's departure.

Next came the questions about 'A' and 'B''s statements and I went through the details of what had been alleged and how it could not have possibly happened in the way it had been claimed. I pointed out the various inconsistencies in their stories and why I thought the allegations had surfaced in the first place. I was clear, direct and unambiguous in all my responses, if, at times, a trifle overenthusiastic and verbose. At one point, the judge interrupted proceedings with the following advice to me:

'Mr Warr, I do not want to dampen your obvious enthusiasm

and willingness to answer all the questions put to you, but it might help your case if you give the barrister the opportunity to finish asking the question before you start answering it.'

I noticed a chuckle from some members of the jury.

I then went over the facts of my never having taken junior PE lessons; indeed, I emphasised there was a discrete PE department at St George's and I gave the court some names I recalled – a Mr Anderson was in charge during my first year and a Mr Saunders took over the department during my second year. They had their own staff and I wasn't one of them because my job was to teach French, Latin and some German. The only sport I was involved in was running the 1st XV rugby team, I stated, which comprised the very senior pupils and certainly not eleven-year-olds. I emphasised, once again, that when I was on the games field with my senior group, all juniors would be having academic lessons in the classroom. After senior games I, with any other teachers who had also been out on the field, would make a cursory check to ensure there was no misbehaviour in the shower area. This is all we had time for because the staff also had to wash and change before the next lesson, which commenced shortly after games had finished.

'B''s change of statement to allege I taught games to the juniors at weekends was also summarily dismissed by me because there were no lessons at weekends at St George's when I taught there, a fact that would be confirmed by other teachers later in the trial. Even if there had been weekend lessons, I would not be teaching *junior* boys out on the games field.

I also debunked 'Y''s allegation that I had supervised junior showers after evening prep, explaining that the junior teachers on duty, along with the matrons and house parents, supervised the juniors' evening routine, while, when I was on duty, I was assigned to a senior dormitory in a separate part of the school, where supervision of the boys' evening ablutions was not required.

The prosecuting barrister then probed me about the alleged treasure hunt incident, which had culminated in a number of pupils being caned in Slade's study. I pointed out the discrepancies in 'A', 'B' and 'Y''s accounts, which differed in fundamental details – 'A' and 'B' claimed, while they were messing about on the ornamental gardens in front of Slade's study, Slade himself had rapped on the window and beckoned them in for an immediate caning, while I sat and watched (I supposedly just happened to be there at the time); yet 'Y' claimed I approached the three of them out on the gardens and asked them what they were doing. An hour later, 'Y' claimed, the school bell rang for assembly and during this assembly their three names, plus somebody else's, were read out and they were told to report to Slade's study. They were then called in one by one. I was supposed to have been sitting watching as they were caned, flexing my own cane across one knee. All four ('Y' claimed there was an extra pupil involved) were then told to return for a second beating. How can versions of an incident they all claim to have remembered in detail differ to such a degree, I asked?

'So, you have never watched as Derek Slade caned pupils?'

'Not that I can remember but, of course, I may have done because an incident of caning was so common in the early 1980s; I may well have forgotten. I can tell you one thing for sure, however. I would certainly have remembered the incident had Slade asked them to pull their trousers down. That I would definitely have remembered.

That did not happen ever with me in the room. And the idea Slade passed on a jokari bat to me while hitting "B" is simply preposterous.'

Questions were put to me about what I usually wore at the school. During the school day, I said, I usually wore formal attire, which included a black gown, as the ex-pupils had claimed. I repudiated the claim, however, that I would walk around the school swishing a cane. This, I believed, was lifted by the allegers straight from the television series I took part in, *That'll Teach 'Em*. I also rejected the allegation that I would throw objects at the pupils during lessons if they misbehaved. I explained that throughout my career by the force of my personality I never had to deal with disruptive behaviour during my lessons, and certainly not on the odd occasions I taught junior pupils!

I once again stated forcibly that I had never caned anyone in my life and I knew why caning was playing such a prominent role in this trial. It was because the three accusers and the police were trying to link me to Slade, thereby creating prejudice in the minds of the jury. If you don't have real evidence, introduce prejudice – that was my message to the courtroom.

The questioning by the prosecution came to an end mid-afternoon and Judge Goodin decided that it would be prudent to suspend proceedings for the weekend, rather than interrupt the defence barrister's questioning of me. I felt the day had gone as well as could have been expected. I remember, as we all left the courtroom, Kim Riley, the BBC presenter of *Look East*, thanking me for speaking so loudly and clearly from the witness box.

I decided to return to my London flat for the weekend and, en route to the station, I purchased the local evening paper, the

Evening Star, to see how the day's events had been reported. I was once again sorely disappointed. The front-page story was, for the most part, another repetition of the allegations that had been made against me in the first place. Little, if any, reference was made to what had actually been said in court that day. This was no forensic analysis; indeed, the piece could have been written by someone without even turning up to the trial.

It was good to get back to my home in London. I had got through the worst and the end was in sight. Mr Gowan had told me that we were ahead in proceedings and yet the defence case had hardly begun. He reckoned there would be a verdict either on Tuesday or Wednesday.

The next day in court, Monday 20 October, would comprise me finishing my testimony, followed by the appearance of eight character witnesses who had driven from various corners of the country to speak on my behalf. On the drive to court, Chris Herbert had told me that I had to be less impetuous in the witness box, calmer. He told me to pause for two seconds after each question before answering. I did my best to follow his guidelines but it was a challenge for me, I have to admit.

At 10 a.m., I was standing in the witness box as my own barrister stood up to question me:

'Mr Warr, in 1975, nearly forty years ago, you were detained in a supermarket in Twickenham, south London, with a piece of cheese and some coffee, to the value of 67 pence, for which you had no receipt. Is that correct?'

'That is correct. I had been drinking in a nearby pub and was sent in by a group of my friends.'

'For which you were issued a warning.'

'Yes.'

'Have you any other criminal convictions?'

'No.'

(Of course, this need not have been brought up because it had no specific bearing on whether or not I'd touched an eleven-year-old boy inappropriately in the early 1980s. However, I was keen that the barrister did mention the incident to let the jury know about my past error and that this had been my only black mark.)

Mr Gowan then took me through the various allegations that had brought me to the court. I answered as clearly and lucidly as I was able and, for the most part, I allowed him to finish asking the questions before I started my responses.

After I had finished answering my barrister's questions, I made my way back to my seat in the glass cage.

The chief investigative officer, DCi, was then called to the stand and she was asked by my barrister what attempts had been made by the police to contact any of the PE teachers mentioned by me in the various interviews; Mr Anderson, for example. She answered that she was unsure and asked to leave the courtroom to consult her superior at Suffolk Police Headquarters via telephone. After a brief adjournment, she returned to announce that, despite efforts, they were unable to track down Mr Anderson (who I subsequently learned had been taking part in online discussions with regard to St George's during those recent years).

It was now time for my character witnesses to come into court, one by one: two ex-teachers and two ex-pupils of St George's, followed by two ex-pupils, one ex-teacher and an ex-parent of RHS.

The first was David Harding, a former colleague and senior master at St George's, who had travelled from Stoke-on-Trent to give evidence. He confirmed that he worked closely with me in the senior part of the school, that I coached the senior rugby team, that I taught Languages and certainly not PE. He confirmed that he, I and Dr Steven Land, the deputy head, were in charge of the most senior dormitory, in the senior side of the school.

Then there was Valerie Land, a former colleague and junior teacher at St George's. She had travelled all the way from Gwynedd in West Wales. Valerie was 'A' and 'B''s tutor at St George's. She stated that at no time did either of them express any concerns about me to her. She also confirmed 'A' and 'B''s PE and games teachers were Mr Anderson and Mr Schoeberl. She stated that I certainly was not a teacher of theirs. She described me as an exemplary professional.

Michael Callander, former senior pupil at St George's and a member of my successful 1st XV rugby team, stated that I was a senior languages teacher and senior rugby coach. He proceeded to give an account of all the activities I organised for the senior boys, taking them to pop concerts, ice skating and suchlike. He had heard of no adverse rumours about me.

Russell Clash, former junior pupil at St George's and in the same academic year as 'A' and 'B', was a keen sportsman at school and is currently the physiotherapist at a professional football club. He described me as an exceptional teacher: firm, fair and totally honest. He stated that I did not teach any of his contemporaries PE or games. After PE lessons he said he remembered going into the shower room but could not recall any teachers coming in at that time. He stated that there was a small room for the PE staff in the changing room and the teachers – Anderson, Saunders, Cartwright and McGuinn – would remain in the room and shout at the boys to hurry up and get changed. In the evenings he said showers were supervised by the four matrons or house parents. He said: 'I can categorically state that during my time Mr Warr didn't take any PE with the juniors and I never missed a single lesson because it was my favourite subject.'

Dr Andrew Doyle, a former colleague at RHS, told the court that he started his teaching career at RHS and explained that on account of his youth and the fact he lived in a flat in one of the boarding houses, he learned a lot of the opinions of the pupils. He said: 'It is no exaggeration to say that Simon Warr was widely considered to be the best teacher in the school. He insisted on high standards and it was precisely this quality that accounted for much of his popularity. Many of the academically weaker pupils, or those with behavioural problems, would actively request to be in Simon's classes. Simon's tutor group respected him immensely and considered themselves lucky to have him as a tutor.'

Dr Mark Hambly, former pupil at RHS and my Head of House when 'C' was a junior pupil, stated that I was one of the most energetic and flamboyant people he had ever come across. He stated I carried this through to the running of my boarding house, Hawke; that I was determined throughout to make Hawke the best boarding house in the school, which it proved to be year after year, both academically and on the sports field. My commitment to insistence on high standards meant the pupils who were not prepared to abide by my regime could find themselves on the wrong side of me, which resulted in a stern dressing down.

I used a raised, powerful voice to keep the house running smoothly. He said I kept my personal and professional life separate. He said he never experienced or heard of any accusations or rumours of inappropriate behaviour.

Rufus Purnell, a former pupil at RHS and a close friend of 'C', was Head Boy of the school and in that capacity would become aware of any irregular situations within the pupil body. He was also a regular visitor to Hawke to speak to 'C', whom he considered a good friend. He stated that 'C' had never made any complaints to him about feeling threatened or intimidated by me, and nor did any of the other pupils. Rather, 'C' would have only complimentary things to say. Rufus said that 'C' was obviously happy to be in the house and was also evidently proud to be a Hawke boy, as it was generally considered to be the best boarding house in the school. He told the court he had heard 'C' calling me by my nickname but it was done in jest, as was my reaction. He concluded by saying: 'Mr Warr was a staunch anti-bullying campaigner. He also dedicated his life to not only teaching pupils to the highest possible standard in the classroom but also teaching them the values of self-discipline and respect and the value of hard work.'

David Watson, parent of a former pupil in my boarding house, is a retired Commander in the Royal Navy. He told the court that in his professional capacity of Commanding Officer on Her Majesty's warships, he had to be adept at the judgement of, and reporting on, character, ability and integrity of naval personnel of all ranks. From the first time he met me, he said, he was struck by my obvious ebullience and boundless energy, my diligence and, above all, by the highest regard I manifested in the welfare, both personal and educational, of all the boys in the house. He and his wife Penny were indebted to the fact that I set up a Hawke Parents' Society, which would have biannual meetings, in Portsmouth and Plymouth, during the school holidays. He stated that he had consulted his son, who knew 'C' well, about the possibility of any inappropriate behaviour on my part and his son was adamant that he knew of no evidence of any inappropriate or indecent behaviour by me towards anyone. He finished off his testimony by stating: 'Simon has always exhibited the highest standards, both professional and personal, including impeccable moral values.'

My barrister concluded by reading out a number of testimonials which had been sent in by various ex-colleagues and ex-pupils. These are a sample from those he had received:

Nicholas Ward, headmaster of RHS 1995–2004, and former Chairman of the Boarding Schools' Division, stated: 'I quickly recognised Simon Warr to be an outstanding boarding school teacher … particularly through his commitment to boarding school life … excellent classroom teacher … I quickly marked him out to be someone who not only inspired children to achieve great things but who was also an excellent role model for other staff … firm but fair … high standards … Mr Warr's name often came up as (the pupils') favourite teacher … first-rate boarding school master.'

Howard Blackett, headmaster of RHS 2004–12, now rector of Peterhouse College, Zimbabwe, stated: 'Simon Warr is a highly experienced school master with many years of outstanding service … he brought energy, enthusiasm and fun … demonstrated a level of commitment which is very rare indeed … a school master of exceptional ability.'

Don Hawkley, ex-colleague at RHS 1983–2012, stated: 'Simon Warr is an outstanding linguist … … inspires pupils with average ability to gain above-average grades … kindled a lifelong love of (foreign) languages in many more able scholars … … coached senior rugby and cricket … meticulous (theatre) director … I have worked closely with Simon over many years … has never been anything but normal, proper and professional.' He finishes by stating 'I would not hesitate to trust the education and pastoral care of my own children to Simon a second time, should it be possible to turn the clock back.'

Jake Motion, ex-pupil of RHS and now a teacher as Head of Science, stated: 'I always found Simon Warr to be an inspirational character … a constant example of the sort of teacher who I, as a parent, would want my children to learn from. I was recently asked why I had chosen teaching as a career. My answer began by describing the inspirational French, Drama and senior school sports' teacher who is Simon Warr … high standards (demanded of) his pupils … I struggle to recall any disciplinary incidents in his class or during his time on duty in the boarding house … held in incredibly high esteem by (my) peers and is regularly invited along to former pupils' reunions.'

Danny King, senior ex-pupil of St George's, 1980–83, stated: '… inspirational teacher who taught me to the highest standards, earning my respect. This was the view of the majority of my peers … with the highest set of ethical morals and principles and he never crossed his professional and personal boundaries … Mr Warr was not a PE teacher; there was a separate PE department, nor did he take any games lessons for the juniors or coach them in any sport … I am a youth worker who deals with vulnerable children and young people, as well as being a single parent to a son with disabilities. Bearing this in mind, I would certainly not wish to support anyone about whom I had even the vaguest suspicions concerning his or her integrity. In fact, I would have been honoured if Mr Warr had taught my own son, as he was such an inspiration to me.'

All that was left now were the two summaries, first from the prosecution and then from the defence barrister. The judge would finish proceedings by addressing the jury, so guiding them precisely in what they needed to focus upon during their forthcoming deliberations.

As the clock approached 3 p.m., Mr Thompson, for the prosecution, stood up to address the jury. He conceded immediately that the Crown no longer challenged the view that I had nothing to do with junior games during my time at St George's. However, he did appeal to the jury that, although what had been alleged did not fall into the most serious of criminal allegations, more than one former pupil of St George's had accused me of acting inappropriately and it had caused both much obvious distress, as had been evident as they stood in the witness box. He then spoke of 'C' and how brave he had been to come to court after all this time because, as 'C' stated, 'he felt it was the right thing to do'. Mr Thompson appealed to the members of the jury to think carefully about what had been alleged and return the correct verdict of guilty on any counts they felt had been proven.

Thus concluded day six.

At approximately 10 a.m. the next day, Mr Gowan, for the

defence, started the proceedings and spoke for nearly twice as long as Mr Thompson had done the previous afternoon. During this hour and a half addressing the jury, he dismantled the prosecution case, as limited as it was, bit by bit. He tore their ill-thought-through allegations to shreds. By the time he had finished, I knew in my heart of hearts that this whole unfortunate saga was reaching, at last, its conclusion, and I felt pretty confident that I would soon be walking out of court a free man with my reputation still in one piece, if inevitably tarnished. How could I possibly be convicted of such a ragbag of inconsistencies and impossibilities?

CHAPTER FOURTEEN

THE VERDICTS AND THE AFTERMATH

Justice is truth in action.

— Benjamin Disraeli

All that was left to be done before the jury retired to discuss what they had heard was the summing up by His Honour Judge Goodin, which began at approximately 11.45 a.m. on that Tuesday morning and concluded at 3.04 p.m. (there was a ninety minutes' break for lunch). The judge reviewed all that had been presented in court and guided the jury on how to reach their conclusions about each of the seven charges. It was obvious to all in the court that he had serious concerns about each and every one of the counts. He questioned the veracity of Counts 1 to 5 (at St George's) and he was doubtful that even if the acts described in Counts 6 and 7 had taken place, that they reached the threshold that could be deemed a criminal offence.

When he had finished, I left the courtroom and met with my barrister in one of the interview rooms opposite.

He spoke first:

'It's now twenty past three and the court will adjourn for the day around four fifteen, so it looks like, with seven counts to consider, we're not going to get closure on all this today; it'll probably be tomorrow morning sometime, maybe the afternoon.'

'Do we have to wait around?'

'Yes, you must, just in case.'

'How do you think the summing up went?'

'He's certainly on your side and I'll be very surprised if there are any convictions. If there are, because of the length of time you've been on bail and on account of the weakness of the allegations anyway, there'll be no custodial sentence.'

Thank goodness, I thought. That stated, even a spell in the slammer couldn't be as bad as what I'd had to endure for the last two years.

I left the room to meet up with my 'support team', friends and colleagues who had been in court all day, every day, throughout the trial. I noticed a few were missing.

'I think some have popped into town for a coffee and to stretch their legs,' I was informed.

I sat down with my colleague Chris and we discussed the summing up and the trial overall. He was adamant they could not possibly convict on what we'd heard. Indeed, after listening to all that had been said in the court since the opening day, he was perplexed as to how the whole matter had reached this stage. Nevertheless, I was under no illusion about the natural stance that members of the public (i.e. the jury) automatically take in these cases. They would be loath to acquit if they had even a smidgen of doubt in their minds.

As I sat and pondered on the events of the trial I was now utterly convinced that cases involving historical sex abuse, particularly when children are involved, are the *crimen exceptum* in our justice system. The 'equality of arms' between prosecution and defence no longer exists and I felt I had been obliged to prove my innocence.

We were interrupted at a quarter to four by a Tannoy message, the contents of which to this day are firmly imprinted upon my mind: 'Could all those in the case of R v Warr please report to Court 14. All those in the case of R v Warr please report to Court 14.'

I saw my barrister rushing into the courtroom, his gown billowing behind him. I followed and, as we entered, I heard a court usher say: 'They're in', which I took to mean the jury had decided upon all the verdicts.

How could they have done? I thought to myself. There are seven counts and they've been deliberating for little more than thirty minutes. They would also have had to appoint a spokesperson and, I presume, go to the lavatory, within this short space of time.

Soon, the courtroom was packed, some of my supporters rushing back from town after receiving a phone message to say the verdicts were in.

I entered my cage for the final time.

We waited for what seemed an age for the door to be opened by the court usher and for the twelve good men and women to file in. I did not look across at them for fear of seeing stern expressions on their faces, making me jump to unnecessary conclusions.

The clerk rose to his feet: 'Could the jury spokesperson please stand?'

A young gentleman in the back row got to his feet.

'Have you reached unanimous decisions on all seven counts?'

'We have.'

'On count one, how do you find the defendant – guilty or not guilty?'

'Not guilty.'

'And that is the decision of you all?'

'It is.'

'On count two, how do you find the defendant – guilty or not guilty?'

'Not guilty.'

'And that is the decision of you all?'

'It is.'

'On count three, how do you find the defendant – guilty or not guilty?'

'Not guilty.'

'And that is the decision of you all?'

'It is.'

'On count four, how do you find the defendant – guilty or not guilty?'

'Not guilty.'

'And that is the decision of you all?'

'It is.'

'On count five, how do you find the defendant – guilty or not guilty?'

'Not guilty.'

'And that is the decision of you all?'

'It is.'

'On count six, how do you find the defendant – guilty or not guilty?'

'Not guilty.'

'And that is the decision of you all?'

'It is.'

'On count seven, how do you find the defendant – guilty or not guilty?'

'Not guilty.'

'And that is the decision of you all?'

'It is.'

Then the judge spoke:

'Thank you, ladies and gentlemen of the jury. It is never an easy thing to do to sit day after day listening to evidence but I feel you have all acquitted yourselves very well. Thank you very much. Our whole court process, so valuable to any democratic, free country, could not function without the jury. You may leave.'

I burst into tears as the members of the jury filed out, attempting to thank each one as they passed me.

Then Judge Goodin addressed me: 'Mr Warr, you are free to leave.'

I had waited 672 days for this moment and it had all been wrapped up by a jury in less than half an hour. I felt both elated and bemused: excited that at last that burden that I had carried upon my shoulders since the day of my arrest was now lifted, but also perplexed: so, it *was* that obvious I was telling the truth. After the police's complete refusal to entertain such a notion, I was beginning to doubt anybody (who didn't know me) would believe me. As my supporters gathered around me outside Court 14, I continued to cry, letting out not far short of 700 days of frustration. People were talking to me but I wasn't really listening. I remember Don Hawkley, my ex-colleague of thirty years and who had supported me throughout, bringing me a sugary drink from the dispenser: 'You look pale, old chap. You need some energy.' He didn't realise just how indebted I felt to him, not for buying me a drink, but for his, and his wife Sarah's, unwavering belief in me from the outset. It was people like Don who had helped me to put some perspective on the whole nightmare.

As more and more people gathered around me, I regained my *compos mentis* and smiled: 'Thanks, everyone.' I was then beckoned into an interview room by my barrister.

'According to the usher,' he said once we were inside, 'a number of jury members were in tears back in the retiring room. They felt very emotional on your behalf.'

'Matthew, thank you for all you have done for me.'

'It has been a pleasure working with you. Don't forget, when you speak to those press people, emphasise: 670 days on bail, less than forty minutes to decide you are innocent. This speaks for itself.'

I rang my brother Nick, in Wales, who had been waiting patiently by the telephone for news, to tell him the verdict. He had wanted to attend the trial but I'd forbidden him.

As I left the interview room, I was approached by Kim Riley, from BBC *Look East*, who asked if I would be able to do a piece for camera for the evening news. I told him I'd do one at BBC Radio Suffolk where *Look East* had a camera studio, and he said he'd set it up for five o'clock.

A journalist who had been covering the case for the past week for the *East Anglian Daily Times*, coincidentally a newspaper I had written a weekly column for since 2007, then approached me for a few words. I obliged:

> I went overnight from being pretty much a happy-go-lucky character to a very dark place. I suddenly lost my job, my home, my community at RHS, my peace of mind and my reputation. This case was brought to court on the shirttail of Derek Slade's trial and there have been repeated unsuccessful attempts to suggest I was a friend of his. These allegations were no more than malicious lies issued for potential personal financial gain. I treat the accusers and their brazen lies with the unalloyed contempt they deserve. Unfortunately for me, it has taken a long time for this case to come to court. The trial was due in April but because some documents hadn't been prepared in time, I was made to wait another six months. I now feel relieved it is over and that my reputation is intact.

The paper ran the following front-page article: 'TWO YEARS OF HELL THEN CLEARED IN 40 MINUTES. Ex-teacher: "My ordeal after being falsely accused of child abuse".'

A friend drove me the short distance from the courthouse to

BBC Suffolk, where I was interviewed for both local radio and television. As I entered the newsroom, I was greeted with a burst of generous applause from my colleagues. I had missed the place, certainly. No sooner had I entered than I was whisked into a studio to give an interview for the BBC Radio Suffolk drivetime programme, presented by my friend Stephen Foster. Minutes subsequently, I recorded a piece to camera, which was to go out that evening on *Look East*'s news programme. I repeated during both interviews what I had said to the *EADT* journalist at the courthouse. The final question that Stewart White, the *Look East* presenter, put to me was how I felt about my accusers who had made the false allegations: I took satisfaction in saying that I was not at present going to waste my feelings on them, merely treat them with the contempt that they and their lies deserve.

After I had finished, I was driven to a reception which had been organised at Chris and Catriona Herbert's beautiful mansion in Holbrook, where most of my RHS supporters had gathered. An ex-colleague, a giant bear of a man, John Dugdale, who was Head of Technology at RHS, telephoned me from his home in France (it was school half-term holiday) and I remember him weeping down the line, telling me how relieved he was that the liars had not won the day. John is ostensibly a scary school master but, just below the surface, he is one of the kindest people I have ever met. I thanked those present for their unassailable support and, after a few glasses of orange squash, I made my way over to my other group of supporters, from BBC Radio Suffolk, gathered at James Hazell's home in east Ipswich. I was feeling on top of the world.

The next few days were a whirlwind, as I gave a number of

interviews to the print press and on national radio stations. After outlining the preposterous allegations once again, I emphasised all the ways I thought the justice system could be improved, and all the ways it had failed me, given throughout this book, including a reduction on the length of bail time; a statute of limitation on historical cases, the cessation of putting a defendant in a courtroom cage; and, most importantly, the need for impartial, balanced, intelligent, inquisitorial investigations, in which the police side neither with the CPS nor with the defence.

The weekend following my acquittal, I resumed my duties as a sports' reporter with BBC Radio Suffolk. The reception I received at the various local football and rugby clubs I visited on match days was almost overwhelming. I remember one particular occasion, the second match I covered, in December 2014, as I walked into the clubhouse, all the fans stood up and applauded me. I was taken aback. Football supporters can be harsh and unbridled in their criticisms and it doesn't take much imagination to consider their reaction to someone they considered to be a paedophile.

BBC's *Newsnight* invited me on to their current affairs programme early in November, to discuss the issue of length of bail. I appeared along with a high-ranking police officer, who put the exaggerated length of bail time down to financial cuts. This puzzled me on two counts: first, I was under the impression that the child protection branch of the force had been ring-fenced; and second, according to a recent study, in the decade up to 2010 police funding went up in real terms by 50 per cent. I argued that, according to Magna Carta, the blueprint for our justice system, 'justice delayed is justice denied', and that there ought to be a time limit of, at most, two months that someone could be bailed without being charged. In my case it took the police nine months to charge me and a further thirteen months for the case to come to trial (a recent study revealed that 5,930 people in England and Wales have spent more than six months on pre-charge bail). I spoke about how someone on bail is forced to live his or her life under a cloud of suspicion and that police bail had morphed into 'police officer justice'. Those suspected of having committed a crime can suffer from arbitrary restrictions on their freedoms. A range of conditions can be imposed: restriction of movement, removal of passport, computer, mobile phone, diaries; personal correspondence is read or removed, as are personal bank details.

I spoke about how people are usually suspended from their job and, in my case, this included banishment from my principal home because it was set within the school grounds.

If there'd been more time on *Newsnight*, I could have mentioned how the accused is powerless when on bail prior to being charged to do any of his or her own detective work because there are so many restrictions about who can be contacted. In my case, had I not been banned from all contact with both the community of St George's and of RHS, I could have taken some steps during those initial nine months on bail to convince the police investigative team that I could not possibly have carried out the alleged abuse. *They* were not prepared to follow the leads I had given them, so I could have done so instead. In practice, all I did was sit on my hands and hope the police would at least talk to some of the people I had mentioned who might be able to help. I hoped in vain.

And what happens when someone has been bailed for months on end and is not then charged? Or, as in my case, what happens when someone is taken to trial on no evidence whatsoever, just the words of three complainants from a career which stretched over more than thirty years, and a jury takes barely forty minutes to dismiss all the allegations? Does anyone apologise? Is there any restitution? As the police side with the complainant throughout the investigative process, of course there will be no restitution, as that would compromise their own position. After being treated by the police like a common criminal, having had my life and repu-tation trashed, I was then expected to carry on as if life was back to normal. If just one of these investigative officers could spend a single week living on bail, with its commensurate pressure, they would not leave suspects languishing so long. I will never get back those six hundred and seventy-two days.

Even though, as the weeks passed after the trial, I felt so relieved that my nightmare was over, what was nagging in my mind was what I needed to do now that the prosecution had not only failed to prove their case but, more than this, it had become evident to anyone sitting in the court that the accusers were lying.

The following day I received a telephone call from my NAS solicitor, Jeremy Guy, informing me the Suffolk Police wanted me to collect my confiscated possessions from them. I was to travel to Bury St Edmunds police station and I did so on Friday 14 November 2014. It was strange being in the same room as the DC who had been pursuing me for nigh on two years, but we managed to negotiate the process civilly, ticking off the various items that had been taken in those dawn raids in December 2012.

What did puzzle me was why a collection of adult, legal porno-graphic films were retained by the police. I didn't make a fuss at the time because I was just glad to get out of that police station as soon as possible.

As I was about to leave, I asked the DC whether I would at least receive an apology from my accusers. Her immediate response was 'That's not going to happen.' I realised then the police had absolutely no intention of challenging those liars and if they were to face any justice it would be the result of my starting private civil proceedings. I have read an official police document, dating from 2011, since the trial, in which 'A' is reported 'to have exhibited concerning behaviour before giving evidence against Slade', while '"B" has a history of mental issues'; yet, still, no attempts were to be made even to re-question the two about their allegations against me.

The question of whether someone who makes an allegation that turns out not to be true should be called to account is a hotly debated topic. During a period of seventeen months leading up to May 2012, there were a total of 5,651 prosecutions for rape and a mere thirty-five prosecutions for making false allegations of rape. According to the Director of Public Prosecutions of the time, Keir Starmer, 'false allegations are relatively rare'. What he meant, of course, was that prosecutions for making false allegations are rare, indeed, almost never happen, in this country. Everyone knows that just because a defendant is found not guilty, that does not necessarily mean the complainant was lying. However, there are times when it is obvious from a weight of evidence that the accuser is telling lies. Surely, in this sort of case, he or she should face prosecution? I feel so strongly about this that in August 2016

I launched a petition to Parliament, publicised on my Twitter account @bbcsimonwarr. These are the reasons why:

> This petition calls for a Parliamentary debate to review whether current laws relating to the offences of perjury and perverting the course of justice are fit for purpose and that they are being pursued with vigour by the Crown Prosecution Service in cases of false allegations of abuse.
>
> False allegations of sexual and other types of abuse have a catastrophic effect upon the lives of those who are accused. Furthermore, making such allegations, whether motivated by a desire for vengeance, attention or compensation, also casts doubt on genuine complaints of abuse and undermines public confidence in our justice system.

My mind is not so closed, even after the awful experiences I had to endure since my arrest, as to think that all false complainants should automatically face legal retribution. But, surely, there must come a point when we realise that there are many people who have latched onto the current obsession with historical abuse, with its link to generous compensation and to becoming the centre of attention, who use it to their own advantage.

Even in the cases where a not-guilty verdict is speedily returned, there is little chance of a comeback against the anonymous liars. It is perilous to pursue private action. One of Chris Grayling's (Secretary of State for Justice 2012–15) many dreadful legacies is a rule that requires the government to pay compensation only if an exonerated defendant can prove *beyond reasonable doubt* that he did not commit the offence. Proving a negative *beyond reasonable doubt* is a pretty tall order. Furthermore, the cost of bringing such a case to court is prohibitive for all but the rich. I firmly believe it should be the responsibility of the state to prosecute those people who make obviously false allegations of abuse and it should not be left to those defendants cleared by a jury. Why should someone who has survived a lengthy criminal prosecution then have to risk his or her life savings to secure justice, not to mention the psychological demands in having to do so?

I was fully aware that my risk in pursuing a private action would be the loss of a substantial tranche of my hard-earned savings and, in our present system, even if I won, the liars who accused me might have no assets, so I would not be reimbursed whatever the outcome. But justice should be done and, in any supposedly open, fair society, liars and perjurers should face the full force of the law. I was not holding my breath.

CHAPTER FIFTEEN

COMPENSATION FOR THE COMPLAINANTS

There is sufficiency in the world for man's need but not for man's greed.

— MAHATMA GANDHI

Being accused of historical child abuse can shred a person's life. I would be one of those labelled a paedophile if my accusers had invented a more plausible and intelligent story. So, I was lucky that the liars were careless. I have considered the possibility of them alleging that these supposed acts of indecency occurred in my private room or in the dormitory in the dead of night. They, of course, couldn't prove the abuse took place but they don't need to in our current judicial system. I certainly wouldn't have been able to prove it didn't and, therefore, under the weight of prejudice which surrounds this type of alleged offence, there would have been a good chance of my being found guilty of at least one of the seven counts.

Liars are prepared to make these false allegations because they realise they don't need to prove what they are alleging and, disturbingly, they know there is little, if any, chance of them ever facing justice if their lies are uncovered. For the accused, it is 'the perfect storm'; for the accuser the perfect situation.

I consulted a number of friends early in 2015, and more than one barrister, about whether or not I should pursue my accusers in the courts, and all seemed to be of the opinion it was better to move on with my life. I fully understood their reasoning, it seemed the intelligent thing to do. However, I had lived through the nightmare and I had felt so upset not only having to deal with the cornucopia of lies but also having to read the emotional hogwash that these liars had spewed forth with only the slightest encouragement. It was stomach-churning just to read 'B''s obvious lies in 2011 of how I had affected his childhood, of 'not being able to get over the abuse suffered at the hands of Slade and Warr'. It is outrageous and belittling to those who have suffered serious abuse when complainants talk of having their 'life ruined' or 'it will be with me until the day I die' or 'the effects of what happened to me are still with me' following minor allegations of inappropriate behaviour. They present their case as if they have been unable, are still unable and will continue to be unable to function properly.

If you put in to Google, as I did in early 2015, 'child abuse compensation', you are presented with page after page of adver-tisements from a cornucopia of legal firms:

Child Abuse Compensation

Abused as a Child? Representing Victims of Child Abuse

Child Abuse – You Deserve Justice

Financial Compensation – Citizens' Advice

Make sure you get the maximum compensation possible

Thinking about Claiming?

Child Abuse Compensation – 'could be huge'

Child abuse Survivor?

If you have a legal system that does not insist that allegations need to be proven beyond reasonable doubt, and you couple it with very generous payouts, probably more money than many of the prospective complainants had ever dreamed of, then it is inev-itable the temptation to make a false claim will be too attractive for some to resist. If you are part of an 'operation', with the full backing of the police, then it makes it even easier for that person.

Further to this paying out of vast quantities of money to vic-tims of even comparatively minor abuse, the Criminal Injuries Compensation Authority guarantee lifelong anonymity to those receiving compensation and this includes payments even to those who make allegations of abuse which are not tested in, or rejected by, a court of law. Some are paid money *before* a trial. All a com-plainant needs is a police crime reference number and the path is open. Thus, I have no idea whether or not my accusers received any compensation from the plethora of lies they invented about me and I'm not likely ever to find out. Add to all this media deals with accusers *before* any trial with regard to interviews in newspapers/

magazines *subject to the defendant being found guilty*, all strictly under wraps, of course, and you can imagine that the likelihood of the complainant telling the truth, the whole truth and nothing but the truth, is severely tested.

CHAPTER SIXTEEN

MORE PRESSURE
TO BEAR

Real courage is grace under pressure.

— ERNEST HEMINGWAY

My feelings of contentment and relief which I enjoyed over the Christmas period of 2014, a time I remember as being one of pure, unbridled joy, were soon to be interrupted, however, when not long into the New Year I received a recorded delivery letter from the National College for Teaching and Leadership (NCTL). It read:

Dear Mr Warr,

On 9 October 2014, NCTL, on behalf of the Secretary of State

---

for Education, received a referral about you from the Royal Hospital School, in relation to your conduct.

In accordance with the Education Act 2011, the Secretary of State is able to prohibit teachers from the profession for reasons of unacceptable professional conduct, conduct which might bring the profession into disrepute or conviction, at any time, of a relevant offence.

In executing this role as the regulator for the teaching profession, the NCTL has considered the referral and has decided that a formal investigation should be started in relation to the following matters...

The NCTL then proceeded to accuse me once again of the very offences upon which I had been tried and found not guilty in a court of law – they repeated the false allegations of my inspecting 'A' and 'B' inappropriately after showers at St George's School; and of attempting to remove pupils' towels and to pinch pupils' bottoms at RHS.

I re-read 'In relation to my conduct'. What conduct? I had been found not guilty! Or were they referring to some of the innuendo to emerge from the two years' investigation? I sat down in the lounge absolutely dumbstruck. So, it still wasn't over. I thought I had proven beyond reasonable doubt that my accusers were liars. I also wondered why the school to which I had devoted nearly all my professional life had decided to refer me to the NCTL a few days *before* the criminal trial. Why could they not have waited for it to run its course? Judging by the tone of the letter, the NCTL seemed to have little faith in the criminal court process. I could have understood its attitude if the police had convinced them I was guilty but I had managed to secure an acquittal on the basis of lack of evidence. But the police must have been fully aware by the conclusion of the trial that they had been supporting and encouraging a couple of liars and that there was no truth in any of the seven allegations. All the NCTL needed to do was to read the transcript of the trial and they would have their answer.

So, as a member of the teaching profession, I was to have the whole case reopened. I had enjoyed a brief period of happiness, gradually finding my former *joie de vivre*, but it seemed the nightmare was not yet over.

I appreciate the NCTL is under pressure to ensure all those working in schools are thoroughly vetted but they must also treat each case on its own merits. They must have known that the allegations were summarily dismissed by the jury and, besides which, I had decided not to resume my teaching career. If I decided to do so at any point in the future, a compulsory enhanced CRB check would inform any prospective employer of my ordeal.

The NCTL followed this up with a second letter, which arrived on 1 May 2015, which informed me that they would be pursuing my case formally and that I might need to answer, once again, to the allegations. I was told that they did not need to reach a threshold of 'beyond reasonable doubt' but just 'the balance of probabilities'. In other words, they had *carte blanche* to bar someone from teaching just because he or she *might* have committed an offence. What's more, they had, once again, libelled me by including the allegations which had been dismissed by the jury almost immediately. (When I complained to the NCTL that they were libelling me by repeating the allegations, their response was: 'You don't seem to realise what we do here.')

The letter told me the whole process would take a maximum of twenty weeks, which I thought a particularly long time considering I had already had over two years in limbo.

I had invited a Swiss friend of mine, Roman, to visit London for a couple of weeks and he was due to touch down at Heathrow the following day. I wasn't sure I was in the right frame of mind to entertain anyone but it was too late to cancel his visit. Besides, it would have been grossly unfair on him. I'd just have to 'wing it', to put on a happy, relaxed front, while my insides would be churning with frustration. I'd got used to this.

As it turned out, he lifted my spirits. I told him what had been going on and he, who knew me well, was totally supportive, as had been all my family and friends since my original arrest.

Later that month, May 2015, I received another recorded delivery letter and it took me a good few minutes to pluck up the courage to open it. What was going to land upon my shoulders this time? More bad news? More questions to answer?

Disclosure and Barring Service

27th May 2015

PERSONAL

Dear Mr Warr,

We wrote to you on 8 October 2013, and explained that you had been referred to the DBS by the Royal Hospital School, following your arrest on historic [sic] allegations of abuse.

We also explained that we were making further enquiries and would write to you again about how we intended to proceed.

We have now concluded our enquiries and have carefully considered all the information received. On the basis of this information we have reached our final decision is that it is not appropriate to include you in the Children's Barred List or the Adults' Barred List.

We have informed the National College for Teaching and Leadership, in confidence, of our decision.

I had forgotten they had written to me back in 2013, a time when I was beside myself with worry and anxiety, so at that time I would not have taken in properly the contents of one of a number of menacing letters I had received. I had felt under siege. This latest communication came as a bit of a surprise and I was relieved to read the contents. However, I was unsure whether or not the DBS had now made a concluding decision about all this. I was puzzled by the final sentence: 'We have informed the NCTL'. Was that, then, the end of the matter? Or did I now have to wait for a third party, the NCTL, to decide whether I was guilty or not? Was the DBS telling the NCTL I didn't have a case to answer? Or was the NCTL an independent body? Could I now finally get on with my life? Or did I have to wait for yet another agency of the state to make a decision about my future?

CHAPTER SEVENTEEN

FIGHTING BACK

Pressed to the wall, dying, but fighting back.

– Claude McKay

I soon became aware that my experience of injustice was certainly not unique. I received emails from others who had been falsely accused and dragged through the courts. I attended the trials of a number of people who were facing a similar ordeal to my own, having learned of their plight from an organisation called FACT (Falsely Accused Carers and Teachers). This organisation was set up in the year 2000 by a group of former members of staff of St George's School (coincidentally) in Merseyside, a school that had become the focus of yet another police trawling 'operation'.

This one had even included the football manager David Jones (who was subsequently acquitted after a criminal trial). FACT held weekly meetings and its purpose was to bring to the attention of the local MP the appalling assault on fairness and justice that police trawling perpetrated. FACT is still helping and supporting all those who are being hauled before the courts on account of false allegations. One of its present committee members, who happened to live in Ipswich, had acquainted himself with me at the time of my trial at Ipswich Crown Court. Since then we had kept in touch and he now invited me to Cardiff Law School (coincidentally, my home city) to attend the annual FACT Conference in May 2015, and, furthermore, I was asked to make a speech to open proceedings.

When I arrived I was met by many kind people; what's more, those who had had to experience a similar nightmare to my own. I was no longer spinning on my own solitary planet, grappling with feelings no one else could understand. These were people who viewed me as a partner, a soulmate. Many spoke of their own suicide attempts. I had felt thoroughly ashamed of myself for even contemplating suicide back in late 2012, but, having spoken to other members of FACT, I recognised that this reaction to having been accused of child abuse was quite common.

At the meeting of FACT I received so many complimentary words about how impressively I had dealt with my anguish that I came away from the conference reinvigorated. I am convinced that confronting such evil with so much fortitude has made me a better person.

I opened proceedings with my speech which outlined the horrendous experience I had been forced to endure over a period of

672 days. If this can happen to someone who couldn't possibly have committed the alleged crime, what chance is there for those who cannot prove their innocence?

I finished the speech by saying that I had always believed in the integrity of the British police force, that they were doing a difficult job in challenging circumstances to the best of their ability. I had considered the British police force to be probably the fairest and most trustworthy in the world. My parochial experiences of the past two years had utterly destroyed that faith, although I was aware there are many, many good coppers working hard to keep us safe.

I received a standing ovation.

It was extraordinary listening to some of the other accounts of blatant prejudice being meted out in the name of justice. One particular individual I spoke to, an ex-policeman, gave me details of how he had been targeted by the police after he had criticised publicly some of the force's practices. Months later, I attended his historical abuse trial at Southwark Crown Court, where he was cleared unanimously by a jury as speedily as had happened at my own trial.

Also attending the FACT conference, as a guest speaker, was Barbara Hewson, who was almost a sole national voice of caution in the aftermath of the Jimmy Savile revelations and the resultant 'Operation Yewtree'. I cannot remember ever meeting someone who is so strong in standing up for what she believes to be right and proper and just, even if this is in direct contravention to the prevailing mood (no matter how many enemies she makes by doing so – and she certainly has!). Ms Hewson called into question the legal and moral foundations of the whole 'Operation Yewtree' and the way it confused a zealous crusade with due process. Unsurprisingly, she soon became another target for the latest witch-hunt, which forbids even intelligent discussion around claims of abuse. Ms Hewson was referred to online as 'vermin', 'a fucking animal', 'a whore', 'a cunt', 'a paedo-loving slag', and, of course, 'a witch'. She was even threatened with rape. The bigotry and visceral hatred directed towards her exposed clearly the raw fears and the insecurities of the hate-fuelled, untutored mob, who are frightened of, or more likely, incapable of, open discussion and reasoned argument.

Ms Hewson was attempting to convey the message that the frenzy that gripped this nation post-Savile had more to do with disorientation among adults than child protection. She claimed that the non-stop excavation of allegations of abuse from decades ago confirmed that British society can only understand the moral categories of good and evil – hence its thirst for grotesque moral dramas that pit the alleged diabolic paedophile against the sacred child.

I would say that there is a strong argument to suggest that now religion plays an ever decreasing part in the lives of the citizens of this country, we have substituted paedophiles for the devil, and children, our only representation of purity, for Christ. This is why the police have virtually *carte blanche* to treat even suspected child abusers in whatever manner they choose, knowing that the public will be on their side, no matter what they do.

No one took any of those vile trolls to task for being so offensive to the distinguished barrister Ms Hewson, who refused to be bullied and intimidated.

Anyone who is the target of an allegation, or anyone who even attempts to question the integrity of an allegation, will be hounded and often threatened with reprisals. This impulse to punish and hurt someone for even being accused of a crime or for merely expressing a view that contradicts mainstream opinion reflects the sort of society which brutal dictators run in some parts of the world. We feel good about the fact that here in the UK we are more culturally developed, more sophisticated as a country, compared with, for example, Zimbabwe. But, in some aspects, we are not. There are so many individuals merely accused of abuse who have been hounded and humiliated by the vitriolic nastiness that has come their way. The threat that is whipped up in the media against anyone accused of child abuse or anyone who wants a reasoned debate on the topic is directly linked to the frenzied witch-hunt that has predictably ensued.

Eilis O' Hanlon, a journalist at the *Irish Independent*, wrote about the vile criticism directed towards Barbara Hewson: 'The vehemence of the reaction against Hewson demonstrates that she was certainly right to compare the public mood around the issue (of historical abuse arrests) to witch-hunts, since it is the nature of witch-hunts to shout down opposition.'

Even the NSPCC criticised Barbara. Initially they tried to gag her: Matt Hopkinson, the NSPCC's chief press officer, told her to 'reconsider her stance'. They even contacted her chambers to advise them to disassociate themselves from her viewpoints. In other words, 'Ms Hewson holds views which are not aligned to those of us here at the NSPCC and, in our opinion, this should not be allowed.'

Anyone can criticise Ms Hewson and offer cogent arguments as to why, in their opinion, she is wrong. I disagree with some things she has said. But she cannot, and must not, be bullied into toeing some accepted line. I consider Ms Hewson to be a courageous defender of civil liberties and the rights of the defence. She has integrity and courage. She does not call victims liars but she targets liars who falsely claim to be victims. She finds it repugnant, as surely any right-minded, intelligent, decent person would do, that some seem to be able to make false allegations of child abuse with total impunity.

When the magician and recently departed entertainer Paul Daniels questioned the validity of some of the allegations made against Jimmy Savile, he was denounced as 'a disgrace' and accused of 'belittling victims'. He retreated. Well, if I'd had the chance to meet Mr Daniels before he died, I would have told him that I totally concur with his point of view. I know from first-hand experience that there are some who will take full advantage of the prevailing mood or culture and use it for their own personal advantage. These people damage further those who have been genuinely abused.

Another person I met at the FACT Conference was Susanne Cameron-Blackie, better known as the blogger 'Anna Racoon'. After leaving the now infamous Duncroft School, in Surrey, she studied for a law degree at Aberystwyth University, eventually gravitating to the position of Lord Chancellor's Visitor for Wales. Susanne first became involved in the deconstruction of the various false allegations emanating from Duncroft School when she realised that the first 'brave victim' to waive anonymity was the occupant of the bed opposite hers at the school. She was puzzled how the platinum-haired DJ Savile managed to carry out in their dormitory his repeated alleged abuse on the girl opposite without she herself ever waking up or hearing about it the following morning.

We also enjoyed a talk given by 'Barristerblogger' Matthew Scott, a criminal barrister who covers murder, serious sexual assault and violence. He has considerable experience in defending allegations of rape and child cruelty.

Chris Saltrese, another guest, has probably been one of the most effective and articulate opponents of police trawling. He was the lead solicitor in the Waterhouse Tribunal of Inquiry, representing teachers and care workers at the infamous Bryn Estyn care home in North Wales, which is the subject of Richard Webster's excellent review of the whole 1980s scandal, *The Secret of Bryn Estyn: the Making of a Modern Witch Hunt*. It was Chris who prompted me to buy the book and it opened my eyes to the appalling number of miscarriages of justice with regard to unproven historical abuse allegations that have taken place here in the UK since the 1980s.

Finally, a guest speaker I met that day was Professor Felicity Goodyear-Smith, who is an academic head in the Faculty of Medical and Health Science at the University of Auckland. She has published extensively, including a book entitled *First Do No Harm: The Sexual Abuse Industry*. In the 1990s, she helped run FACT's equivalent in New Zealand, COSA (Casualties of Sexual Allegations), which was set up following a huge wave of allegations based on 'recovered' memories, fuelled, of course, by compensation payouts, which required no corroborative evidence. Her new book is entitled *Murder that Wasn't*, based upon the case of a man who was wrongly prosecuted for child sex abuse and murder.

I found the whole day enlightening and I met a number of people who had suffered, or were still suffering, the same inexorable mental pain that I'd had to endure throughout 2013/14. I knew exactly what they had gone through, or were still going through. I wouldn't wish that feeling of hopelessness and depression on my worst enemy. I recognised the desperation in their eyes, those effects of sleeplessness, night after night, which they were forced to endure, just like I'd had to. Those faces I saw had the same drawn expressions which I had confronted in my bathroom mirror during those 672 days.

In July 2015, I went to see a new play, *An Audience with Jimmy Savile*, at the Park Theatre in Finsbury Park, written by Jonathan Maitland and starring Alistair McGowan. I thought his portrayal of Savile was superb; indeed, we seemed to be watching the real man walking about the stage, so convincing was McGowan's portrayal of Savile's well-known mannerisms. Needless to say, in the play all the allegations were put across as undisputed facts and, as I was leaving, I was asked to give money to a charity that helps people abused in their childhood. I asked the lady collecting whether she was sure all the people she was representing were real victims and her response was that nobody invents having been abused and that she was very angry I had asked her such an impertinent question.

'You don't understand,' she told me forcibly, 'abused people do not invent stories and are just not listened to in this country.'

I had much to tell her but felt, if my initial remark had caused her so much irritation, she was not of a mind to have a reasoned debate on the subject.

How could she possibly believe that, here in the UK, in 2015, people were not being even listened to when they alleged abuse? My experience had been the exact opposite: they were not only listened to but also believed far too readily.

CHAPTER EIGHTEEN

―

MANACLED
TO LIES

*It takes twenty years to build a reputation and
five minutes to ruin it.*

― WARREN BUFFETT

No laws have been put in place since the arrival of the internet to take into account the publicity surrounding people who are the target of malicious allegations, particularly sexual ones, which are subsequently proven to be false. In the times before the internet, someone who was accused falsely of a crime was cleared in a court of law and the reporting of the trial was forgotten about within a week, at the most. There used to be a saying pre-internet: 'Today's newspaper is tomorrow's fish and chips' wrapping paper.'

―

Nowadays, if someone is accused falsely, those details are with the accused forever. They will follow the person around digitally like a conjoined twin. And no agents of the state are prepared to do anything about it. A barrister representing me has done all in his power to have the references to my nightmare deleted from the net on the grounds of fairness and justice but he has come up against a solid wall of resistance. The result is 'A' and 'B' are still having a deleterious effect on my quality of life. While they hide, I am totally exposed, as details of my *anni horribiles* are laid out for anyone to read at the touch of a screen.

I was trying my best to supplement my pension, and my modest salary from the BBC, by applying for a variety of media opportunities which were advertised on the website *Star Now*. Time after time I would be contacted, only for initial enthusiasm to meet me suddenly to peter out. I knew this couldn't be unconnected to what was still awaiting anyone as soon as they typed my name into Google. Nobody would take a chance on someone who had been even *accused* of child abuse. I therefore sent, via my lawyer, a formal letter to Google to request that the references be withdrawn now that I had not only been found not guilty, but also the allegations had been proven to be lies. In the letter, my lawyer made reference to articles on the BBC website, the *Ipswich Star*, the *East Anglian Daily Times* and the *Bury Free Press*, all of which gave detailed reports on the whole case and my eventual acquittal. *The Independent* had a report on charges relating to the allegations, including a photograph, and personal information about me posted in September 2013. However, there was no subsequent reference to the fact that I had been found not guilty of the charges in October 2014.

Can you imagine them ignoring the story had I been found guilty of even one of the seven charges?

I contacted the Head of Online at the BBC about the references to the trial; I asked my editor at BBC Radio Suffolk for assistance and all seemed powerless to help. The facts were being reported and the general public had a right to know, evidently, that these liars had damaged my reputation.

Google's response to my barrister's letter was that they were not prepared to take down the references as they believed it was in the public interest that they remain: 'The URLs in question relate to matters of substantial interest to the public regarding your client's professional life.'

How can references to damned lies, invented by a couple of rotten misfits, be of substantial interest to anyone, apart from somebody writing a book or thesis on 'Cruel Opportunists'?

My lawyer then wrote to the Public Commissioner and asked for reasons why Google were refusing to remove the search engine results containing information about my arrest and trial. He received the following response:

> You contacted Google on 4 September 2015 to request removal of links resulting from a search on your client's name, Simon Warr. You explained that your client wanted these results removed because they relate to allegations of historic [*sic*] sex offences, for which Mr Warr was acquitted on all counts. The continued availability of these search results is affecting your client's psychological well-being and impacting upon his ability to secure employment.

OUR DECISION

We have considered the factors which are relevant to this removal request and we have decided it is likely that the search results comply with the DPA (Data Protection Act). We do not, therefore, expect Google to remove the links.

The Court of Justice of the European Union judgement does not intend to protect against *any* negative information appearing in search results. The judgement states that internet search providers can be required to remove search results displayed if the data is inaccurate, irrelevant, no longer relevant or excessive in relation to the purposes for which it was processed and in the light of the time elapsed.

You have acknowledged that the information returned in the search results is factually accurate ... In addition to this, the information is published in a legitimate journalistic context ... We recognise the importance of search results in making journalistic content available to the public ... We acknowledge that freedom of expression is a fundamental right in our society and having access to information about individuals that play a role in public life is more relevant than the reporting of information about ordinary private citizens. We note that your client is a public figure, being a writer and contributor to radio and television programmes, hence there will be a stronger public interest in his experiences.

From the information available to us, it appears that Google's processing of personal data to present the search results complies with the DPA in this case.

Yours sincerely, etc. etc.

So, there it was: the powers that be who govern these things had decided that, even though it had been proven beyond reasonable doubt that I had had my reputation tarnished by a couple of fantasists, it was fair game for their lies to be inextricably linked to me for years to come, thereby punishing me over and over again. The fact that I was a 'minor celebrity' (I know, ghastly phrase) was one of the reasons I had been targeted in the first place. I have absolutely no doubt that if I had been an ordinary teacher, living a quiet life somewhere, 'A' and 'B' would have hardly been able to remember me, so this 'minor celebrity' tag had already cost me dear. I seemed to be paying a second time.

In eighteenth-century Britain, those found guilty of certain offences were branded with an iron so that they carried their criminal record with them forever; nowadays it is the search engines which provide the service and you don't even have to have committed a crime.

My last resort would be to take my case to court, under section 10 of the DPA. My teaching career had been damaged irreparably; I was tied to debilitating search engine articles, thereby damaging future employment opportunities in other areas; my reputation was continuing to be tarnished in the eyes of those who didn't know me; and I was being threatened by the NCTL, who were conducting their own investigation.

Whether guilty or innocent, anyone accused of child abuse will never throw off that connection with the accusation. I believe the search engines, the Commissioner and the police are all influenced by the nature of the crime which was alleged against me. If it had been practically any other type, the likelihood is I'd never have been charged on such flimsy 'evidence' and, if I had and been taken to trial and found not guilty, the search engines would have been more sympathetic to my plight. I have heard of other people who have actually been found guilty having their references removed from the internet.

I'll give a couple of examples of the prejudice I am forced to deal with on a regular basis. Last year (2015) I was asked to present a section of a TV show on which I had appeared prior to my court ordeal. I knew the film company knew nothing about what had happened to me because a producer asked me how I was and asked me what I'd been doing since we last spoke. He then offered me the chance to do some presenting on camera on their behalf. The weeks passed and travel arrangements/dietary requirements were discussed and finalised. However, a few days prior to filming, the whole project was pulled. I was given no reason why but it didn't take much working out. Perhaps I'm just being paranoid.

This year I was contacted by representatives at ITV to take part in a television debate. During the introductory conversation I was asked if I had a criminal record and I said no. Some days later they telephoned back and I was then asked whether I had been arrested within the past five years. Quite what business it was of theirs, I don't know, but I told them what had happened in 2012. The reader will not be surprised to learn that the offer to appear was withdrawn.

When is someone in authority going to wake up to the fact that nowadays, because of the internet, people's lives are being repeatedly damaged through no fault of their own but just because they have been the target of some lying opportunist? For politicians, fairness and justice are inextricably linked to prospective votes at the next election. Their sole concern is currying favour with the masses. If my plight had any racial undertones, you can bet your last pound some politician would be fighting the cause on my behalf. But I'm an alleged child abuser and standing up for me could jeopardise votes; certainly most unlikely to win any!

And once the police storm your property, you will be immediately named and shamed publicly – there will be no going back. These agents of the state care nothing for the trashing of a potentially innocent person's name if it could conceivably lead to further complainants coming forward. K. Harvey Proctor, in his book *Credible and True*, states:

> The politicians … are currying favour with the electorate – what are they doing to redress the balance between the alleged victims who can keep their anonymity and the alleged abusers who cannot? When will innocent before being found guilty be more than just a totem of a supposedly liberal society? Who are the guardians of our liberty now?

Why are the powers that be so reluctant to address the obvious imbalance? Harvey Proctor goes on to say:

> The only people deemed more unpopular than the media, journalists, police and politicians with the general public are paedophiles. So they are all pursuing the issue to try to get on the good side of the people of this country and rehabilitate themselves from their past lapses.

It was now August 2015 and the new football season had started and I was back doing what I very much enjoyed, commentating on sport. I had to do all in my power to try to move those references off the first page of search engine results and the only way I was going to do that was by my future accomplishments. After some six years of helping to host a Saturday morning phone-in programme, as part of the *Mark Murphy Show* on BBC Radio Suffolk, entitled 'The Warrzone', a weekly discussion about a current topic to hit the news, in 2015 this was replaced by a weekly feature called 'On the Warr Path', now part of the *James Hazell Show*, who had taken over the Saturday morning slot. Each week I was sent out and about to take up some challenge: archery, dancing, speed cycling, being an auctioneer, rowing, golf, learning to play the oboe, etc.

Life seemed to be returning to something like it had been prior to my arrest, although, of course, I was no longer teaching. People often used to say to me that, because I put so much of myself into my teaching career, I would be lost without it. Strange to state but I hardly missed it. Indeed, it was pleasant not to feel so tired so regularly. I was enjoying my radio work all the more because I wasn't always in a rush to arrive at the studio after morning lessons or in a hurry to leave to get back to school after covering a match on Saturday afternoons. I had every reason to hope that if I worked hard I could rebuild my reputation within the media and gradually drive those search engine references onto page two and then, with luck, beyond.

CHAPTER NINETEEN

CREDIBLE AND TRUE OR INCREDIBLE AND FALSE?

There is no crueller tyranny than that which is perpetuated under the shield of law and in the name of justice.

— CHARLES DE MONTESQUIEU

I know that the police become exasperated when the epithet 'witch-hunt' is used to describe their method of trawling for evidence of historical abuse and blind acceptance of the claims of any complainants. They believe that such an emotive expression does the complex and important issue of child abuse investigations no good at all. Witches don't exist, it is claimed, but paedophiles do. Nevertheless, witch-*hunts* did exist and they took place at

---

a time when magic and the supernatural were part of the current culture and when some groups in society were part of an organised demonic cult. Once beliefs of this kind convinced the minds of the most learned in the land, the empirical evidence upon which it was based became all but irrelevant. In the days of the Salem witch-hunts, there was no requirement for reliable evidence or proof because the alleged crime itself was so appalling in the eyes of that society. The balance of justice was tipped in favour of the complainant. Once this *modus operandi* took hold, inevitably innocent people were condemned.

Because of modern-day society's repugnance towards the topic of child abuse and our disgust that someone like Jimmy Savile was able to perpetrate such abuse with impunity throughout his life, once again we have created an atmosphere in which an allegation is sufficient to condemn. We know that paedophiles definitely exist, so it is not difficult for complainants to convince others they are telling the truth. On many occasions, of course, they are but, on the other side of the coin, to ignore the temptation in our current climate for fantasists and opportunists to proffer their evil lies is dangerous.

Child abuse is a very real problem in our society and I am fully aware, having been educated in a boys' boarding school in the 1960s/'70s, teachers have in the past managed to avoid prosecution despite having abused children in their care. I was one of those children. But, as Barbara Hewson states, 'two wrongs do not make a right'. Just because we are angry as a society that paedophiles have avoided justice over the decades due to a hierarchical British culture which promoted a society in which 'children should be seen and not heard', this coupled with a lax approach towards child abuse by law enforcement, these are not reasons nowadays to attack and destroy accused individuals on the basis of no evidence whatsoever, but just on the words of complainants. We have reached a time in our society when even the learned men and women of the judiciary are frightened into aligning themselves with the collective historical abuse insanity which grips Britain. When this febrile atmosphere includes unsubstantiated rumours of the involvement of senior political figures in sex rings, including one ex-Prime Minister, then the insanity becomes even more potent.

Part of the blame for the creation of this modern culture rests with those gullible police officers and their collective embarrassment over past failures. How can we reach a point in our history when a senior officer, Detective Superintendent Kenny McDonald, the head of 'Operation Midland', stands outside the home of a former Prime Minister and, before there has been any meaningful investigation following absurd allegations made by 'Nick', he states confidently that he believes Nick's allegations to be 'credible and true'? It can safely be claimed that we had, at this point, reached a position when the making of a modern-day witch-hunt was all but complete.

But it is not just the police, as agents of the state, who are to blame for this modern madness. Part must be ascribed to those who have turned a blind eye to the growing culture of false historical abuse claims for fear of being hounded themselves. Look what has happened to Barbara Hewson. It is pretty chilling to read some of the adjectives, listed in the previous chapter, which were used against her by the nasty, vitriolic, untutored mob. Sometimes it takes enormous courage to stand up for what is right and just and honest.

As I write this chapter, on Tuesday 12 April 2016, the front page of the *Daily Mail* reads: 'Dragged Through Hell by Rape Police.' It is the story of four young men who were charged with rape following an allegation made by one young woman. The men were kept on bail for over a year. The charges were eventually dropped after it was discovered that the complainant had made dubious claims concerning an alleged rape in another trial. The accused were angry that detectives working on the case had 'cherry-picked' evidence to support their case, while 'airbrushing' out anything that suggested that they were innocent, the same thing that happened in my case. The accused men stated that they were viewed as 'guilty until proven innocent', *presumed guilty*, just as I was. They spoke of the 'devastating' effect the arrest and being charged had had on their lives, just as my life was ripped apart.

Once again, it begs the question why, in a supposedly just democracy, were the four young men kept on bail for thirteen months before being charged? And why were seriously critical notes about the integrity of the accuser omitted by the policeman who was recording the evidence? Detectives were also said to have 'buried' damning text messages sent by the accuser to one of the defendants.

Yet again, we have a case in which evidence favourable to the defence, which casts grave doubts on the allegations under scrutiny, is concealed. This is exactly what happened in my case, the police not bothering to check whether the fundamentals of the allegations against me had substance. What's more, they still pursued me through the courts even after realising that, at best, the accusers had got even their basic facts wrong.

Can someone explain how this can happen and, when it does, no one is called to account? Neither the liars themselves nor the agents of the state are required to explain themselves. Surely, a point must come when bare-faced lies by an accuser and/or selective and weighted investigations by the police are exposed.

Reports of the shocking experiences of precisely those people my petition seeks to help protect are almost a weekly event at present. Within a few days of the previous article, I now read the headline: 'Private school teacher cleared of sex abuse left ruined by £195,000 legal costs.'

This is the story of geography teacher Kato Harris, who was accused of raping a teenage pupil in a school classroom. He was cleared by a jury in just twenty-six minutes. Despite the serious doubts about whether the accuser was telling the truth – she alleged that he would invite her into his classroom at lunchtime for chats, prior to attacking her – Mr Harris himself, the deputy headmaster of the school, has been left 'crushed by stress'. Friends of Mr Harris have now set up an online appeal to help pay his costs. His accuser has walked away free and has lifelong anonymity.

There are many innocent people who, as a result of police trawling operations, are spending time behind bars. Hundreds of complainants have come forward having been encouraged to do so by the compensation culture and/or as a means of stepping out from a hitherto miserably dark, unproductive life. Some have done so as a result of 'the recovered memory movement', in which therapists encourage people to make false retrospective allegations of sexual abuse by teachers and carers. This particular therapy played a principal part in the now discredited Cleveland abuse scandal in 1987 and in the Orkney satanic abuse scandal in 1991. The NHS's 'Lantern Project' uses a technique called 'unstructured therapeutic disclosure' (UTD.) This is where 'victims' of alleged sex abuse are given the details of the effects of sex abuse suffered by the actual counsellor and the 'victims' are then strongly encouraged to re-live their own abuse. History professor Philip Jenkins, of Baylor University, North Carolina, wrote the following in the *American Conservative*:

> … one simple statement has achieved the status of a religious
> creed: victims never lie about child abuse. Children don't lie,
> nor do adults reporting their childhood sufferings. If you doubt
> this fact – if you use a word like 'alleged' victim, then you are
> an accomplice to that abuse … … Doubt is the devil.

As the journalist Richard Littlejohn would say – 'you couldn't make it up'.

Often, when false claims make it to a court of law, they are camouflaged as spontaneous complaints but are frequently anything but. Some have been imagined or have even been prompted by some well-meaning counsellor, social worker or police officer. Sometimes there are elements of truth in the allegations and, if there are, they are soon swamped by exaggerations and lies.

'Nick', the prolific internet fantasist, seems to have been the perfect story teller; he succeeded in convincing some top agents of the state hook, line and sinker into believing his claims of historical abuse and murder and, as a result, 'Operation Midland' was set up. It must surely be the first time a murder investigation has been set up without any bodies and without anyone knowing who had actually been murdered. 'Nick' is a convincing fantasist, that's for sure, who, if the newspapers are to be believed, may have netted the grand sum of £50,000 in compensation before any alleged perpetrator had even been charged with a crime.

With regard to our *modus operandi* of investigating historical sexual abuse allegations, what is at stake is the presumption of innocence itself. In the case of State v Coetzee, in the South African Constitutional Court, Mr Justice Sachs said the following:

> There is a paradox at the heart of all criminal procedure in that, the more serious the crime and the greater the public interest in securing convictions of the guilty, the more important the constitutional protections of the accused become. The starting point of any balanced inquiry, where constitutional rights are concerned, must be that the public interest in ensuring that innocent people are not convicted and subject to ignominy and heavy sentences outweighs the public interest in ensuring that a particular criminal is brought to book. Hence the presumption of innocence, which serves not only to protect a particular individual on trial, but to maintain public confidence in the enduring integrity and security of the legal system.

I contest that in modern-day Great Britain, when historical sex abuse is being investigated, Mr Justice Sachs's wise warnings are being ignored. In these cases, the presumption of innocence until proven guilty has been abandoned and, in its place, there is now a presumption of guilt. Criminal trials can become absurd pretences, determined by prejudice rather than by proper evidence: 'enduring integrity and security of the legal system' has been well and truly jettisoned.

Today is 11 July and Gerard Singer, the teacher who was dismissed not long after my arrival at St George's in 1981, has been jailed for twenty-one years at Ipswich Crown Court for historical abuse against eight boys in his care. As is patently clear from my reaction to learning of his inappropriate relationship with 'Nicholas' all those years ago, I believe Gerard Singer is unfit to be a teacher and deserves punishment from the state. However, after watching the unfolding of 'Operation Racecourse', I have developed serious doubts about the process of law in this country with regards to the handling of these historical sex abuse 'operations'. One of the detectives who has been involved from the start of 'Operation Racecourse' announced on the steps of Ipswich Crown Court today as I write (11 July):

> This trial brings to a close one of the biggest child sex abuse investigations carried out by Suffolk Police. I would personally like to thank all those that [sic] gave evidence in this matter for their patience and the trust they put in us. Some of them were spoken to as far back as 2009 and have waited a long time for this matter to come to court. I hope that now these matters have been dealt with it will help them to deal with the awful events that took place at St George's School. They should feel very proud that they have helped to bring to justice a man who

has been a sexual predator and a risk to young boys for more than three decades.

It all sounds so unimpeded, so glib, as if 'Operation Racecourse' has been the ultimate example of dedicated, effective policing. There is no mention that one person they arrested committed suicide before he came to court and another teacher they arrested was proven completely innocent of a series of preposterous lies, yet had his career wrecked, lost his home, his good name and he came close to taking his own life. 'A' and 'B', proven liars, were supported and even encouraged throughout by police officers conducting this 'operation'. That ex-teacher is still waiting for these liars to be brought to justice or, at least, an apology from them or from the police officers concerned and is expecting to wait for a very long time.

Furthermore, one has to consider the cost of my investigation, in terms of both taxpayers' money and police officers' time. All that money and time and effort could have been used in bringing real abusers to justice. The primary focus of 'Operation Racecourse' seems to have been: let's arrest and charge as many teachers from St George's as we can and, thus, keep the funds to support the 'operation' flowing in.

After my third interview at Bury St Edmunds' police station in August 2013, answering to 'C''s allegations of bottom pinching and towel swiping, remember what the investigative officer DCi said to me – she wanted a decision made by the Crown Prosecution Service on that day (it was now late afternoon) whether to charge me or not, as she was flying out to Greece for a holiday the next morning. I asked her how the CPS, who were based in Chelmsford, Essex, could possibly come to a decision about whether 'C''s allegations should amount to me being charged, as they didn't have access to my replies to those allegations. Her shocking response was: 'They will proceed based on what I tell them.'

So there you have it. If anyone ever tells you that the police and the CPS act independently in investigations, you know that this is not the case.

CHAPTER TWENTY

CHANGES WHICH
MUST SURELY COME

Alone we can do so little; together we can do so much.

— HELEN KELLER

On 9 May 2016, now 1,240 days after my initial arrest, I received another letter from the National College of Teaching and Leadership (NCTL) informing me that they had now spoken to the individual who had made the first allegation against me in 1993:

> The panel noted that further information had been obtained
> from another student at Royal Hospital School, SC [I'll refer
> to him as]. The panel noted that the Presenting Officer held

---

a telephone conversation with him on 8 March 2016, in which
he disclosed details of an alleged incident of a serious nature.

This, of course, was 'C''s best friend. What did the NCTL expect
him to say? 'Oh, by the way, I told a pack of lies to the police in
the lead-up to the court case of 1993 and when I became seriously
worried as I was standing in the dock that the defence knew precisely what had happened on the night in question, I decided to
change my story at the eleventh hour'? Or was he going to stick
by his initial lies? What was the point of the NCTL pursuing this
nonsense, anyway, I wondered, even if what he was claiming was
true (which it most certainly was not!)? What he alleged supposedly
happened over twenty years ago and it had had no adverse effect
on my role as a teacher in the interim. If it were a 'serious' issue,
why was it not attended to at the time, after the case to which I
referred in Chapter Two had been thrown out of court in 1994?
Are the NCTL going now to pursue every teacher who has been
merely *accused* of abuse during the last forty years? This latest
'assault' on me certainly represented an abuse – effectively, I was
to be re-tried on two cases both of which had been summarily
dismissed and there had been not a smidgen of fresh evidence since
the acquittals. How could there be? Both cases were based on lies.
Besides which, how could I possibly have a fair hearing after all
these years? I was prejudiced because I no longer had access to the
1993 complainant's court testimony, for starters.

Despite all this, the 1993 allegation was added to the NCTL's
'consideration sheet'. Here was another example of 'if you don't
have any hard evidence, add as many allegations as you can'. At the

time of writing I am considering my options – sue the complainants for malicious falsehood? Contact my MP? After all, the NCTL are supposed to be representatives of the Secretary of State.

I didn't have to wait long for the NCTL to make their final decision:

> After considering the information provided, it was the deci-
> sion of the panel that the National College for Teaching and
> Leadership should close this matter with no further action …
> Therefore the case will not be progressed further by the NCTL.

I have finally managed to extricate myself totally from the historical allegations/lies and I can now make untrammelled efforts to bring my principal accuser to justice.

As I write this latest chapter I read in today's newspaper the case of a man who alleged he was abused by his house matron when he was a pupil at a Sussex school in the 1980s. She has just been cleared by a jury on all five charges in just over an hour. What is most concerning, even more than the fact that there is plainly a significant doubt the boy was ever abused (and certainly not by the matron), is, prior to the case even coming to court, the complainant had already started proceedings to sue the school (i.e. their insurers) for £120,000 compensation. Let's just suppose he was abused; I believe it is still wholly inappropriate he should be visiting a civil firm of solicitors and signing a civil action affidavit *before* his case had even come to trial.

Because of the vast number of false historical allegations which have been forthcoming in recent years, it is no longer possible to know who is telling the truth and who is not. We have created a situation in which people who have been genuinely abused are doubted, as others fear they may be lying. I partly blame the compensation culture, powered by the voraciously greedy PI lawyers, for the mess. The scandal perpetrated by opportunists like 'Nick', and, to a lesser extent, by 'A' and 'B' in their lies about me, leaves a mess which means anyone who has genuinely been abused could well be deprived of justice.

Daniel Finkelstein wrote a powerful opinion column in *The Times* on 18 May 2016. It was titled 'Destroyed by false accusations of child abuse' and his thrust was, if we're not careful, our certainty about tackling the legacy of Savile will simply create thousands of new victims, i.e. the falsely accused. The article was prompted by the recently published study by Oxford University's Centre for Criminology, entitled *The Impact of Being Wrongly Accused of Abuse in Occupations of Trust*. While stating forcibly that it is right and proper that all allegations of sexual abuse, whether historical or present day, are investigated, Lord Finkelstein argues that, as we rise together as a society to combat this social ill, we must not at the same time sweep away any inconvenient truth. He says that the complainant must be treated with respect and the allegation taken seriously but this does not mean he or she should be automatically believed, which would defy common sense. This could lead to the investigative officers trying to fit the facts to the story, rather than test the story with the facts. As the police trawl for as many complainants as possible, it matters little that further allegations vary in nature, as long as there is a common alleged perpetrator. And, Lord Finkelstein states: 'We all, let's face it, find the fact that someone has been accused of a large number of crimes pretty compelling.' He says many think that 'the impact on the abused child is too grave for us to worry all that much about the suffering of those wrongly accused.'

The study, he says, describes the terrible toll on those who are arrested but not charged, are acquitted after a trial or have their conviction overturned – dismissed from their jobs, saddled with huge legal bills, homes lost, as well as the serious psychological impact.

Many reading this may think I am exaggerating the negative effects of being found not guilty, but I know the damage is done before the trial and, often, before a suspect is charged. There is anger, anxiety and frustration that you, the accused, are being treated as a common criminal and you are powerless to remedy the situation. There is also the gradual realisation that the agents of the state are not out to uncover the truth but to railroad you into court. These are people whose job it is to root out the guilty and protect the innocent. I have tried in this book to convey the feelings of despair and hopelessness with which an accused person has to deal.

It is now June 2016 and the singer Cliff Richard has just been told he will not be charged for historical abuse, having had his home raided in the full glare of the media 672 days previously. (That number of days is exactly the length of time my ordeal lasted.) The headline in today's paper is a quote from Sir Cliff: 'Police treated me as guilty until proven innocent and it's a disgrace.'

Here is another lamb to the slaughter – well known, not married, rumoured to be gay – it fits perfectly the profile of a modern-day historical abuse sitting duck. Sir Cliff is just the type of person whom any malignant opportunist, supported by the agents, sees as fair bait. I contend that the 2014 raid of his home by the police, who had forewarned the BBC so they could film the disgraceful event, would shame a totalitarian state.

Sir Cliff goes on to say:

> They [the police] made me feel as if I was having to prove myself, rather than them trying to find that I was definitely guilty … I was not accepted as innocent, they assumed I was guilty … My lawyer told me that the police treat accusations as evidence … I was hung out as live bait.

I have been informed by a good friend of Sir Cliff of the circumstances in which the supposed 'football stadium abuse' took place and it is so unbelievable that if it were written in a novel you would stop reading it there and then on the basis of it being the imaginings of an immature mind rather than an accomplished author. Indeed, if someone related to any sane adult what was being claimed he or she would be puzzled as to why the story was being entertained by agents of our state. The police, evidently, considered the allegation to be strong enough to raid the 75-year-old's home (in the full glare of publicity of course), thereby forever tarnishing his impeccable reputation. It does not make you proud to be British. What followed was the usual trawling, as part of 'Operation Kaddie', for further 'victims' to come forward and a number of oddballs duly obliged, including known fantasists, a mentally ill blackmailer, a serial rapist and a sex offender. After the decision was made by the CPS not to charge Sir Cliff, the original complainant exercised his right to have his claims reviewed, which meant another four weeks of misery for the singer. Twenty-seven months after that appalling stunt at his home, the whole case finally reached an overdue conclusion.

In the aftermath Sir Cliff is arguing for two things: a) a statute of limitation, that's to say some sort of time limit within which someone is permitted to make an allegation of historical abuse (is it fair that someone has to defend him or herself against an offence that supposedly happened more than thirty years previously? It is a difficult (almost impossible) task to refute if the liar has the intelligence to invent a plausible story); and b) anonymity before a suspect is charged.

The singer is puzzled as to what would motivate anyone to smear him with such vile allegations as touching up a teenage boy. I hope he has the opportunity to read this book and he should then have a clearer picture.

An even more shocking case in the news at the moment is that of 66-year-old David Bryant, an ex-fireman who in his pretty illustrious career has received a number of commendations for bravery. He was imprisoned in 2013 after 53-year-old Danny Day had alleged that Mr Bryant and a colleague at the fire station where they all worked had raped him when he was fourteen, over the fire station pool table. (It was subsequently revealed that there was no pool table in the fire station in those days.) Mr Bryant was found guilty and sentenced to six years in prison. However, Mr Day was not satisfied with the sentence and set about an appeal to have the prison term of his 'assailant' extended, which it duly was. Mr Day waived his right to anonymity and offered himself up for various newspaper interviews and immediately and unsurprisingly launched civil proceedings against both Mr Bryant and Dorset County Council, demanding 'aggravated damages' between £50,000 and £100,000. Of course, once someone has been convicted, these enormous payouts are a mere formality. He was prepared to allow Mr Bryant to rot in jail. I presume my own accuser would have done the same, had his lies been more intelligently thought through.

As it transpired, Day was no more than a narcissistic, cruel fantasist, and it was his unfettered greed that brought his downfall. In order to maximise his payout, Day claimed he used to be a champion boxer, with a record better than Muhammad Ali. He claimed he was unable to participate in the 1984 Los Angeles Olympics because of the trauma of the rape. It was all fabrication. Once a proper, thorough investigation (I presume the initial one was anything but) was carried out, it revealed that the complainant had to seek medical help from his GP between 2000 and 2010 for a condition which can be best termed 'being a chronic liar'. So, only by the skin of his proverbial teeth was an innocent man finally acquitted following the appalling lies of a greedy fantasist, up until this point viewed as one of those ubiquitous 'survivors'. Unsurprisingly, Mr Bryant's conclusion of the entire scandal was: 'There are serious questions about how allegations of historical abuse are investigated and dealt with.'

This could be regarded as an understatement in view of the fact poor Mr Bryant spent two years of his life in jail. But, in modern-day Britain, to exacerbate matters, the trauma will never be over for Mr Bryant because search engines will refuse to delete references to his ordeal. This will be the first thing new acquaintances and neighbours will read about when he offers them his name. As he is both happily married and retired, perhaps this does not bother Mr Bryant too much, but what of the thousands of people falsely accused of child sex abuse who are comparatively young and still have to find gainful employment? What about the accused's children, with the same surname? They will all be manacled to the appalling allegations in perpetuity. If Mr Day's narcissism had not reached such epic proportions that he waived his own anonymity, he could have continued his life totally divorced from the appalling scandal. And this is all meant to pass for justice.

I have been asked repeatedly in media interviews since the trial why, in my opinion, would someone invent such a cruel, fictional account of what had supposedly happened to him all those years ago. There is no better answer to this than that given by Richard Webster in his book *The Secret of Bryn Estyn*, which states that the complex motivations which may impel individuals to make false allegations of historical abuse are often felt more acutely by those who have spent their childhood away from home, as did 'A' and 'B' in my case. Ex-boarders and residents of care homes can feel they have been subjected to invisible emotional wounds which are pronounced when living away from Mum and Dad. Had they been at home, they could have rebelled like all other teenagers. But, in a strict, almost militaristic environment like many 1980s boarding schools, certainly St George's, they felt powerless when faced by both teachers and older boys. Now is their opportunity to redress the balance; and what better way to express one's general resentment about having had to endure such a controlling environment as a child than flexing one's proverbial muscles thirty years later?

This is an opportunity to reverse the power relationship. Adults who make up stories of historical abuse can incite and sustain the kind of emotional attention which they crave and which has been absent from their lives hitherto. For some people the act of making a false allegation of abuse can bring a feeling of real satisfaction.

Prisons are filling up with frail elderly men who have been convicted for alleged offences, often from decades ago. Some of these will die in prison, while their families and friends live in despair. Others have been imprisoned for crimes which never happened. Surely, the idea that reliable evidence is required to prove a case before the state convicts and takes away a person's freedom is as fundamental as the rights to live in safety and free of prejudice that, as an example, were absent in South Africa before the 1990s.

Historical child abuse is a repugnant crime and there is consequently a dread among those who have to make judgements about allowing a suspected pervert potentially to avoid justice. This can have an effect on their mindset when considering the evidence available. We must be aware of this danger. A witch-hunt must never affect the dispensing of justice. I hope that a journalist reading this book will start a campaign to restore the foundations of our once world-respected justice system and put an end to the moral panic and the biased investigations that have become part of modern life here in Britain. Not only will it put a stop to innocent men and women going to prison or having their careers wrecked, it will also help ensure that genuinely abused people have their claims properly and thoroughly investigated. As Bob Woffinden, a miscarriage of justice expert, writes in *The Nicholas Papers*:

The malfunctioning of the criminal justice process is not only destroying thousands of lives quite unnecessarily but is also costing the country hundreds of millions of pounds, equally unnecessarily. It should always be remembered that the judicial system in England and Wales now pits a tiny, seriously under-funded and perpetually handicapped defence team against a prosecution which has all the powers of the state, regularly augmented by all the powers of the established media.

During the course of this book, I have given details of all that I perceive to be wrong with the current *modus operandi* of investigating allegations of historical abuse. If nothing else, there are a few things which need immediate attention if we are to restore the reputation of the once world-respected British judicial process:

1) The police must investigate totally independently of the Crown Prosecution Service; it is illogical to side with the complainant and investigate in a partial manner. If they continue with this biased approach to their work, not only will people continue to risk being found guilty of crimes they didn't commit, but the police will not be in a position subsequently to prosecute those who make palpably false allegations. Police investigations are not supposed to be adversarial exercises. Police procedures are meant to be impartial and it is their duty to inquire. Their goal, as agents of the state, is to seek the truth, on whichever side it may lie, by detective work and not to believe or disbelieve either the complainant or the defendant. One can only infer from my own case that the police suspended common sense as they 'believed the unbelievable and imagined the unimaginable'.

2) Police trawling has to cease forthwith and there should be an immediate ban on advertising for complainants. These trawls can lead to criminal trials that are no more than cruel charades, the outcomes of which are determined not by evidence but by overwhelming prejudice. Indeed, all the evidence suggests that the majority of the many thousands of allegations that have been collected by police trawling operations are false. There will always be a danger that innocent people will be convicted when verdicts are based solely upon multiple complainants. No one should have their life ruined through prejudice as opposed to the truth. How can a defendant receive a fair trial when it is based upon 'evidence' that is grossly contaminated? Often facing multiple counts, that defendant may be guilty of none; he or she may be guilty of some. The strong possibility in our present system is he or she will be found guilty of all. In many of these 'farcical' trials, genuine complaints can become surrounded by a large number of false allegations. We then expect the jury, twelve ordinary citizens, to separate the wheat from the chaff. As a consequence, the chance of 'roulette justice' is highly likely. If similar *allegation* evidence is to be used in any criminal trial, it is imperative to establish before the trial that there has been absolutely no opportunity for the complainants to confabulate. If there has been an opportunity, then the 'evidence' is worthless.

3) We must bring an immediate end to the handing out of large sums of compensation payments. Sexual abuse claimants should not be regarded as immune from the temptations and incentives, particularly financial, that drive human beings generally. We have created a culture in which cash motive and the compensation

culture are making a mockery of justice. Instead, any complainants should have full access to whatever counselling or psychiatric help which is deemed appropriate and the convicted perpetrator should face a lengthy stretch behind bars. This should provide more than adequate support and fairness for anybody who has been abused in all but the most heinous of crimes.

4) Given the nature of the crime and the stigma that is attached to it, I feel it imperative that those accused should remain anonymous, at least until they are charged. I know from first-hand experience that just to be arrested is damaging to one's life and is exacerbated beyond measure by the surrounding publicity. The advent of social media and instant communication makes this issue even more pressing.

5) I believe it is now time to enforce a statute of limitation in all but the most heinous crimes.

6) It is imperative that a Committee of Inquiry is set up to consider what further safeguards need to be put in place to protect teachers and carers from false allegations. At present the impact that a false allegation has on someone employed to educate or care for children is devastating. Teachers and carers have never been so vulnerable.

What is vital is that we don't inadvertently bring about some kind of ethical collapse: in a bid to safeguard the lives of innocent children, the investigative *modus operandi* must not now be a weapon for destroying the lives of innocent adults: alleged historical child abuse must not be treated as a *crimen exceptum*.

I understand why it is so easy for the police to be so rigorous in their single-minded determination to prosecute those accused of child abuse. This determined action against alleged sex offenders will generally win favourable publicity and bureaucratic rewards. After all, the police know they are on to a winner if they are seen to be protecting the most vulnerable in society, particularly from sex perverts. And what better way to secure professional advancement and maintain a generous budget? Post-Savile, at a time when police budgets are being severely cut, the child protection branch has received enhanced powers and resources. Thus, they themselves have a vested interest in justifying their crusade by the constant production of statistics indicating that historical child abuse is widespread. The statistics fall in line with public expectations and exaggerated claims are accepted as truisms. The police certainly have a vested interest in justifying their modern crusade. Child abuse provokes intense heightened emotion. It is not a subject in which one can purport to have little interest without appearing to be lacking in humanity. The emotional content includes anger and hatred, not only in those who are the victims but also for those involved on the periphery and, indeed, ordinary people who have no connection at all with historical abuse (the internet trolls). The police know they have the general public on their side and, consequently, do whatever is required to bring any suspect to account. They don't even realise that their trawling method for fresh 'victims' is sowing the seeds of the allegations they are harvesting. It needs to stop.

CHAPTER TWENTY-ONE

THE IMPACT OF BEING WRONGLY ACCUSED

I n a new study, *The Impact of Being Wrongly Accused of Abuse in Occupations of Trust: Victims' Voices*, Carolyn Hoyle and her team at the Oxford University Centre for Criminology highlight:

> There has been a cultural shift towards believing allegations of abuse, and the presumption now is in favour of trusting those who present themselves as victims. It is important that all agencies, particularly the police, are alert to the needs of those who claim to be victims of abuse, but not to the extent of overlooking those who are victims of wrongful allegations.

After extensive research, interviewing many victims of false allegations, the team found these victims 'felt disregarded and that they and their immediate family were left to suffer the ignominy alone'.

The research started from a position of full and unequivocal support for the progress that has been made in recognising the problem of sexual and physical abuse of vulnerable people at the hands of those who should care for them. On this basis, the team conducted in-depth interviews with thirty 'legally innocent' people who had suffered the trauma of having been arrested or even charged and sent to trial. They addressed in the interviews:

– Employment and financial damage (including anger at having a hitherto successful career wrecked)
– Physical and mental health repercussions
– Effects on family and close friends
– Damage to reputation
– Loss of faith in the British criminal justice service

I was able to tell the research team the profound negative effects that I suffered, including depression, panic attacks and even suicidal thoughts. Being labelled a paedophile (many people are not interested in the fact it is only an allegation) leads to social withdrawal, fear and extreme anxiety. I felt so low mentally that, at one point, I even considered not bothering to fight the claims. Also, at the back of my mind was the dread there could be further lies propounded. After all, the agents had given credence to a pretty preposterous account of abuse in a shower room offered by someone I didn't even know, so what chance had I of evading the false claims of other malicious liars whom I had dealt with among the thousands of children I had taught during a 35-year teaching career? I have upset plenty of people during this time, for sure!

One of the difficulties I found hard to deal with, and the research team found this to be a common problem among those interviewed, was being unsure 'who knows what'. Whenever I met someone during that lengthy time on bail, be it an old friend, an ex-colleague, a neighbour, even one of my tenants, I was never sure if I should explain what had happened or just hope they were unaware and keep quiet: it was a constant problem and caused a lot of anxiety. One thing is for sure, anybody who has been accused of child abuse will find it hard ever to make new friends (not to mention find employment) in the future, even if that person is acquitted.

Inevitably, the insensitivity of the investigative team, coupled by the barrage of abuse emanating from the foul-mouthed trolls, led to feelings of isolation and alienation. One thing which did help me enormously was meeting all those others in a similar position to me at the FACT Conference in Cardiff.

Carolyn Hoyle and the research team at the University of Oxford were prepared to hear about the damaging effects that being 'labelled a paedophile' have on an accused person but even they were surprised by the extent of the damage. They heard how the false allegations affected every aspect of the accused's life – psychological, material and physical. The team found that this damage is all the greater when the accused is able to cast serious doubt upon the allegations at an early stage of the investigation but is simply ignored.

The research stated that in a 2015 survey by the Association of Teachers and Lecturers, of 685 members, 22 per cent had been the subject of a false allegation. This was blighting careers and exerting enormous pressure on the teaching profession as a whole. This can only lead to fewer and fewer top graduates considering teaching as their chosen career and current first-rate teachers abandoning the profession.

The research concludes with the words of warning that, in our campaign to bring those abusers to justice, we have now created a new tranche of victims, whose suffering is as intense as those who have been genuinely abused.

Being falsely accused elicits stifling anguish and misery, but it is not only the innocent person who is damaged by these unwarranted arrests, it is also those who have been genuinely abused who never find justice because so many resources are used up chasing innocent people. Those who make false, malicious claims and those who have created the climate for these claims to be made should hang their heads in shame.

I'd like to think that none of what I have said in this book is other than common sense. If the steps outlined in the previous chapter are considered carefully, we can bring to an end the present *modus operandi* of investigating historical abuse here in the UK and restore a fair system of justice, which has been revered around the world for centuries. We must not continue to allow contaminated, prejudiced, unsubstantiated 'evidence' into our courts of law and the police must start investigating historical abuse allegations impartially and thoroughly; it is not their duty to believe or disbelieve either the complainant or the accused. It is their duty to investigate.

At the start of this book I told the reader about Chris, who has struggled through life following the abuse he suffered as a child, indeed barely into his teens. He feels angry that there are people who have hijacked the understandable concern we as a society have for those who have suffered life-changing abuse by lying and fantasising in a bid to seek financial or psychological rewards for themselves. He considers these crimes disgraceful and, in his mind, nothing will palliate the pain they cause those who have been really abused. He thinks it is imperative that these dishonest opportunists are not allowed to damage people like him even more.

I leave you with those wise words of Richard Webster concerning the modern-day child protection movement: 'In its zeal to believe *all* allegations, it has betrayed the very children it seeks to protect.'

AFTERWORD

I am a supporter of Cardiff City football club and our club manager from 2005 until 2011 was David Jones. I recently read his auto-biography, *No Smoke, No Fire*, which focused particularly upon his court case of 2000 for alleged historical abuse in a children's home. The case collapsed in court after a number of complainants, all with a criminal record, failed to turn up and the one who did had told someone he was only making the complaint against Jones to pay for his transgender operation. The judge said to David Jones at the con-clusion: 'You leave this court as you entered it – an innocent man.'

After the trial, the *Daily Mail*, a newspaper you wouldn't imme-diately turn to after being falsely accused, had the following to say:

> Major questions hung over the way child abuse cases are inves-tigated last night after the trial of soccer boss David Jones dramatically collapsed. Crucial witnesses failed to turn up to face defence claims that they had invented their stories in the hope of winning pay-offs...

Lawyers involved in a series of similar cases on Merseyside say that Jones is not the first innocent victim of the system of trawling, where police investigating allegations about a children's home contact other former residents to ask if they have complaints.

As lawyer Chris Saltrese stated after Jones's trial:

> The English legal system assumes a man is innocent until proven guilty. But, in this case, that burden has effectively been reversed. A defendant facing allegations from five, ten or fifteen complaints has a mountain of prejudice to climb.
>
> Unfortunately, most defendants in these cases are not successful in doing so. I think the conviction rate in these types of cases is 90 per cent, which is disturbingly high. Sheer volume will prevail. Jurors are loath to acquit where they think there is a scintilla of evidence that the offence may have been committed.
>
> There may be (many) innocent people in jail. I know of up to twenty people who I think are innocent who have been convicted. The national position doesn't bear thinking about.

The general consensus back in 2000 was it was a good job the liars who accused David Jones had not thoroughly thought through their invented stories. The same was true with regard to my accusers in 2012. It would have been so easy to send both David and me to jail. The accusers didn't need a smidgen of evidence, they just had to invent a plausible account of what could possibly have happened thirty years ago. All the police then required was a number of former pupils to say similar and, bingo, they have a likely conviction.

And this passes for British justice.

'History is the study of the past, in order to understand the present and, so, prepare for the future', to paraphrase William Lund. Where historical child abuse investigations are concerned, this continues to be ignored.

'Let my accusers be cloaked in shame' (Psalm 109), for they have surely diminished the legitimate cause of all those who have truly suffered abuse.

ACKNOWLEDGEMENTS

I would like to thank the following people:

All those who supported me at Ipswich Crown Court in October 2014 (mentioned in this book). I will never forget your courage and generosity of spirit. You had nothing personal to gain and potentially a lot to lose.

Also:

> Nick and Ava Warr
>
> Philip McConnell
>
> Michael Simmonds
>
> Marc and Sarah Godfrey
>
> Don and Sarah Hawkley
>
> James and Karen Hazell
>
> Graeme and Brenner (BBC radio)
>
> and Roy McLean.

Bless you all.